Managing Information for the Knowledge Economy Series
Series Editor: Angela Abell

information architecture

designing information environments for purpose

edited by **Alan Gilchrist** and **Barry Mahon**

facet publishing

Published by
Facet Publishing
7 Ridgmount Street
London WC1E 7AE

Facet Publishing is wholly owned by CILIP: the Chartered Institute of Library and Information Professionals.

First published 2004

British Library Cataloguing in Publication Data
A catalogue record for this book is available from the British Library.

ISBN 1-85604-487-4

Typeset from author's disk in 10/14pt University Old Style and Zurich Expanded by Facet Publishing.
Printed and made in Great Britain by MPG Books Ltd, Bodmin, Cornwall.

Managing Information in the Knowledge Economy is a unique new series that provides current thinking and practice relevant to the management of information in knowledge-based organizations.

Contents

Contents

Acknowledgements

Chapter 3 is a revised and extended version of a piece that originally appeared in *Exploit Interactive*, 2000.

Chapter 6: Thanks to Sabina Kruse for the freedom to use Henkel KgaA, Germany, as a case study.

Chapter 9: Thanks to Nina Coton of the UK Home Office and Nigel Owens of the UK Cabinet Office Strategy Unit for their help in preparing this chapter.

Chapter 13: Thanks to the UK Department of Trade and Industry for permission to use the Department as a case study.

Chapter 15: Thanks to the United Nations ReliefWeb and PeopleSoft.com for the freedom to quote from the experiences of the author in working for them.

Chapter 16: Copyright, Marylaine Block, reproduced by kind permission.

Chapter 17: Thanks again to PeopleSoft.com for the freedom to include them as a case study.

Editors and contributors

Bob Bater is Principal Associate of InfoPlex Associates, which specializes in the design and development of systems for the organization and use of knowledge and information. His most recent series of articles - for *Managing Information* in 2002 - examined how a new generation of software applications can support knowledge transfer when considered from the viewpoint of complexity theory. Bob is a Member of CILIP.

Rob Davies of MDR Partners is an independent project manager, consultant and researcher, with wide experience of the library and information policy area and of associated technical and service developments. He is project manager for the SeamlessUK project. Recently he has been the project manager of the EU-funded PULMAN and ISTAR projects, and co-ordinator of the PULMAN-XT project. He has conducted a number of major studies for the British Library and the Library and Information Commission (LIC) in the United Kingdom, and has worked on libraries and learning resources projects for the Asian Development Bank, DFID, World Bank and the European Commission European Development Fund.

Cathy Day began working for Essex Libraries in 1979 and held a number of information service posts. She was Deputy Area Librarian for the Brentwood area, and later was responsible for Information Services in the South Group covering libraries over a wide area of Essex. Since 1998 Cathy (with Jo Morris) has been part of the Community Information Network Team for Essex County Council and has worked on the Seamless Project since its inception, responsible for developing the SeamlessUK thesaurus and metadata application profile.

Stella G. Dextre Clarke is an independent consultant specializing in the design and implementation of knowledge structures, including thesauri, classification schemes and taxonomies. Acting for the Office of the e-Envoy, she developed the GCL (Government Category List) described in this book. She is the convenor of a working group that is currently revising the British Standards for construction of thesauri. Stella is a Member of CILIP.

Mike Fisher of the Neil Cameron Consulting Group has an engineering degree and is an IT consultant to professional services organizations. Mike joined the law firm Freshfields in 1982 and led its systems development for over 15 years. More recently Mike led the development of an information model for the post-merger Freshfields Bruckhaus Deringer.

Janice Fraser is a founding partner of Adaptive Path, a world-leading user experience firm. She has worked in high-tech media as a designer, writer and educator for over a decade with clients around the world. She teaches design at conferences around the world, and is on the faculty of San Francisco State University. Her clients include the United Nations, PeopleSoft, Intel, News International and LineOne.

Alan Gilchrist's information management consultancy firm has recently celebrated its 25th year. He is also a senior association consultant with TFPL Ltd. He has published widely and is co-author of the extensively used manual *Thesaurus Construction and Use*, now in its fourth edition. He is a Certified Management Consultant, an Honorary Fellow of CILIP and editor of the *Journal of Information Science*.

Angela Greenwood has been working for the past three and a half years as a knowledge management expert in a global management consultancy company in southern Europe. Before this she gained a BScEcon in Information and Library Studies at the University of Wales in Aberystwyth.

John Gregory has managed the MarketTracks intranet contract for the US Postal Service for the past four years. Specializing in online information retrieval, he has set up systems for government agencies, universities, foundations and corporations in the Washington DC area. He holds a BSFS from Georgetown University's School of Foreign Service and an MSLS from the Graduate School of Library and Information Science at Simmons College.

Manfred Hauer has a diploma in Information Science, Sociology and Political Science and now teaches at universities of applied sciences in Austria, Switzerland and Germany. He has been Manager of AGI – Information Management Consultants since 1983, a German-based company developing software in information and knowledge management, using programmers in India. The company focuses on indexing, machine indexing, retrieval, workflow management and design and implementation.

Sabine Kruse has been working at Henkel KGaA in Düsseldorf (Germany) since 1988. She is currently Manager of Library Services at the Henkel InfoCenter. The Centre provides the Henkel group worldwide with scientific and business information. Sabine is responsible for the library, document delivery centre and periodicals department.

Catherine Leloup was trained as a telecommunications engineer. For about 15 years she has been undertaking projects as a specialized consultant in information management and systems for large French and other European companies. Her main skills are in the fields of document and content management.

Liz MacLachlan is currently Director of Information Policy and Services at the UK Department of Trade and Industry, responsible for information content services. Her most recent achievement is the DTI's successful electronic records and document management programme. Liz sits on CILIP Council and has published and spoken on project management, change management, information audit and Electronic Records and Document Management (EDRM).

Barry Mahon holds an MSc in Information Science. He ran an information service for industrial users in Ireland before being seconded to the EU in

1978 to manage the first telecommunications network dedicated to online information. From 1991 to 1996 he was Executive Director of Eusidic, the European Association of Information Services. He now works as a freelance consultant, specializing in knowledge management, particularly on new software products and their effect on information delivery. He is an associate consultant at TFPL and also the Executive Director of ICSTI, the International Council for Scientific and Technical Information.

Ruth McLaughlin has been working for the past three and a half years as an information specialist in a global management consultancy company in southern Europe. She completed her MSc in Information Science at City University, London, and before that had worked in Japan and England.

Jo Morris spent ten years working for EEV Ltd, a leading UK electronics company, where she was an information scientist, then becoming Head of Library and Information Services. Since 1998 Jo (with Cathy Day) has been part of the Community Information Network Team for Essex County Council and has worked on the Seamless Project since its inception, responsible for developing the SeamlessUK thesaurus and metadata application profile.

Peter Morville is President of Semantic Studios and co-author of the international best-seller *Information Architecture for the World Wide Web*. He is widely recognized as a founding father of information architecture and a passionate advocate for the importance of findability in shaping the user experience.

Mary Rowlatt is Strategic Information Manager for Essex County Council where she is part of the e-Government team. She is responsible for leading and co-ordinating the development of a county-wide community information network and building an Essex portal – *Essex Online*. Within the Council she is also responsible for information and knowledge management, and web services. She has a particular interest and expertise in interoperability, distributed information services and the use of metadata and thesauri, and is a member of the office of the UK government e-Envoy's Metadata Working Group.

Elizabeth Scott-Wilson was born and educated in Christchurch, New Zealand. In 1988 she co-founded the Records Management Branch Consulting and Training Service for National Archives of New Zealand and in 1997 she founded SWIM Ltd, New Zealand's leading independent information management consulting company. She now leads the Advisory and Knowledge Services team at The Stationery Office in the UK.

Camille Sobalvarro is the creative director and chief information architect of PeopleSoft.com. With equal passion for business and user-centred design, Camille has played an integral role in shaping and implementing PeopleSoft's web strategy. Prior to joining PeopleSoft in May 2000, Camille worked in design management at publishing Fortune 500 and other start-up companies.

Derek Sturdy is the Managing Director of Granite & Comfrey, a company he set up in 2000 to do the actual work of knowledge management. Previously he ran the Primary Law division at the legal publishers Sweet & Maxwell, where he developed major electronic publishing initiatives; before that he was the Sales and IT Director of Legal Information Resources, which provided electronic abstracting and indexing databases.

Amy J. Warner of Lexonomy currently works as an independent consultant advising organizations on information architecture and taxonomy design. She was formerly affiliated with Argus Associates, where she was Thesaurus Design Specialist. She holds a PhD degree from the University of Illinois in library and information studies, and has written many articles and a book in her areas of expertise.

Bob Wiggins of Cura Consortium Ltd has worked in information management as a manager and latterly as an independent consultant for a wide range of private and government organizations in the UK and abroad. He is the author of *Effective Document Management - Unlocking Corporate Knowledge*, published by Gower.

Preface

A brief history of information architecture

PETER MORVILLE
Semantic Studios, USA

W hat we recall is not what we actually experienced, but rather
a reconstruction of what we experienced that is consistent
with our current goals and our knowledge of the world.

Memory, Brain, and Belief by Daniel L. Schacter and Elaine
Scarry, Harvard University

History is written by the writers. And as websites, blogs and search tools transform our information landscape, history will increasingly be chosen by the readers. In the past decade, I've had the good fortune to have played a role in the emergence of information architecture as a discipline and a community of practice. As a reader, writer, user, architect, activist, manager and entrepreneur, I have experienced first-hand the tumultuous childhood and adolescence of the profession. It was fun. It was painful. It was exciting. It was a lot of work. And it's over. For better or worse, information architecture has entered a new stage of maturity. So, before senility sets in, I'd like to tell you a story about what really happened. Of course, built upon the imperfect foundation of false memory, this story is horribly biased and tragically flawed. My only hope is that you, gentle reader, will also find my story to be interesting, persuasive, and perhaps a little contagious. After all, like I said, history is chosen by the readers.

The Argonauts set sail (1994)

Immediately after graduating from the University of Michigan's School of Information and Library Studies, I joined a start-up internet training firm named Argus Associates. I didn't want to be an entrepreneur. I simply couldn't find any jobs in established companies where I could design information systems.

Argus was owned by faculty member Joseph Janes and doctoral student Louis Rosenfeld. As employee number one, I had a difficult first year. I worked mostly alone, for little pay and no benefits. I lived in a cardboard box in the middle of a busy road. Okay, I exaggerate, but these truly were tough days to be an 'information architect', particularly since we didn't yet have a label to hang our hats on.

We did do some interesting work though. We taught people to use state of the art internet tools such as Gopher, Archie, Veronica, FTP and WAIS. We created a guide to nanotechnology resources on the internet. And, as NCSA Mosaic launched the web as a multimedia medium for the masses, we began to design websites.

We found ourselves using the architecture metaphor with clients to highlight the importance of structure and organization in website design. Lou got a gig writing the *Web Architect* column for *Web Review* magazine, and I soon joined in.

In 1996, a book titled *Information Architects* appeared in our offices. We learned that a fellow by the name of Richard Saul Wurman had coined the expression 'information architect' in 1975. After reading his book, I remember thinking 'this is not information architecture, this is information design'.

And so, while some folks adhered to the Wurman definition, we became evangelists of the LIS (library and information science) school of information architecture. We argued passionately for the value of applying traditional LIS skills in the design of websites and intranets. We hired 'information architects' and taught them to practise the craft. We embraced other disciplines, integrating user research and usability engineering into our process. And, along the way, we built one of the world's most admired information architecture firms.

A polar bear is born (1998)

Lou pitched the idea of an information architecture book to Lorrie LeJeune at O'Reilly in 1996. She didn't bite. But a year later, she called us back. At industry conferences, Lorrie kept hearing web developers complain about a pain with no name. Users couldn't find things. Sites couldn't accommodate new content. It wasn't a technology problem. It wasn't a graphic design problem. It was an information architecture problem, we explained, and so began the book.

In February 1998, after countless nights and weekends spent writing, the O'Reilly book on information architecture was published. Sales began slowly but grew steadily as increasing numbers of people discovered the name for their pain. Jakob Nielsen called it 'the most useful book on web design on the market' and Amazon named it 'Best Internet Book of 1998'. Information architecture had arrived.

A community takes shape (2000)

In April 2000, a very special event took place at the Logan Airport Hilton in Boston, Massachusetts. Lou worked closely with Richard Hill of the American Society of Information Science and Technology (ASIST) to organize the first annual Information Architecture summit, bringing together people from universities, libraries, web consultancies and Fortune 500 firms to share perspectives.

The energy at this conference was incredible. This was the first large scale gathering of the information architecture community in history. And we were at the pinnacle of the internet revolution. Stock valuations and salaries were going through the roof. We were all overworked, living on internet time, but loving it all the same. The SIG-IA discussion group spun out of this event, and a community was born.

Back in Ann Arbor, business was booming for Argus Associates. We created a new community-oriented business unit called the Argus Center for Information Architecture and organized a wonderful IA2K conference in La Jolla, California.

Along the way, we had become a 40-person company with roughly $4 million in revenues and a world-class client list. Information architecture had lifted us to heights that were exhilarating and just a bit terrifying. At such times, life is great, provided you don't look down or ahead.

The valley (2001)

We all know what happened next. The bubble burst. A few trillion dollars disappeared into thin air. Budgets were slashed. People lost jobs. Companies folded. As a firm specializing in this new-fangled, near-invisible thing called information architecture, Argus was a canary in the coal mine for much of the IT industry, and it all happened real fast. After seven profitable years, it took only five months to move from feeling the pinch to closing the company.

Upon announcing that Argus had ceased operations, we received hundreds of heart-warming messages from all over the world. People told us how our book had changed their lives, giving them the confidence and credibility needed to jump-start a new career. This outpouring of support was truly the silver lining in a dark cloud.

But many saw the fall of the house of Argus as an ominous symbol for the entire profession. We tried to combat this pessimism, but it was tough to sell a positive, long-term vision while many in the community trudged through the valley of shadows.

Emergence (2002)

2002 was a big year for information architecture. We emerged from the valley with new strength and maturity. We connected top-down and bottom-up. We reached out to our colleagues in user experience, visual design and content management.

Boxes and Arrows (http://boxesandarrows.com/) burst onto the scene, triggering a wonderful cross-disciplinary resurgence of writing and discussion. We launched the Asilomar Institute for Information Architecture (http://aifia.org/), an international professional association dedicated to advancing the design of shared information environments.

And we collectively published an impressive array of new books. In *The Elements of User Experience*, Jesse James Garrett explored strategy and structure within the context of user-centered design. In *Information Architecture: blueprints for the web*, Christina Wodtke brought Richard Saul Wurman back into the story, unifying the LIS and RSW schools of thought. In *Information Architecture: an emerging 21st century profession*, Earl Morrogh tackled the history and future of the field. And, of course, we completed a second edition of *Information Architecture for the World Wide Web*, featuring a heavier, wiser polar bear.

Tomorrow's architects (2094)

So, where do we go from here? How will the landscape of information architecture change between today and 2094?

Certain trends are already visible. For instance, the leadership of the discipline is becoming increasingly international. This book, edited by Alan Gilchrist and Barry Mahon of TFPL, is but one example, injecting a distinctly European perspective into the global dialogue that will shape the future of information architecture practice.

On a higher plane, a strange blend of social, economic, environmental and technological factors will shape our future in an unpredictable manner. Today, as an information architect, I earn my living in ways I could barely have imagined just ten years ago. If I'm still around in 2094, I expect to inhabit a radically different world. That said, I bravely and perhaps arrogantly predict the practice of information architecture will be alive and well on its 100th birthday.

Well, that's my story. You decide whether or not to make it history. And if you disagree with my bold prediction, let me know; let's make a long bet (http://longbets.org/) and I'll see you in 2094. In the meantime, read this book, become a better information architect, strengthen the practice, foster findability, make the world more usable and, whatever you do, don't forget our bet. I intend to collect.

Introduction

BARRY MAHON
TFPL Ltd, UK

ALAN GILCHRIST
TFPL Ltd, UK

I n this paper we argue that a core ontology is one of the key building blocks necessary to enable the scalable assimilation of
information from diverse sources. A complete and extensible
ontology that expresses the basic concepts that are common
across a variety of domains and can provide the basis for special-
ization into domain-specific concepts and vocabularies is essential
for well-defined mappings between domain-specific knowledge
representations (i.e. metadata vocabularies) and the subsequent
building of a variety of services such as cross-domain searching,
browsing, data mining and knowledge extraction.

Towards a Core Ontology for Information Integration, *Journal of
Digital Information*, **4** (1),
http://jodi.ecs.soton.ac.uk/Articles/v04/i01/Doerr/

This extract illustrates well the area where information architecture is
expected to be applied. While in no way criticizing the paper, the complexity of the description is, while academic in nature, a good example of the
range of real issues to be addressed in trying to integrate information generation, organization and use in organizations (in this case, in the
comparatively more esoteric area of ontologies).

In the context that information is now recognized as a valid and valuable resource in the management of an organization, the function
described as information management has grown from being a library,
filing or computing function – or, in some more progressive organizations,

a documentation function – to a mainstream management activity. With this recognition new concepts have arisen. One of these is information architecture (IA).

There have been essentially sterile arguments about a precise definition of IA, which will not be rehearsed here, but we may be allowed to quote two of them. In our research report for TFPL (Mahon, Hourican and Gilchrist, 2001) we created a pragmatic definition – 'a coherent set of strategies and plans for information access and delivery **inside** organisations'. The Asilomar Institute for Information Architecture (AIfIA) defines information architecture as 'the structural design of shared information environments', and we have no quarrel with this. We choose to emphasize in our discussions on IA the architecture aspect, the process of designing for purpose.

In that sense, implementing IA is a pragmatic activity. The result will not be seen as a whole, except by the architects, but will be used by many requiring information as part of their work. IA is a work in progress, given the rate of change in modern organizations, but with an overall plan and vision, its aim being to provide the relevant information to the right people at the right time.

This volume is a snapshot of the IA situation in mid-2003. Morville says in the Preface 'we [staff of Argus Associates] became evangelists of the LIS (library and information science) school of information architecture' referring to 1996. We have always tended to take the LIS view – even before we began to look at IA, in dealing with the management issues arising as a consequence of the widespread introduction of IT and associated networking in organizations. That is not to say we have always felt that LIS had all the answers but there were, and are, skill sets in LIS that lend themselves efficiently to IA. This volume attempts to describe how LIS skills can fit with other technical and skill requirements to achieve the overall objective: the efficient use of information.

Although we have chapters in this volume on information modelling and associated activities, we are not so naïve as to think that anyone starts from a clean sheet when implementing IA. Even brand new enterprises have other priorities, although some, for example those in the leading edge IT area and pharmaceutical companies looking for drug approvals, need to install formal information control systems. Everyone would like to 'stop the world' as the management issues become problematical but few, if any, can.

Therefore we have conceived this volume as a tool that can provide inspiration, examples, advice and experience for those who are either implementing IA or contemplating it.

The driving force behind the move to IA is the fact that all, or almost all, the information in an organization is now digital in creation and use. Thus the boundaries that traditionally and for pragmatic reasons existed between different kinds of information have been eroded. This drive is accelerated by the move to networking, originally justified as a means of sharing resources but more and more justified today as a means of co-ordinating functions. Thus the roles of records managers, archivists, and library and information personnel are converging, not necessarily in terms of their specific skills but because the basic commodity they deal with is or can be handled in a common fashion through IT facilities.

The other pressure behind IA is the need to 'get organized'. As more and more information is electronically created within organizations and is fed in through e-mail and other electronic means, the phenomenon generally described as information overload or, to be more precise, a feeling shared by users and systems administrators alike of loss of control of information, has become prevalent. The simplistic approach to dealing with this is to assume that the IT investment can be put to use to deal with it. Thus enterprise management suites such as SAP and other organization-wide applications have been introduced, with some success it must be said, to deal with the 'flow control' aspects of organizing information – primarily those related to financial management. Attempts have been made to extend these approaches to more generalized information control but, to date, there has been little success.

One of the reasons why generalized enterprise management tools have not been applicable is that such systems do not lend themselves to dealing with unstructured data. Control systems generally deal with information as structured records, information such as stock levels, production capacity, sales, and so on. Much of the 'other' information in organizations, which is recognized now as being of importance, is unstructured, such as messages from the market, technical developments, economic changes. These information types are generically described as business information or business intelligence. Their management has traditionally been in the realm of LIS professionals. The need for IA has arisen because of the need to integrate this latter information into the other types of information in use in the organization.

Unfortunately, this fundamental mismatch has not inhibited some software producers from claiming that they have created solutions to the information overload issue. Some of the offers work for some of the problems but, as can be seen in the case studies in this volume, they are not panaceas.

Some of the papers in this volume are complex. The activity of actually implementing IA is far from trivial, combining serious analysis with future proofing and flexibility. The other element that becomes clear from the work described here is that few attempts to develop integrated, coherent information spaces work the first time; several iterations are needed and should be planned for. The overall impression one gets is that practitioners should not try to 'stop the world' in the sense of re-engineering the information processes completely but should not be afraid to start at the bottom of the problem and get agreement on what to do. Tackle the relatively easy wins, but have a wider plan, in short – an information architecture.

Reference

Mahon, B., Hourican, R. and Gilchrist, A. (2001) *Research into Information Architecture: the roles of software, taxonomies and people*, London, TFPL.

Reading guide

We have tried to make this book as practical as possible. We felt at the outset that information professionals would welcome a compilation that attempted to put many of the daily topics faced by professionals in context. Consequently we have mixed direct information on techniques and technologies associated with information architecture with case studies, written by professionals, which tell the story as it is (or was) with commendable honesty.

While we are not so presumptuous as to suggest how you should read this book, we do not expect that it will be read from beginning to end like a novel! So, we thought we would provide you with a short guide to what you might want to do.

- Few if any professionals get the chance of creating an IA from scratch, but many organizations are now finding that their initial forays into 'content' and its control lead them to reassess their situation – it could be the right time to suggest an appraisal of the basics. For those of you who need to read yourself into this may we suggest you read Part 1, which provides two complementary views of how to set about designing a system and a case study of how to ensure it remains relevant.

- Unfortunately organizations don't always do things in the right order from an information professional's point of view. Typically this applies to buying software for dealing with IA-related matters. More often than not the information professionals find themselves entering the software selection process at a late stage, if not after the event! For those who need to be aware of the pitfalls we suggest you read Part 2, where you will find some practical guidelines, a checklist of what to look out for and a good example of how an existing software environment can be adopted and adapted to an organization's needs.

- There are always new technical developments and it seems that the rate of invention of new ways of dealing with information moves at warp speed. Much of what is written is intended for the IT professional and is couched in terms that assume a significant knowledge of 'how to' at the code-writing level. In Part 3.1 we attempt to demystify this. We have tried in the introduction to provide a practical take on what has become probably the most commonly used buzzword in IA – 'metadata' – and in the rest of Part 3.1 we provide practically written contributions on some of the most important contemporary technical developments so that readers can evaluate their relevance to their own situation.

- Many of the questions we get in TFPL concern taxonomy so, if you are interested in taxonomy and how to go about creating one, then we suggest you read Part 3.2. This provides some valuable background information and two contrasting case studies, which provide very practical advice.

- In the end the success of any information system will depend on the quality of its interface. It has now become *de rigueur* to use the web when looking for information. In Part 4 there are three contributions that will help readers to avoid having to give negative answers to the question posed on the front cover of *EContent Magazine*, June 2003 edition: 'So, you've built it, now what?'

We had thought of providing a 'further reading' section, as many compilations of this kind have. Not wanting to avoid the work involved, we reviewed the many, many references we had noted in the course of creating this book and came to the conclusion that there was so much material that any selection would be invidious. Our own experience is that many of our sources were relevant at the time of writing but then quickly overtaken by new developments. So, by the time you read this book, many of the references that we might suggest, while not obsolete, would be partially or completely out of date.

Finally, we want to thank TFPL, CILIP and Facet Publishing for the opportunity to do this work. We would not be honest if we said it was all plain sailing, but it was interesting.

Part 1

The design environment

Preface to Part 1

This section is concerned with how to create an IA, identifying the components of an information model. The first two chapters show different ways of achieving this, through modelling the information processes. Fisher's contribution is based on a departmental or functional solution and follows what might be described as a 'classical' method of creating the model. However, as he points out, there is no 'classical' solution that fits all requirements and flexibility is needed to ensure that the result is acceptable and workable. Leloup's chapter is concerned with the same process but from the starting point of rationalizing an existing web-based information system, which appears to have been constructed without a model and led to difficulties in operation. This illustrates another facet of the need to be acceptable and workable: modelling to make a system work.

Of note here is that in both cases the model was tested on a subset of information objects. This reinforces the recommendation we made in our general introduction that an IA framework should be tested with a view to aim for easy wins while not overlooking the wider plan.

The case study by Rowlatt puts the two contributions exactly in context. It is not specifically concerned with design but rather with development from a number of designs, the attempt to link different systems into a coherent whole. Although the Rowlatt experience is based on co-operation between different bodies, many of the issues that arose will be similar to those that prevail inside an organization.

We draw the conclusion that modelling in one form or another is essential in order to be inclusive, but that it is not worthwhile to try to implement all the items identified in the model at the same time.

B. M.
A. G.

Chapter 1

Developing an information model for information- and knowledge-based organizations

MIKE FISHER

The Neil Cameron Consulting Group, UK

Why now?

For information- and knowledge-based organizations, *knowledge* is part of the tangible value of the firm. *Information* is one of the key elements of knowledge and is therefore one of the key assets of the firm.

Knowledge, as a product or a service, can be sold and bought but it can also be wasted, under-used, used inconsistently, damaged or lost. The challenge is to maximize its value while reducing its negative aspects.

Business and commerce is being conducted in an ever more dynamic fashion using electronic means to communicate, interchange information and collaborate with individuals and groups within organizations as well as outside. The ease with which information can be created, extracted and transmitted with up-to-date software, e-mail and communication links has built up expectations of the ability to exchange information faster and more frequently between the parties who are involved in the business collaboration process. This is taking place against a backdrop of many more complex transactions and projects involving an increasing number of parties with a need to create, provide, contribute, review or use information.

Information models help organizations deal with the information overload caused by these trends and allow the increasing volumes of information to be disseminated, digested and managed effectively. Information modelling is typically being undertaken by information- and knowledge-based organizations to manage their internal information but greater benefit can be achieved by considering information needs beyond an organization's boundaries.

Many information- and knowledge-based organizations have already invested in information systems that cover many areas of business and practice. It is often the case that organizations have adopted a limited view, only focusing on the specific domain of the system being implemented. Furthermore, information systems have sometimes been implemented without considering the wider context of the business processes that these systems are meant to serve. Much of what is being discussed here is based on the experience of a large international law firm but the general principles are likely to be equally applicable to other professional services and information-based organizations.

Information- and knowledge-based organizations have an opportunity to improve individual and organizational effectiveness and productivity by rationalizing the information managed within their existing systems; this will provide more clarity, consistency and improved information flows, thus unlocking additional benefits hidden within their existing IT investment. Benefits can be achieved with little additional investment in technology by focusing on adding value and bridging the content held in existing information systems.

Knowledge and information created and used in organizations varies from the highly structured (such as that found in database-driven information systems) to the completely unstructured (such as that found in documents held by individuals or groups within an organization). The often significant volumes of semi-structured and unstructured information can present a greater challenge to manage than structured information as it has been created with far less focus on the business process. This has created barriers to the effective use of information since it is held in many different and inconsistent structures and formats even when relating to the same subject matter.

Organized and structured knowledge can reside in the information systems that cover almost all areas of the business, such as document management, practice management, client relationship management, marketing, websites, extranets, deal–case–project collaboration and support, human resources and professional know-how. These different information systems have often been developed with varying focus and motivations, in different parts of the organization or at different times. Organizational growth through mergers has also been a contributing factor to the diversity of systems.

What is an information model?

An information model provides a layer of commonality to bridge differences between systems and makes it easier to manage and use information in a consistent way. The variety and complexity of information in use today within large organizations makes it difficult 'to see the wood from the trees', hence the need to create a level of abstraction to make it easier to understand the complex information relationships that exist. The information model is the abstraction of the information requirements of an organization; it provides a high-level logical representation of all the key information elements that are used in the business as well as the relationship between them.

The nature of the process of developing an information model involves a change from less well defined information requirements to a rationalized and optimized definition of these needs. It is why an information model consists of an 'as is' view (an audit) of the organization's information as well as a 'to be' view (a blueprint) giving direction and guidance for the future development of information systems.

The information model addresses two key aspects of the information environment: the 'static' view covering the structures of information (elements and the relationships between them) and the 'dynamic' view, which focuses on processes, essentially the information life-cycle describing how information is created, managed and used.

An information model is created as a set of documented information structures, information processes, standards and guidelines for implementation. If desired, it can also be presented in formats that could be used by software engineers for the design of technology solutions.

Positioning the information model

The creation of an information model should be viewed in the wider context of an 'enterprise IT architecture'. 'Architecture' is a term used in many different contexts. Here, it is defined as: 'The fundamental organization of a system embodied in its components, their relationships to each other, and to the environment and the principles guiding its design and evolution' and an information architecture (see www.ogc.gov.uk/SDTooklit/reference/deliverylifecycle/setdir/enterprise#arch.html).

An enterprise IT architecture aims to avoid situations where (new) business solutions do not fit with the existing technical environment or (far worse) where the changes in technical environments do not support business changes. Both can result in a waste of time and money, and failure to achieve the expected benefits.

An enterprise IT architecture links together the four technology focus areas for a business: the external business environment, business architecture, information systems and technical infrastructure. It provides a clear overview of the technical and business environment and their interdependencies. It enables core business users and information staff to understand fully their IT services and allows IT managers to understand their clients, both internally and externally.

By providing a common blueprint, an enterprise IT architecture enables the bridging of the gap between business and technology, in the context of the implementation of IT applications. It provides a common way to rationalize the business processes and provide a smoother implementation path for any necessary changes in the business and technical environment by using a common reference.

An information model developed in the context of an enterprise IT architecture can be extended to provide a link to the software engineering stage of information systems. This is done by the static and dynamic view of information (the structure and process) being produced in the form of a UML (Unified Modelling Language, an industry standard notation for software design) object model, which is one of the key building blocks in modern software engineering methods.

The process – information modelling in action
Introduction

The constituent parts of an information model depend on the specific objectives of the organization for which it is created but it will generally have two views: a 'static' view covering the structures of information elements and the relationships between them and a 'dynamic' (behavioural) view that focuses on processes and describes how information is created, managed and used. Many of the concepts and forms of notation have been derived from methods and tools that are used in the software engineering field and two broad approaches are possible: the 'information centric' approach

and the 'business process centric' approach. Focusing on information structures rather than on an information life cycle can help gain greater acceptance
for the information audit by avoiding the natural resistance created when
looking at 'what people do'. For clarity both aspects are outlined below.

The static view focuses on the following elements:

- *a classification scheme or taxonomy:* a predetermined catalogue that
segregates elements of information into subgroups that are mutually
exclusive, unambiguous and, taken together, include all possibilities
- *controlled vocabulary and thesaurus:* the vocabulary of a classification
or taxonomy scheme, formally organized so that the *a priori* relationships between concepts (for example as 'broader' and 'narrower') are
made explicit
- *metadata:* information that describes information, usually limited to
the formal information elements, author, date, and so on
- *data standards:* the rules and conventions set to ensure consistency in
the way information is maintained and used
- *a logical data model:* a model that shows the relationships between different types of information.

The dynamic view focuses on:

- *a business process model:* to define the information needs of, and interactions between, the main business tracks (core business processes as
well as supporting processes)
- *an information process model (or information workflow model):* to define
the activities in the life cycle of information sources
- *a data flow model:* to define the transitions and various states of information during its life cycle.

Overview

As with any information project, or indeed any project, the setting of clear
objectives and the creation of detailed plans are essential to the project's
success. Although there are no precisely prescribed steps and route to follow there are a number of techniques and tools available. The choice
depends on the specific objectives set by the organization. Each step in the
process has a number of possible 'deliverables' that document the identified

facts and design decisions and lead the project to the next step. Together all these 'deliverables' make up the tangible and visible product referred to as the information model, which can then be used for the implementation of the desired improvements in the organization's information environment.

The creation of an information model requires an active involvement of individuals from within the organization since a good familiarity with the subject matters being studied is essential. By its nature, the creation of an organization-wide information model spans different functional groups. Thus, it is essential that there is a consistent approach throughout the project to ensure that a unified view of information is achieved. This consistency can be achieved by setting up a core team that leads the project from start to end. That team introduces the common methodology for the project, guides subject matter experts in each of the information domains and facilitates the various steps of the process.

It is also important to ensure that the core team members, including the project manager, possess a high-level understanding of the overall business and specific information domains being studied and that they are proficient in the information modelling methodology being used (see Figure 1.1).

Defining objectives

It is essential that the objectives and scope of the information modelling project be defined at the outset. This is necessary since the nature of the subject matter can easily expand in area and depth of coverage and therefore an agreement on clear boundaries for the study will avoid the project losing focus. It is possible that the objectives and scope may change as the project progresses but any remodelling should be undertaken in a controlled and transparent way. Often it is appropriate to develop a high-level information model spanning all the business activities areas of the organization (but in lesser detail) in order to identify specific information areas where there is a greater need or benefit (e.g. legal know-how, business development) so that it is possible to prioritize the review of specific areas in more detail.

It is helpful for the project objectives to be distilled into a few high-level concepts that can be used throughout the analysis and design steps as a yardstick to assess the state of the current information sources and identify the areas with the greatest potential for improvement during the design stage. Examples of such high-level objectives are:

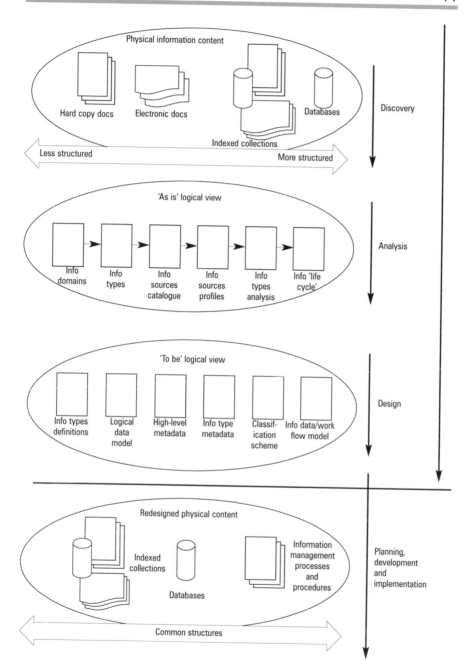

Fig. 1.1 The Information modelling process – key steps

- the removal of inconsistency between information sources
- reducing duplication in information maintenance
- ensuring that out-of-date information is not used
- providing links between related information
- allowing information to be personalized to individual users' needs based on their professional profiles and interests.

Identifying information domains

When the development of a high-level organization-wide information model is undertaken it requires the identification of the information domains that exist in the organization. This ought to be done even if the information model is being created for a specific sector, as it helps to set the context for the area being studied and identify its boundaries between domains. Information domains are not necessarily required to reflect the departmental structure of the organization but it is often easier to start by identifying the information sources created, managed or used in specific groups and departments.

The process of information domains identification is a relatively simple one and involves listing the main areas of the business activities in the organization including the main tracks of the core business (e.g. real property, employment and intellectual property in a law firm) and the support functions such as business development, finance, human resources, training, knowledge management, information technology and others.

To assist any prioritization of the information domains that may be necessary and to provide initial hooks for use in the discovery step it is helpful to identify the main information types or entities and systems that the domain is concerned with. The human resources, training, finance and legal know-how domains in a law firm are used to illustrate this (see Table 1.1 – the shaded areas highlight possible overlaps on 'people' information).

Such a high-level mapping of the information domains detail can be used to identify the areas in which an organization is likely to gain the greatest benefits from rationalization and integration of information. Table 1.1 shows several instances of personnel information managed in different information domains.

Table 1.1 Identification of main information type or entities and systems

Information types or entities

Human resources domain	Training domain	Finance domain	Legal know-how domain
Partners' details	Qualifications	Payroll	Authors' details
Associates' details	Continuous professional development (CPD) details	Fee-earners' charge rates	Users' areas of interest
Trainees' details	Courses/Seminar attendees	Fee-earner time recorded	Internal sources: • information banks • newsletters
Permanent employees	Courses/Seminar presenters	Clients	
Non-permanent employees	Courses/Seminars material	Projects	
Fee earners		Bills	External sources: • CD-based • hard-copy
Lawyers		Credit control information	

Systems

Human resources domain	Training domain	Finance domain	Legal know-how domain
A centralized human resources system	Training management system	Payroll system	Library management system
Other local human resources systems in one or more international offices	Non-database training records	Time recording system	Information bank index
		Billing system	Precedents documents collection
		Accounting systems	

The discovery step

The essence of the 'discovery' step is to gather the raw information to enable the creation of an 'as is' view of the information model (in the analysis step). It serves as a detailed record of the current information environment.

The discovery process is carried out for each information domain separately but if several domains are being studied they can be carried out in parallel. The discovery process can be carried out by people who operate within the information domain being studied. However, it is essential that a common methodology is used for all the domains to ensure that the material produced can be analysed with consistency.

The discovery step involves the collection and documentation of the raw facts and details about the information structures and processes and the creation of an information sources catalogue.

Using a small group of subject matter experts in each domain, a catalogue is created that lists the following:

- *information type:* as part of the information domain identification
- *information sources names, title or description:* the identification of specific databases or information collections
- *the information sources owner:* the person who is responsible for the maintenance of the information source content
- *information sources reference number:* in order to be able to identify and track each source throughout the information model development; this will prevent ambiguities during the analysis and design steps when the amalgamation and reorganization of information sources is being considered.

It is likely that as part of the information domain identification a hierarchy of information types is identified. This can be introduced into the information sources catalogue by grouping the sources, for example, for the legal know-how domain grouping sources as internal or external.

Further details are obtained in the next stage of the discovery process. Each of the designated information source owners is asked to provide detailed information about each information source. This can be achieved via questionnaires or interviews. The level of detail to be provided depends on the specific objectives of the project. The detail required falls into two major categories:

- *the 'static' view:* covering the structures of information and the relationships between structure elements
- *the 'dynamic' view:* focusing on the information processes and 'life-cycle' (how information is created, managed and used).

A possible way to manage the scope of the project is to deal with the 'static' aspect (the 'what') of the information model first and tackle the 'dynamic' aspect (the 'how') at a later stage.

It is important to note, however, that details of any new information required by the user community and how existing information is used (or not) is vital for the design of a future oriented information model. As the design of an information model is usually carried out by information specialists (in organizations that are large enough to be able to have such specific roles) it is therefore beneficial to carry out a 'user needs survey' in parallel to or at the end of the discovery process.

The level of detail that is gathered from information source owners should be determined in advance in order to achieve uniformity in the details that are gathered. The exact details required for each information source depends on the nature of the organization, the type of source and the specific objectives of the project. Table 1.2 illustrates the details that might be gathered.

Table 1.2   Gathering details of information sources

Detail	Example
Information sources assigned unique reference	0555
Information type	Information Bank Index
Information source's names or reference	Employment Group Information Bank
Information source's owner	The Information Bank Manager (information officer of the Employment Group)
Sources description	An index of individual items grouped by subject matter
Any stakeholders in addition to the owner	Professional Support Lawyers (PSLs) in the Employment Group
The information users	All lawyers in the Employment Group; selected clients and other contacts who receive edited versions of relevant material

continued

Table 1.2 *(continued)*

Detail	Example
The primary entity the information relates to	Item unique reference number
Other key entities or related information sources	Subject matter file reference • Item abstract author • Items in the Employment Group's monthly newsletter
The format of the information	A database
Details about the 'searchability' of the information source content	Index is searchable via a customized intranet search screen (by subject matter, item title and abstract text)
Information category or type	General legal know-how collection
Internally/externally generated content	Internal
A description of the information life-cycle	• Lawyers submit candidate content to the to the Information Bank • Professional Support Lawyers (PSLs) review and edit content and produce versions for the Information Bank and newsletter
Details of any data entry standards used (to ensure internal consistency in the information source)	• 'Area of law' classification assigned from an agreed pick-list • Citations to legislations and cases follow a standard format
Details of the technology used	Microsoft Access database
Content volume, volume growth rate and usage statistics	• Current volume: 30,000 items • Volume growth rate: 200–300 items per month • Usage statistic – not available
The internal structure of the content, if there is such a structure	• Unique reference • Subject matter collection • Document type • Document date • Author • Abstract author • Language

continued

Table 1.2 (*continued*)

Detail	Example
	• Source
	• Document reference
	• Area of law
	• Legislation
	• Citation
	• Client/matter reference
Content examples	*An example of a representative record could be given*
Comments on the relevance to the project's design concepts	Duplication – many items in this index are also maintained in the employment group newsletter index.

The opportunity of the questionnaires and/or interviews with information owners should be used to identify further information sources that have not yet been identified by the project team. The net should be cast as widely as possible including sources held as electronic documents (whether in an organized folder structure or not), organized or informal hard-copy collections, collections of relevant e-mails, web pages with structured or unstructured information, and so on.

The analysis step

During the 'analysis' step the 'as is' view of the information model will be distilled from the raw details gathered in the discovery process. This highlights the areas for improvements and serves as an input into design of the 'to be' view of the information model.

The analysis step involves using techniques to distil the commonality and diversity that exist throughout the information environment being studied. It is likely that some of the attributes of a well designed information model may already be present in the existing information sources but there is also likely to be a diversity of approaches to the design resulting in an overall inconsistency. Much of the design of an information model involves the introduction of uniformity to the model and ensuring consistency of information management.

The first task is to identify the main information types that exist within the domain being studied. This would have been attempted initially in the domain identification step and is expanded on in the discovery step, during which it is likely that similar or identical information classified and organized in different ways is identified. The objective is to identify no more than about ten information types for each information domain. The basis for setting the information types depends on the domain to which they apply. For example, for legal know-how they may relate to collections such as precedent documents, seminar material or newsletters. Additionally a short definition of each information type is written.

The next task is to analyse each information type group in order to highlight both the commonality and variations that exist. The following areas are tackled:

- what constitutes the information source
- the major sub-divisions or groups within the source
- the attributes or fields of the information items (if they are identifiable)
- any significant issues and features.

A matrix is a useful format to represent the detail of the analysis and an example is shown in Figure 1.2, which refers to a precedent collection.

The matrix in Figure 1.2:

- shows a consolidated picture of how a specific information type is managed across the organization
- identifies variations in approach to what is essentially the same information as that shown in the shaded area of the above example
- identifies where any controlled classification/taxonomy vocabulary is used.

The design step

The 'design' step produces the 'to be' view, which is the blueprint for future information management in the organization. It sets the standards to be followed in the rationalization of existing information sources and for any new sources to be set up in the future.

This step brings together all the preparatory work carried out in the previous four steps and is characterized by the collaborative nature of the process. The core information modelling team leads a series of workshops with the information sources owners and other information domain stake-

Feature or attribute ✓ – Present ✔ – Present and uses a controlled vocabulary pick-list	Source no. 1	Source no. 2	Source no. 3	Source no. 4	Source no. 5
Format — A physical collection only				✓	
A physical collection with an index	✓	✓	✓		✓
Database index	✓	✓			
Non-database index			✓		✓
Group — Organization wide	✓				
Department wide		✓	✓	✓	✓
Sub-division by industry sector	✓				
Sub-division by geographical region			✓		
Attributes — Reference number	✓	✓	✓		✓
Document author	✔	✓	✓	✓	✓
Language	✔				
Document sate	✓	✓	✓	✓	✓
Document title	✓	✓	✓	✓	✓
Document system reference	✓				
Document name		✓	✓	✓	✓
Source document	✓				✓
Related document			✓		
Cross reference		✓			
Related guidance notes				✓	
External author					✓
Document type	✔	✓			
Related documents	✓				
Area of law	✔		✔		✓
Client reference	✓		✓	✓	
Matter reference	✓		✓	✓	
Issues/ Features — Duplicates content from another information type			✓		✓
Multilingual classification	✓		✓		

Fig. 1.2   Matrix of attributes of a precedent collection

holders, to achieve a consensus on the desired design. The information model design could include some or all of the following points, which may be developed over time:

• an agreed list of information domains

- an agreed information types list and definitions
- a high level logical data model to link information types across domains
- agreed metadata for all information types across information domains
- agreed extended metadata for each information type within the information domains
- a taxonomy, thesaurus or controlled vocabulary to provide, between them, consistency of concept structures and labelling across domains as well as at a more detailed level within each information domain
- an information process view describing the 'life-cycle' of each information type.

Planning, development and implementation

Once the 'to be' information model is defined, a programme leading to the gradual implementation of the model will be initiated, but this is not covered in detail here.

The implementation process is likely to consist of some of the following:

- the reorganization or consolidation of existing information sources to fit with the standard information types
- the creation of database indexes to record metadata for previously unstructured information sources
- the procurement and/or development of software to enable integrated access to, and management of, content.

Methodologies and tools

The development of an information model is of little value if it does not serve the operations of the organization and if it is not possible to implement it in real world business processes and software solutions.

It is therefore of no surprise that many of the techniques and notation forms used in the development of an information model are derived from, and have links to, the world of business process design and software engineering.

The link between business process modelling and information modelling

Business process modelling can be defined as the creation of a simplified view of the business process. It is carried out to enable organizations to focus clearly on the different aspects of a business. In many stages of a business process generally and in most (if not all) stages of business processes in professional services organizations, information constitutes the input, output or the 'consumed resource' of business processes. In business process modelling an 'outside in' view of information is taken by viewing information as an input, output or a resource.

In information modelling an 'inside out' view of information is taken by focusing on the information 'life-cycle' by determining how, when and by whom information is created, maintained and used.

The link between information modelling and software engineering

Modern software engineering methods are based on designing software systems around 'business objects'. These objects represent the things that the business creates, interacts with and uses, such as clients, projects, transactions, bills and so on.

There is a close correlation between these real world objects and the information that represents them and is held in information sources such as databases. The object-based analysis and design methodology is widely used today in the establishment of systems requirements and their realization in component-based system architectures. One of the key elements of that methodology is the development of an object model that represents all the 'business objects' used in an organization.

The object model encompasses the static (structural) and dynamic (behavioural) aspects of each 'business object' in a form of 'attributes' and 'operations,' respectively. A completed object model is one of the necessary building blocks for a systems design.

An object model is an additional 'deliverable' from the information modelling phase into the software engineering phase. This can be created using details from the 'to be' information model design such as the information types, their metadata, their life-cycle and the logical data model that describes the relationship between information types.

Further useful 'deliverables' from the information modelling are XML schemas that allow the structure and relationships between information types to be read and understood by software.

The notational form used to document an objects model within the object based analysis and design methodology is the unified modelling language (UML). The standard for this notational convention is controlled by the Object Management Group, which is a software industry body chartered to promote standards for object-oriented software.

Metadata standards

It is possible for organizations to develop their unique metadata for their information types; however, there are many metadata schemas that have been developed for industry-specific needs by various bodies representing the joint interests of many similar organizations. It is essential that the relevant industry metadata standards are reviewed as part of the information model development to ensure that the organization's metadata is aligned with them. A few examples of such standards are listed below:

- PISCES is an electronic data exchange standard, based on the industry standard XML, developed for the UK property market.
- Digital Object Identifier (DOI) is a system for identifying and exchanging intellectual property in the digital environment (see also Chapter 10).
- Open Archives Initiative (OAI) develops and promotes interoperability standards to facilitate the efficient dissemination of scholarly content.
- Dublin Core is a metadata format agreed on the basis of international consensus, which has defined a minimal information resource description, generally for use in a world wide web environment (see also Chapter 9).
- Resource Description Framework (RDF) is currently under development within the World Wide Web Consortium (W3C) and provides a framework for metadata in different application areas, for instance resource discovery, content ratings and intellectual property (see also Chapter 8).
- IMS Enterprise – Learning Resources Metadata Information Model is used for use in the e-learning environment.

The coal face

The earlier sections of this chapter have proposed a methodology for the development of an information model applicable in a professional services organization. This methodology is based on practices and tools that are commonly used in the information and knowledge engineering world but which were adapted to fit the needs of law firms and similar professional services organizations.

However, there is plenty of scope to adapt the methodology to fit the specific objectives of the project. This section discusses how the methodology was applied in practice to legal know-how in law firms.

The legal know-how domain

Legal know-how is one of the most suitable areas for starting the creation of a firm-wide information model as it directly supports the core business of a law firm and has links to all other information domains. Many would argue that this is also true of most other information domains that exist in law firms, namely human resources, finance, practice management, business development and IT. These, together with the information domains of the core business (e.g. corporate, litigation, real property and so on), were the high-level information domains that were identified for the firm-wide audit.

Legal know-how discovery

The experience at law firms, which is likely to be true in other busy organizations, has shown that it is essential to create a project momentum at the early stages. This was achieved by selecting a core team from within the first domain being reviewed, the legal know-how domain, and carrying out an initial discovery of information sources based exclusively on the team's knowledge of the subject matter.

This has resulted in a substantial number of information sources being documents in an initial version of an 'information sources index' and the ability to present these to other stakeholders within the legal know-how domain for validation of the gathered material and the addition of other less obvious and known sources. The concentrated effort of the core team to create the initial index, both in terms of the time scales and of the methods used, provided an effective start to the project. The presentation of an initial list, provisionally classified into information types, has greatly reduced the workload on the stakeholders outside the core group and provided a clear path to follow.

By way of illustration, in the legal know-how domain, over 100 different information sources were found in a large international law firm at the end of the discovery step. An initial discovery by the core team yielded about half that number. These included, for example:

- standard forms with guidance notes for their use
- information about best practice
- legal opinion collections
- precedents
- general legal know-how collections (typically collections with a computerized index)
- library indexes
- collections of various practice groups' minutes (of internal knowledge sharing and current awareness meetings) containing know-how
- indexes of external information sources
- indexes of transactions
- internal newsletters (both as documents and computerized indexes)
- useful web links (with classification and abstracts of content)
- details on internal staff areas of expertise
- prospectus collections, issued as part of deals the firm was involved with
- details of forthcoming know-how events
- conferences material collections.

Legal know-how analysis

During the analysis step much of the effort went into identifying existing commonalities and differences in the way legal know-how information is managed across the firm. This task required a 'like with like' comparison of information sources and was carried out in brainstorming sessions. The 'correct' tagging of each information source (as being of a certain 'information type') was a key requirement. This was achieved through trial and error, initially classifying all sources into approximately 20 types by the core team and followed by a review process with other stakeholders to arrive at an agreed 'information types' list and the classification of all sources according to that list. Within each information type, the sources were analysed in two ways:

- the form in which the information was held (e.g. hard copy collection, a database, both)
- the way in which the information source was structured.

A common pattern emerged in which a few sources within each information type had more advanced and comprehensive features, for example, highly consistent structure and well developed standards for data entry. These few sources were also those with the greatest volume of material.

Legal know-how design

It was essential that the design of the information model was practical and 'implementable'. Therefore any emerging design had to be developed against the backdrop of the firm's objectives for the project and with reference to the effort required and resources available to implement any changes.

The pattern that emerged in the analysis step (a few, more developed, information sources with higher volumes of content) led directly to a design based primarily on these sources but adjusted to accommodate the more specialized requirements that were found in less developed sources.

This resulted in an information model whose features included:

- an agreed list of 'information types'
- a data standard that specifies that each source (hard copy or electronic) should have an index
- a model metadata (for the index) of each 'information types' to describe the content of sources
- a common and simple scheme for the key 'area of law' classification
- an optional hierarchical classification scheme extension to the simple 'area of law' classification
- a list of entities within the legal know-how domain that reside in other information domains (e.g. internal people information, client's transactions).

Having built a 'model' format for legal know-how sources, the next steps will involve bringing as many as necessary sources nearer to the 'model'. This is a non-trivial effort of migrating, cleansing and enriching existing sources and could involve the consolidation of some sources with others as well as the subdivision of some sources into several sources.

In the case quoted the timescales were not agreed, but clearly this is a long-term exercise, which requires prioritization in order to achieve some easy wins as well as the greatest return on effort. It may also involve more than one iteration, a possibility that has to be built in to the time planning.

Chapter 2

Document, information, data, content

How to model information?

CATHERINE LELOUP
Independent consultant, France

C e qui se conçoit bien s'énonce clairement

Boileau. French philosopher, 18th century

What is easily understood is easily explained
[free translation by the author]

[*Editorial note: 'document' in single quotes is used in this chapter to distinguish the general concept of publishable product from the more specific meaning of paper support.*]

Companies often face difficulties in selecting an appropriate strategy to manage information in a way that will meet all their requirements. What are the frontiers between information, data, document and content? To what extent can electronic documents and their content be integrated with legacy systems and other traditional information systems?

The complexity of such issues probably lies in the variety of available technologies, information structure and user needs. Lack of well proven methodologies to model information as well as the weight of habit and IT history does not help. Even worse, design methods are strongly connected to technologies. A relational method is devoted to building relational databases, whereas object methods handle basic object properties and methods that are specific to the object world.

This chapter intends to formalize a possible approach to modelling information through in-the-field observations, illustrated by a practical example in the banking sector.

Clarifying concepts
Background history

There is general agreement on the definition of data as structured information. In fact, this only refers to information encoding depending on its content in order to ensure that the data is properly entered and stored in digital systems. Indeed, data is either dates, numbers of all kinds, Boolean information (yes or no), text (short or long) or binary data. This is what we have dealt with for a long time. Obviously, compared with the real world, this is a fairly restrictive view of our environment.

Then comes the world of unstructured information, for which there is no definition, only a default one – it is not structured. Indeed, it covers anything that is not data: images, electronic 'documents' produced by proprietary software, e-mail messages, graphics (assuming they were not produced using CAD/CAM software tools), sounds, and so on.

The frontier between structured and unstructured data has been tightly closed for a long time, not only from a technological viewpoint, but also as far as human skills were concerned in the computer departments of organizations. Things were quite simple 30 or 40 years ago: an automated system was complementary to other information sources such as paper documents, individual or shared knowledge. Recent terminology such as content management implies that there has been a slight opening of this frontier. However, this also is very confusing.

The *Cambridge Dictionary of American English* gives the following definitions:

Content	The subject or ideas contained in something written, said, or represented
Data	Information collected for use
Document	A paper or set of papers with written or printed information, especially of an official type
Documentation	Official papers, or written material that provides proof of something
Information	News, facts, or knowledge

Of course, such definitions were established regardless of the evolution of information technology or its possible impacts. However, it is particularly interesting to notice that these definitions mix many different basic concepts:

- the subject
- the medium, e.g. 'paper'
- the communication channel, e.g. 'something written, said, or represented'
- the usage: 'collected for use'
- the source: 'official papers . . .'
- the legitimacy, 'proof'.

A rapid analysis of such definitions in other cultures (for example the French one, which I know the best) shows that such definitions are not shared worldwide. For instance, we call documentation a 'subset of documents collected for a given aim and purpose' and document 'a physical support and the information it contains'.

Does it make sense to look for definitions? Probably not, until recent years. The web and other communication media have changed the rules. Indeed, they reveal to the external world the way internal information systems are built and how they work.

For more than five years now, the computer industry has convinced every company that it should 'go on the web'; easy to say, but difficult to do it properly.

Content, in a web environment, is seen as a part of marketing, a means of directing users to and through a set of constantly changing links. It is a very restrictive view.

Meet our banking company
What is the business problem?

The bank wants to provide its customers and employees with consistent information about its products (a few hundred of them), at the same time, through many communication channels.

How is it done today?

Two different departments (at least) are in charge of publishing information – to the customers on the one hand (marketing department) and to employees on the other hand (organization department or set of departments). Consistency is managed manually and based on the goodwill of each publisher.

Web and other media authors copy information such as tariffs, date of application and reference numbers from the legacy system(s) into word-processed documents and transform them (technically) before publication on the web, on paper, on WAP, and so on.

It is not only a costly method, but it is also inefficient.

How to improve the system?

The only way to improve the system is to implement a common source of information and publish it differently according to each audience's needs. Each audience receives information through different communication channels, but coming from a common source. Do not focus on web technologies only. Paper is still alive. And other media could be developed.

This example shows that it is simply not possible to redefine how information is handled each time the organization faces new challenges, whether new media, new use of information, new audience or whatever.

Therefore, we need some definitions in order to understand what we are dealing with.

Tentative definitions

Logically, definitions should address content first, information next and finally 'documents'. Data is a clear concept in the IT environment.

> Content is an object with embedded rules. Contents are a set of content.

For instance, an address is composed of a street name, a postcode, a town, a city and a country, and each of these elementary components has its own rules. A paragraph is a set of sentences, each sentence being a set of ordered words separated by some special signs and beginning with a capital letter (in the English language convention). A product designation describes an individual product; each product has a different content.

The most difficult thing to define is information. News, facts, opinions, ideas, orders or knowledge could all be some sort of representation of information. However, such a definition mixes content and management rules. Indeed, a piece of news is static information. Knowledge is not.

> **Information is a mix of content and management rules and responsibilities.**

For example, the content 'product designation' is handled under the responsibility of the marketing department, whereas the content 'product reference' is under the responsibility of the manufacturing department. The product designation may change every day with limited controls, whereas changes in the product reference are supposed to be kept to a minimum and are carried out with great care because of their possible impact on the supply chain.

> **A 'document' is a mix of information, publication support and communication methods**

Indeed, 'documents' are made in order to be understandable by human beings. As binary data is not their mother language, information has to be processed before being published in a convenient medium.

A 'document' is not information. There are many ways to provide the same information using different 'documents'. For instance, to be informed about today's weather, you can turn your TV set on and look at the meteorological bulletin (a video scene), ask your neighbour (a sound), search on the internet (the web) or open your window (an image). At an organizational level, documents are highly redundant and probably inconsistent. It is often said that so-called electronic document management systems have failed in many cases. If using electronic document technology just consisted of transforming paper documents into electronic images, a success would have been a miracle. Indeed, depending on the role of an existing paper document – simple information support, proof, initiator of a procedure, and so on – it may become a wide range of things in a digital environment – a record in a database, an event, a message, an electronic document . . . or nothing.

Back to our banking company

The product catalogue content should assemble contents from various origins:

- a content repository (product description, legal information, marketing information, and so on), mainly composed of textual information
- data from legacy systems (tariffs, rates of all kinds).

and should refer to other publications such as procedure manuals or contract forms for the bank personnel. When publishing the catalogue, contents should be distinguished according to their accessibility to end-users (personnel of the bank or customers).

To put it another way, a final product description, whether published on the web or on paper, is the result of a process of analysing the catalogue's contents and arranging them according to publication standards tailored to their intended medium.

Modelling information: the traditional approach

Figure 2.1 illustrates the traditional approach for information management systems.

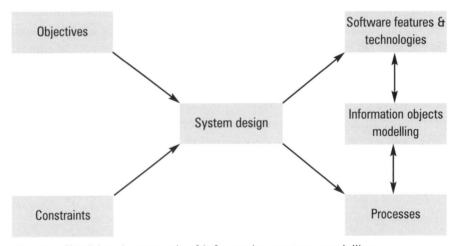

Fig. 2.1 Traditional approach of information system modelling

From the general objectives and identified constraints – technical, human, organizational, etc. – the first step in modelling an information system consists of designing future systems in terms of processes, players and requested software features; then selecting host technologies, such as web architecture or hardware platforms, and enabling the appropriate software. At this stage the information that the system should manage is not described in detail. Information models are generally limited to the description of metadata, files and media to be handled by the systems.

This approach, although widely used, suffers from a number of drawbacks, especially when the system to be implemented deals with 'documents' – and most do. Applying our definitions we have:

- a poor description of objects to be managed
- a future and sometimes mythical system, the design of which is based on existing practice
- a lack of understanding of technologies.

A poor description of objects to be managed

In user specifications, one often finds a description of 'documents' to be handled as office automation files, HTML files and other media-specific file formats. 'Documents' are not only files. Just take a look at an office 'document'. It contains a lot of metadata (we carried out a lot of research work to find out that the only document that has almost no metadata, except a reception date, is an anonymous letter . . .) such as reference, author, title, date, subject, and so on, which are embedded in the file. The file probably includes cross-references to other documents, revision history, authentication items such as approval signatures, and so on. Of course, you can put all that in an MS Word file. But you may encounter difficulties in maintaining the consistency of versions, the validity of cross-referenced documents, just as your webmaster experienced it on your website. Because rules apply – for example version 2 can no longer be produced once version 3 has been published – the approval process depends on the document type, and so on. Some of the rules may be implicit; for example, the date implies the version.

Product description in our banking company

A product description is never unique. It often refers to information that can be applied to several products of the same family, for instance legal or fiscal product environment. It does not make sense to draft the product description from scratch each time. On the contrary, re-use of common information is essential in order to publish high-quality, consistent information, and also to control the updating processes. Significant parts of the product description should be considered as content, which should be propagated from a product family to its individual products.

In the real world, however, it is not that simple. For instance, if the law defines how a minor can subscribe to banking products in general, it is not valid to apply certain information to a given product if a minor cannot subscribe to this particular product, although other parts of the product family may be available to minors. So, propagating content should be monitored by an information system that knows which type of customers can subscribe to which products. Of course, a cut-and-paste facility could do the same, but not at the same price and not with a sufficient level of confidence in the quality of information.

The weight of existing practices

It is very difficult for users to review their current practices; nobody likes change. But what have we done with information for 40 years? We used technologies for what they could do, not for what we needed. Databases were initially implemented to compute figures, then to manage data, and are now used for a bit more than that. Office automation has enabled anyone to produce anything, without the help of any management tool except Windows Explorer, and regardless of the best practices that secretaries have established over centuries. E-mail systems are extremely useful, assuming they are correctly used, but they should not be used as electronic copying machines, with which anyone sends (receives) anything.

Personal computing and legacy systems have not always been good companions.

Corporate imperatives in our banking company

Writing the product description before the product is launched is obligatory, but parts of that description may be in legacy documents and must also be monitored in relation to what is already contained in customer contracts. Information managers must ensure that information is of high quality and complete, especially when it is automatically published on the web.

Generally speaking, existing practice regarding information management is not very good, so companies should capitalize on their know-how, not only on their current available content.

Lack of understanding of technologies

There is a magic formula in the information management field:

New technology + Old organization = Vast disaster

There are many varieties of content management technology. Any vendor will explain how easy it is to create, publish and maintain information content, but they all keep silent on their content models and embedded features. Unfortunately, these are the key to the success of a content management system. XML is not a content model: it is a grammar. It tells you how to write well formed documents, not how to design your own content model; that is clearly the responsibility of the customer, who is the only one capable of making decisions on what should be managed and how.

Qualifying information in our banking company

Everyone knows that editorial items such as tables are represented differently on the web and in paper documents. So, our XML model includes a table 'model'. But publishing the same source information to customers and internal staff requires that content is qualified either as 'public', or not; some items should be emphasized and marked (tagged) appropriately. Figures or links to other products should be managed properly in the corresponding XML model and this must be included as an option in the table model.

Modelling information: an alternative approach

Obviously, the approach should be more structured. Figure 2.2 presents the suggested approach.

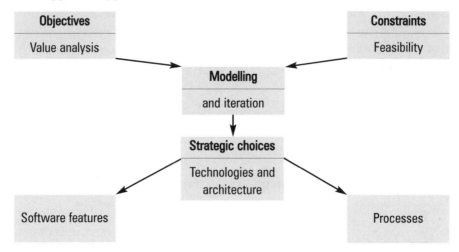

Fig. 2.2   Suggested approach to information modelling

Objectives should be defined in the light of the information needed by the company. Constraints should qualify the feasibility of the future system. Information modelling is the core issue and often requires iterations. Once information modelling has been completed, then the necessary software features and optimal processes should be defined.

Let us describe in detail each step of this approach.

Objectives: the value analysis

The question is: what is the value of this information for the company? This leads to four different questions:

- What kind of information is it?
- What is it used for?
- Who uses it?
- Who manages it?

What kind of information?

The 'What kind of information is it?' is the never asked question, probably because users never ask this of themselves. But it is essential. No one would manage news, facts and knowledge in the same way. From our experience, there are five basic types of information, which show very different levels of structure, management processes, volume throughputs and sharing capabilities. These are:

- *Administrative production* – Basic paperwork, from insurance contracts to administrative declarations, manuals, orders, claims, and so on. It is the field where documents are information supports and process initiators. Exchanges are essential within and outside the company. It concerns a limited but often widely dispersed population within the organization. Forms have gradually changed the working environment.
- *Reference information* – The real information assets of the organization, giving details of its knowledge and know-how. Product catalogues, methodological tools, procedures, operating manuals and quality documents are examples of reference information. This is – or should be – highly structured information, in a limited volume, used by anyone, but managed by few people. Reference information, although often updated, is a long lasting asset. Reference information could be either operating information or knowledge, but they should not be addressed in the same way.
- *Project information* – Information about a project, an activity that has a limited duration of a few weeks to a few years. Volume throughputs are huge at company level, but may be limited at project level. Few people should access all the information about a project, but many should be aware of the status of the project. Information is partially structured. A project could be anything, such as a new product launch, a computing project, a crisis project, and so on. Confidentiality is often a key issue within the organization.
- *Intelligence information* – Used widely in business information and technology surveillance. The complexity lies in the fact that from a raw magma of structured and unstructured content – web pages, professional databases, records, facts and figures, and so on – information specialists produce high value added reports. Input volumes might be very high, but intelligence reports are not very numerous and, depending on

the organization's policy, are more or less widely distributed. Knowledge databases, to some extent, may be considered as intelligence information (for instance research reports).

- *News* - By definition designed for immediate consumption. Pretty unstructured, news often feeds other information repositories, once correctly processed.

Different types of content simply cannot be handled the same way. No one would try to find something from reference information using full-text searching techniques. For example, a fireman in a chemical plant would certainly not search for the emergency protocol 2805-20, which relates to electrical fire, using a complex Boolean search like '[fire or flames or smoke] AND electric AND NOT supplies', because he would know the reference number of the document. In the real world, many people are suspicious about news, and the accuracy of information distributed on the web is often questionable.

What is the information used for?

The second question, 'What is it used for?', identifies what the key information processes are: reading and printing, re-use, sharing, publishing, distributing, relying on them to do something, and so on. There is not a one to one correspondence between use of information and information type, but this question helps to define priorities and constraints.

What is product information used for in our banking company?

A product description has many different uses:

- For the customer, it helps to understand what the product is and to compare it with competitors' offers.
- For commercial staff, it helps to sell and to point out the benefits of a product compared with the competition.

Is it compatible? Yes, but only if the company knows its competitors well. Which means that building a unique catalogue that will be published internally and for the general public does not make sense if the company does not know its competition and that knowledge is not available internally.

Who uses it?

The third question, 'Who uses it?', should help in identifying the actual population of users. Again, we are talking about content, not documents. And the content that is sent out to customers should also be available to the internal staff, in exactly the same way.

What was the concern in our banking company?

Technicians do not write the same content as marketing people. A comprehensive description of a product should logically help to identify commercial benefits for the customer. In the banking industry, it is a matter of money, security and return on investment.

So we had to find a way of translating a technical advantage into a commercial benefit. It consists of changing a given identified phrase by another during the publication process. XML has helped a lot. Further development may offer the possibility to automate this process as a function of the intended audience.

Who manages it?

Despite many conferences and papers, a number of organizations have not yet understood that publishing information is different from producing it. Surprisingly, fundamental rules are disregarded in connection with elec-

How to cope with this in our banking company?

One of the problems we faced was that the existing product information system was designed for internal purposes only. Unfortunately, the content was not protected against the use of 'copy and paste'. And guess what happened? Part of the information was published on the web, by a webmaster who did not succeed in getting the information from the person responsible in marketing on time. So, he did his best . . . but it was not very useful for the customer . . . .

Company information is not an open market. Rights and duties should be clearly set, known and agreed for content production, publication and use.

tronic publishing. Producing information is the responsibility of managing accurate and updated content; publishing is the responsibility of tailoring the same content to various audiences.

This question will certainly raise a lot of other concerns, such as the legitimacy to produce or publish the information, the quality of information, its usability for a given audience, and so on.

Constraints: the feasibility issue

Naturally, human constraints – competences, skills, availability – and technical ones – integration to the IT environment – arise. They are not necessarily the most critical issues. The critical ones are:

- content quality:
  - How reliable are existing contents? Should we migrate or rewrite them?
  - How usable are they? Should we reorganize or rewrite them?
  - How accurate and up to date are they?
- organizational issues:
  - Who will manage the project?
  - Can the manager get enough resources?
  - Has the manager the necessary authority to carry out this project?
  - Who will write the content? Who has the skills?
- cost issues:
  - Who will establish the budget?
  - Would that budget be acceptable?
  - Who pays?

There are no unique answers to these questions. However, before entering the information modelling process, they should be answered. Budgets are often good regulators of the information-modelling process.

Information modelling: the key issues

The key issues are:

- satisfying objectives and constraints
- sharing the same vision among participants in the project

- explaining technologies
- validating future processes.

There is no well proven method. There are methodologies but they are for designers only, not for users, which is why it is necessarily an iterative process. Examples of questions include: Should I structure this content? Would authors be able to cope with it? If not, should we establish a clearing house or a writing house? – But that is related to processes. Could the technologies help?, and so on.

Modelling product information in our banking company

Fiscal information is particularly interesting. In France, there are far more tax rules than varieties of cheese! Basically they depend on your legal status (individual, professional, commercial company, and so on) and the source of revenue (income or real estate, for example). Logically, depending on the product family, a specific rule should apply to each legal status. But we also have more generic fiscal rules, such as death duties, which include various sources of revenue. So, in order to determine which fiscal rule should be applied to a given product, you have to know which type of customer owns the product and which type of revenue is involved, and then apply generic rules such as death duties.

These contents are recorded in a database (and then encoded) and they control the production of the product information sheet. Propagation of contents for a product family depends only on the content in the database, which is uniquely updated and applied to all the products in a product family.

Information quality is ensured by a mechanism that guarantees that a fiscal rule cannot be attached to a product if it has not previously been attached to its product family.

There is no single way to model information content. Logic helps. The company environment is far more essential. A product description in the banking industry has nothing to do with an electrical product description or a drug description. This is probably because market knowledge is essen-

tial. The only efficient way to model information for a given company is
through a joint effort of information designers and market specialists.

Strategic choices

Strategic choices depend on the technologies available. One should select
technologies first and then software products. Some of the considerations
are discussed below.

- *Content model* It is a matter of compromise. Structured textual information requires a content model definition using XML grammar. If you
  want your texts to be processed, then they should be processable.
  XML, well formed 'documents' are processable because the schema(s)
  or DTDs define a logical structure of the 'document', regardless of the
  publication format. Authors must comply with this structure, instead
  of focusing on information presentation as they would naturally do with
  their word-processing tools. Optimistic people call it computer-aided
  writing, and the rest of the world calls it constraints.
- *Content storage model* A true project is an integration project, which may
  include native XML, XHTML, XML export–import capabilities or HTML.
  This means that there will be some specific software developments. It
  is obvious: XML is a grammar not a content model. In other words, it
  tells you how to build structured content, not how to specify it. Other
  choices may lead to the adoption of 'off the shelf' software products.
  HTML is still unstructured information and will never be re-usable as
  it does not show any semantics except title, body and metadata; it is
  'flat' information. XML is a structured information content representation. Then there are cases where re-use of content is not a real issue.
  Standards need to be considered, also; the ad-hoc standard may be
  Microsoft but there might be questions about the strategic factors sur-
  rounding the use of (for example) MS XML as opposed to generic XML.
- *Workflow* Workflow is a technology that aims at automating the circulation of information and tasks among users. The key issue is to
  determine whether the workflow will monitor the distribution of work
  among users or whether each user applies rules to select other users
  who should contribute. In the first case, the workflow is a production
  workflow, in the second, it is an ad-hoc workflow. Corresponding soft-

ware tools have few elements in common except their routing and monitoring functions.

- *Publishing* Is publication automatic or manual? Is the information model powerful enough to be sure that automatic publication will provide error-free results?

What did our banking company do?

We selected XML-based formatting as a strategic choice, for various reasons. One of these was so that it would compute an automatic synthesis of our product description, re-using information from the product description database, generated automatically, just as MS Word does with a table of contents.

We did not implement workflow, because most participants involved were simply not ready to comply with such rules. We just record all steps of the validation process. We publish automatically, in any media, because this was the main objective.

Software features

These are comparatively easy to establish because however you model your content the functions to be managed are always the same. Besides the usual functions such as user management, system management, security management and day-to-day operation, there are 12 end-user functions to be specified:

- creating
- previewing
- formatting
- publishing
- distributing
- storing
- searching
- viewing
- printing
- revising
- archiving
- exporting and importing.

Once the modelling phase has been passed, this is a very simple exercise, which only requires listing what is in everybody's mind. Drafting technical specifications may require time but, once the model has been completed, it is not difficult. It is just a matter of logic and writing ability.

What did our banking company select?

Given that the production of content is monitored by a database, a document management system is useless. Content management systems were evaluated: some were too raw, others too complex to be interfaced.

But as this application is fairly specific the architecture is based on a content repository and most end-user functions have been developed to meet precise needs. When an author decides to write a product sheet, the system searches the database in order to identify applicable subjects and generate a default sheet; this default sheet contains items that are propagated from the product family sheet to the proposed product sheet, depending on the content of the database. The author can accept or refuse this proposal, item by item, taking care of course. Other functions, such as sorting contents, re-generating the default sheet and comparing versions of the same product sheets have also been made available to authors.

Processes

Processes are affected by the information model. There are many ways to build them and many available methodologies to do it. But there are also three key issues, which cannot be ignored:

• *Defining the content* The easiest way to define content is to define content types first and the rest (document, information, data and contents) as content type instances, the results of processed content. Defining content types is the modelling phase output. A content type is a structure model and management rules, such as authoring authorization, lifecycle, and so on. For instance, a content type could be a product designation and another one the set of companion products.
• *Designating an owner for each content instance* A content instance can have any owner; an owner is responsible for the life of the instance. A

different type of owner should be designated for each content type, not the same as for the instance, otherwise it rapidly becomes unmanageable. A content type owner cannot be an individual or a department. It has to be a function in the organization, regardless of which department is concerned. But this raises another issue: the organization's structure or who is responsible for which function. In other words the creation of information types may require the implementation of an organization-wide directory, which should be comprehensive enough to handle such information.

- *Defining production and publication cycles* Normally these cycles can be derived from the information model. However, they should be described carefully especially in terms of responsibilities.

So, contrary to what happens in the traditional approach (see the section on modelling information, above), defining processes is clearly a sub-product of the modelling phase. Indeed, it is very close to it.

Conclusion

One cannot build a rule from a single case. However, information modelling is certainly the key success factor in an information management system. Observation shows that many errors arise in organizations systematically, such as:

- *Addressing information by volume throughput instead of its value* Statistics show that a document entering a company is duplicated 12 times on average. Then the 'copy and paste' activity starts and the same document is transformed into hundreds of variants. But it is too late. No one knows any longer which is the original document, so you can throw all of them away. It is much wiser to teach staff how to use basic office automation tools like e-mail messaging properly rather than to search for an ideal technology that could overcome bad practice.
- *Copying existing practice, because it is easy* It takes a lot of time and effort to understand what existing methods are and, until the analysis is complete, there is no change. When the analysis is completed, no one can change anything. That is a real problem. We did not manage information. We managed what computers are able to deal with; remember that they started from scratch. We constantly adapt to their capabilities, which

are still very limited. Human intelligence should drive their progress, not the contrary.

- *Forgetting processes, because they are complicated and also terribly boring* As a designer you have to play the schoolmaster role towards people who do not think they are learning. Rationalization of passionate behaviour is pretty complex. But the principle that works in general physics, which says that any system naturally reaches its balance point, does not work with human beings.

- *Ignoring organizational issues* Changing the rules of writing and asking a marketing person to write structured documents when he or she feels that their day-to-day work is to compose poetic and attractive documents containing boring legal information is a real challenge. The key message that has to be accepted is that everybody works with the objective of furthering organizational excellence, not for their personal pleasure.

- *Selecting software tools, while forgetting the project's objectives* Comparing software tools is a very simple exercise. You just have to ask a thousand questions and rank them. And then you are lost, because it is a useless task. Software tools all provide similar functions and run on similar architecture. And the missing evaluation question is 'What is your content model and how does it fit my content model; does the software allow for it?' This is the only question that matters.

Recommendations:

- Forget the idea of documents: look at content, regardless of media and communication channels.
- One could build the best model in the world, but if no one can understand it and its value, it is useless. Prototypes can be implemented and improved within a short time (a few weeks).
- Do not focus only on existing processes and content. They result from technologies that have been implemented in your company, not from your ideas.

Georges Clemenceau said that 'war is too serious a thing to be left in the hands of military people'. Information is probably too serious a thing to be left in the hands of IT people.

Chapter 3: a case study

Developing a scaleable information architecture for a cross-sectoral, distributed citizen's information system

The SeamlessUK experience

MARY ROWLATT with CATHY DAY and JO MORRIS
Essex County Council UK
and ROB DAVIES
MDR Partners UK

Background

The SeamlessUK project is developing a powerful citizen's information gateway designed to enable people to find information from a range of local and national sources in a single search. One of the objectives of SeamlessUK is to make it much quicker and simpler for the public to find information on health, education, employment, rights, benefits and government without having to know which organization(s) produce that information. It is funded under the New Opportunities Fund (NOF) Digitization Programme in the UK and runs until the end of December 2003. The project is led by Essex County Council and involves a further eight local authorities and 14 key national information providers, working together to develop a national citizens' gateway, and nine locally branded portals, one in each local authority area. It is hoped that the system will be taken up nationally in the UK.

SeamlessUK focuses on public information – information produced by government agencies at all levels, public sector organizations, voluntary and community groups, and commercial organizations. The service operates in such a way that a search across these distributed, multiple information sources produces an integrated results 'hit list'. The system is standards-based and uses SOAP, XML query, Z39.50 and Harvest. The SeamlessUK metadata application profile is based on the e-Government Metadata Standard (e-GMS), which is itself based on qualified Dublin Core. The project team is developing a number of tools and services including a cross-sectoral citizens' information thesaurus, a metatagging tool, and a 'geocoder' to interpret and map between various geographic information formats. The team is also producing a mapping between the SeamlessUK thesaurus and other key controlled vocabularies such as the Government Category List and other more specialized vocabularies.

An important feature of SeamlessUK is that it has been designed to complement and add value to initiatives already under way. Participating authorities are able to specify their own branding, set up and administer their local information targets and have the option to provide access to SeamlessUK by adding the SeamlessUK 'portlet' to their existing site. In this way we hope to avoid adding to the multiplicity of data sources confronting the citizen and sidestep the 'portal wars' syndrome. It is also important to recognize that, particularly at local authority level, the provision of improved information services must go hand in hand with the delivery of electronic services and improved communication and consultation facilities for the public.

For example, the local portal for SeamlessUK in Essex is called Essex Online and the SeamlessUK portlet provides the search engine for the site. Further functionality is being developed by the Essex Online partnership, which comprises the county council, the 12 district and borough councils and the two unitary authorities in Essex, the Essex Strategic Health Authority, Essex Fire and Police, together with a further 30 public, private and voluntary sector organizations. It will be the community portal for Essex and is recognized by the partners as the central focal point for the delivery of e-services to the Essex citizen. An initial, very limited, website is now live and two new transaction services – e-forms (for ten public services including planning applications) and e-payments (for payment of parking fines, other applications to follow) will be added shortly. Other e-services are being developed.

SeamlessUK builds on the original British Library funded research project, SEAMLESS, which ran locally in Essex from February 1998 to January 2000. This aimed to develop a new model for citizens' information – one that was distributed and based on partnerships and common standards. The team worked with 29 local organizations in Essex, covering a wide range of sectors, to develop the necessary standards and set up a prototype system.

Project partners

Essex County Council is the lead partner, Fretwell Downing Informatics is the technical developer and MDR Partners are responsible for project management, monitoring and evaluation. Current national information providers are a mixture of national charitable organizations, government departments and other similar organizations, which have been chosen because they have good online content. They are listed in the Appendix.

Local authority partners are Essex, Bexley, Bromley, Brighton and Hove, East Sussex, Kent, Lewisham, Medway and North Lincolnshire, giving a target audience of six million people. In turn each of these local authorities has their own group of local information providers, similar to the Essex Online partnership in Essex.

The model is scalable and other authorities interested in joining SeamlessUK are invited to contact the project team. The system could potentially also accommodate regional portals or portals based at a smaller, local community level.

Partnership issues
Working with other organizations

One of the major concerns at the start of the local SEAMLESS project was that other organizations might not want to participate in the project. In fact the opposite proved to be true. In many respects the original SEAMLESS project was an exercise in managing expectations and keeping participating organizations down to a manageable number.

There were, possibly, two reasons for this. First, SEAMLESS arrived on the scene when the time was 'right'. SEAMLESS chimed well with the emerging government agenda for the Information Age, and with many of its key initiatives – partnership working, modernizing local government and empowering citizens. It arrived at a time when organizations were becoming more aware of the potential of ICTs and the internet and were looking for new and more effective ways of working. In this context SEAMLESS seemed to offer them some benefits. Second, the team was effective in publicizing the project locally. The launch gave the project a fairly high profile and also indicated that SEAMLESS had the backing of the county council, which gave the team some credibility to trade on at the start of the project, before it had time to establish its own. After the launch the team made contact with individual organizations, but also took any opportunity to address wider audiences in Essex and beyond.

Similarly, during the SeamlessUK project the project team has deliberately sought to integrate SeamlessUK with the wider e-government agenda, for example by deciding fairly early on that it was not sensible to think of the local SeamlessUK portals as standing alone (and in competition with other local portals) but to seek to integrate and add value to work already under way by offering the SeamlessUK service as a portlet that implementers could add to their existing sites. This approach in Essex has seen the number of local organizations with whom we are working – so as to incorporate their information in the system – rise from 29 to over 45 over the last couple of years.

Partnership building

Not surprisingly the team has found that building, supporting and maintaining partnerships of this size has been an ongoing, and time-consuming commitment. It is clear that nationally (SeamlessUK project) and locally (Essex Online portal) staff will be required to manage both the technical side of the systems and the relevant partnerships.

At SeamlessUK project level there will be a continuing and growing task to be performed in administering the system, the data from the national information providers and the servers, and in developing and maintaining the necessary metadata tools, thesaurus, and so on to support the process. This task will grow as the number of distributed resources making up the system increases. In addition, both the technology and available standards are developing and changing very rapidly in this area and it will be necessary to monitor this continually and adapt the system as necessary. In parallel there will be a requirement for staff to manage and monitor the administration of the local portals and the development of new e-services and facilities. The introduction of new partners as the system expands will require the input of considerable staff time. There will also be a continual need to ensure compliance with the standards adopted, to monitor quality and performance, to provide feedback and evaluation to partners and management, and to market, promote and develop the system.

On the organizational side the team has found it necessary to maintain contact with existing partners (both national and local), to cope with changes in their staff, their information and their systems. For example, even within the short timespan of the much more restricted original SEAMLESS project, five partners launched new websites, two organizations merged and in six organizations the main contact changed. The experience of the SeamlessUK project reinforces this with a number of key personnel changing, responsibilities being moved or split between organizations and organizations undergoing almost continuous development and change to the technology and methods they use to deliver their information. Staff changes can be positive, however, and in many of these cases there has been increased activity and involvement with the project after the appointment of new staff. In all cases the 'germ' of the idea has survived within the organization and the senior management has been keen to maintain its participation in the project.

Governance issues

During the original SEAMLESS project we established a partner board with representatives of the various sectors involved to steer developments. The SeamlessUK project has a project management group made up of the core partners – Essex County Council, Fretwell Downing Informatics Ltd and MDR Partners – which is advised and guided by the other partners via two steering groups, one made up of local authorities and one of the national information providers. In Essex we now have an interesting situation developing whereby SeamlessUK has been integrated into the Essex Online portal. Currently the portal is managed by a steering group made up of senior elected members and senior officers from the authorities involved. However, there is a clear need and growing demand to involve other sectors and groups. For example the County Strategic Partnership and a number of projects working with or representing business interests have expressed strong interest and a desire for a more active role. If the portal is truly to develop into the community portal for Essex there surely ought to be a place for the voluntary sector and a voice for the citizens too. The team is currently working with our partners to develop a strong and sustainable *modus operandi* for the portal.

Technical issues
Distributed vs centralized citizens' information systems

The Essex-based SEAMLESS project began with two models of citizens' information in mind. The traditional, often library-based, centralized database of community information and a new distributed model of citizens' information, which could potentially be led by the public library or by e-government or other relevant staff within local authorities. Citizens' information seemed to be a rather more powerful and active construct than community information in that it consisted of the actual data itself, rather than signposts to the organizations providing it, and it encouraged and facilitated direct interaction between the user and the provider through the provision of interactive services and communication facilities.

At the end of the original project the picture appeared somewhat more complex and fragmented. The team was aware that a number of government initiatives, for example the University for Industry, the Children's Information Service and NHS Direct, were crucially dependent on the development of what were in effect new citizens' information systems, this time quite outside the library sphere, and that some of those systems were in effect distributed systems in their own right. The SeamlessUK project has been working with all these organizations with a view to including their data in the new system, raising a further prospect – that of a group or hierarchy of distributed systems working together.

Impact of local organizations' information systems

The original SEAMLESS proposal assumed a certain level of sophistication in the information systems in use by local (Essex-based) information providers. It was expected that most information providers would be using databases, a significant number would have their own websites, some would be running servers connected to the internet and maybe a few would be running Z39.50 compliant servers.

In reality there was a much more complicated picture. At the time many of the smaller agencies and voluntary organizations had little more than word-processors. The system therefore had to be designed to cope with word-processed documents as well as databases and websites. This problem was solved by converting the documents to HTML to create 'quasi' web pages, which were then loaded onto the SEAMLESS server.

Quite a few organizations had websites but in many cases they were contracted out to external bodies, which not only managed and hosted the site for them but also created the content. We have found during the SeamlessUK project that this remains the case. This adds a further level of complexity to meetings and discussions at local level as the team often has to go through a two-stage process with these organizations in order to get the necessary preparatory work done on their data. It also means that the organizations themselves have to pay to get the work done. This can sometimes be a disincentive – in general it is easier to persuade organizations to commit staff time to the project rather than hard cash.

Some of the larger local organizations, the district councils and the universities, for example, have provided a different challenge. The difficulty here is sometimes in identifying which part of the huge volume of information they produce to include in the project – especially since many of them seem to work in a decentralized fashion and the team has had to speak to a number of contacts in order to get a reasonably accurate picture of what is available.

With the passing of time the scene has changed again. Many of our local information providers are either introducing, or planning to introduce in the near future, content management systems. This has had two major effects. The first is that they are trying to minimize the resources they spend on their existing websites and are thus unwilling to add the SeamlessUK metadata to their pages. The second, and possibly more worrying issue, is that most of the systems they are now buying either do not cater for metadata at all or, if they do, may only be capable of handling it in a very limited way. A key question confronting the SeamlessUK project, at local level at least, is how to cope with this.

The team has offered to create the metadata for key pages in participating websites but despite this most organizations have still been unwilling to incur the relatively small overheads involved in adding the coding to their pages. In the short term therefore the team is investigating setting up a separate database in which to store the metadata outside the web pages and point the system to appropriate pages. It is also developing a web-based interface to the SeamlessUK thesaurus, which should enable organizations to link their content management systems to it as they implement them and make it easier for their staff to add the subject metadata. In the longer term we hope to be able to access the underlying databases, which will be much more efficient for all concerned.

At the other end of the scale SeamlessUK is working with some very large national partners and the team has had to find new ways of accessing their data. For example we are working with a number of these organizations on solutions based on SOAP and XML Query Language. The team is also investigating the possibilities for mapping between the SeamlessUK thesaurus and other common vocabularies, starting with the Government Category List.

Content issues
Duplication of data

The original SEAMLESS proposal recognized that currently many organizations spend considerable time and effort on collecting data to supplement their own core data and that this results not only in duplication of data but an unnecessary workload. The proposal postulated that one of the potential benefits of SEAMLESS could be that this duplication of effort could be reduced because organizations would be able to concentrate on their core data and rely on the system to supply the other information they need. Core data can be defined as data that organizations need and generate as a routine part of their day to day business activities. They therefore ought to be the best source of that data, as they are maintaining it as a normal part of their work, and the data ought to be accurate, comprehensive and up to date.

What we found was that most local organizations tended to adopt a 'wait and see' attitude. They were happy to supply data to the project but were unwilling to change their other information practices until they felt confident that the system would be sustainable. At the same time, even the limited amount of data in the research prototype showed that duplication of data was likely to be problematic. One of the goals of the original SEAMLESS project was to offer users more focused information retrieval and make it easier for them to find fewer, but more relevant, results. Duplication of data in the system is not helpful to users. However, it was not reasonable to expect information providers to stop duplicating the data they need until the system reached some sort of critical mass. This conundrum was not resolved during the life of the research project.

In the SeamlessUK project the team has tackled this in three ways. First, we decided it was necessary to be more proactive and selective in managing the supply of content to the system, based on the outcomes of our user research and resulting content map, which attempts to match user needs to available content. Second, having established that much of the information people require locally is actually (and increasingly) produced by national agencies, such as nhs.uk or government departments, we decided to focus on these definitive sources and deliberately to exclude locally produced variations. This is not to say that the smaller agencies do not also hold valuable core data. However, their unique contribution is more likely to be in interpreting and repackaging the information from the key data providers in a way that suits the needs of their particular client groups or is relevant in a particular geographical location. Third, the team recognized that although it did not wish to disenfranchise or delay the smaller organizations it needed to find a way to minimize both the management overhead in introducing each additional small information provider to the system and the workload for the organizations themselves in creating the relevant metadata, indexing their content and so on. As Essex Library's LIFE database was already available to SeamlessUK as a Z39.50 target, and as it contained records for some 12,000 local organizations, the team decided that the most scalable solution was not to harvest metadata from the potentially 12,000 separate websites but to use the LIFE database as an index. SeamlessUK therefore searches the LIFE database and as the database record contains the URL of the organization's website users can navigate to the relevant pages.

Need for tools

The application of the metadata to web pages, or 'tagging', caused some problems. The research project predated the publication of the e-GIF and associated e-GMS, which mandate the application of metadata by public sector organizations. Consequently most of the local organizations the team were working with were in the position of applying metadata retrospectively to pre-existing documents. Applying metadata in this way is time-consuming and thus expensive in staff time. Some organizations found the prospect of tagging somewhat daunting at first, even though the profile was simplified as much as possible. However, subsequent feedback was more positive. Respondents were very appreciative of the support they have received from the project staff, in the form of tutorials, documentation and one to one support. Most found the process less difficult than they expected once they actually started.

The accuracy and quality of tagging was difficult to control and mistakes may result in poor information retrieval or documents being rejected by the system entirely. The tags, although not difficult to understand, have to

conform exactly to the required syntax, which includes opening and closing brackets and quotation marks around attribute names and variables.
It is very easy to make mistakes, and not very easy to spot them by eye. The
team therefore produced data preparation guidelines to explain to participating organizations what they needed to do to make their data available
to the system. They also developed a metatagging tool, Seamless.dot, to semi-
automate the process. Both of these proved invaluable and have been
updated within the SeamlessUK project.

There was, and still is, concern about how many of the attributes organizations chose to apply. Only seven of the 33 SeamlessUK attributes are
mandatory and there is a danger that this minimum set becomes the
norm, with a corresponding negative effect on the sophistication of searching and display within the system. The production of database reports during
the research project proved more difficult than expected, largely because
of the lack of experience in report generation among the partners. Although
time-consuming, the team has been able to resolve these problems during
the SeamlessUK project, where databases from national information
providers are of key importance, by providing individual support and
guidance as required.

Some of the technically more advanced organizations, however, seem to
have regarded the process as an interesting intellectual and technical challenge and have managed not only to automate it successfully but to build
it into their normal work practices such that it is not seen as a burden at
all. A good example of this is Anglia Polytechnic University, which developed a system that produces tagged versions of their prospectus every time
the prospectus is updated.

Semantic issues

The application of the SeamlessUK profile only achieves interoperability
at the technical level. It ensures that the SeamlessUK system can 'read' the
data from other data sources and that it 'looks' in the right fields for particular sorts of information, keyword and description for example. In
order for the system to work effectively it also has to achieve some level of
semantic interoperability, to ensure that participating organizations are using
a common vocabulary to index their data. This has been partially achieved
through the development of the SeamlessUK thesaurus and the adoption
of place name and geographic data authority lists.

However, one of the problems that has become apparent is that not all organizations are indexing to the same level of detail. This has an impact on retrieval from the system as more detailed indexing leads to improved recall and precision. Originally the project team recommended that all organizations index to the most specific level of detail possible, and then include all the terms above that in the hierarchy as well, but in the real world there was a very real tension between exhaustive indexing and the workload involved.

Subsequently in SeamlessUK the thesaurus has been substantially expanded, overhauled and redeveloped with the assistance of a thesaurus expert and our many partners. It now complies with BS 5723:1987/ISO 2788:1986 *Guidelines for the Establishment and Development of Monolingual Thesauri* and supports hierarchical, associative and equivalence relationships between terms. The search system has also been developed such that it can 'understand' the relationships between terms. Indexers now only have to include the most specific term at the indexing (tagging) stage because the system is able to associate that term with broader and narrower terms, related terms and homonyms at the search stage. This is a significant improvement and reduces the workload for participating organizations.

There is a similar problem with the level to which participating organizations apply metatags to their web pages. Some organizations apply the SeamlessUK metatags to all of their pages, while others apply them only to the higher level pages. Again this affects information retrieval. If all the pages are tagged a search will take the user directly to the relevant web page; however, if only the higher level pages are tagged, the search will take the user to a more general page, which may or may not look relevant to their query. In order to retrieve the required information the user will then have to navigate through the site to find the relevant page. For databases the problem is not so acute as the workload is 'front-ended' rather than ongoing. The intellectual effort lies in creating a mapping between the database structure and the SeamlessUK metadata profile.

Developing and implementing standards

In the original proposal the team had the idea that it might be possible to develop the definitive citizens' information profile. However, it very quickly became apparent that although it might simplify things considerably if everyone adopted the same profile, this was unlikely to be achievable in a real world environment where a number of different profiles were already in use. Therefore our aim became to build a profile that could be 'mapped' to other profiles so that SeamlessUK would be able to achieve at least basic interoperability across a range of systems irrespective of the particular profiles adopted by each.

To this end, the SeamlessUK application profile has been based on a combination of subsets of existing and widely used profiles – Dublin Core and the e-GMS, together with a number of additional SeamlessUK elements, principally to enable us to describe the geographic locality in which a service is available, which Dublin Core and e-GMS do not cater for. In addition to the obvious benefits to interoperability with other systems another advantage of going for established schemes is that they will be maintained and developed over time.

One area where predicted problems did not materialize was with the data itself. Prior to the research project the team had been aware of a number of research projects that had been funded under the e-lib (JISC) and Telematics for Libraries (EU) programmes with the aim of searching collections of distributed resources. However, these had largely focused on bibliographic data – the catalogues of academic libraries, museums and archives. Catalogue data is by nature very structured and the team was not sure that a similar approach could cope with the huge variety of unstructured data found in the domain of citizens' information. However, so far at least, the SeamlessUK profile has been able to accommodate everything added to the system.

Conclusion

So what have we learned? We have learned that:

- Creating a sustainable partnership is crucial but time-consuming.
- Information providers have to understand why sharing information (interoperability) is important.
- Metadata must be made as easy as possible for the information providers to implement – make it understandable and provide tools.
- Implementers should use the fewest possible number of elements and refinements in their application profile BUT they should make sure they have all the ones they need to support the functionality they require.

- Compliance with established standards is essential; and the human side is as important as the technical – provide training, information sheets, help and communication.

However, some five years after we began working with local partners to implement common metadata and some three years after the e-Envoy's Office mandated its use across the public sector some serious concerns about the approach remain. As librarians we understand the shortcomings of free-text searching; however, as we have described, we have found it difficult at local level to achieve a widespread and consistent use of metadata. We have observed that at this level many organizations find it difficult to allocate the human resources required and, when they update their technology, they also seem to find it difficult to acquire software and tools that cater for the metadata approach within their available budgets. The project team feels quite strongly that some of these problems need to be solved if the metadata approach is to be successful. The means have to be found to simplify the process for participating organizations, to improve the accuracy and consistency and reduce the overheads of data preparation.

To this end the team has been testing some semi-automatic indexing products. Although this work is at a very early stage it does seem at the moment that existing tools, or at least those within our budgets, are not able to cope very well with either the range of subject domains the SeamlessUK system covers or with the extremely unstructured nature of citizen's information. Even with the benefit of a good thesaurus, which can be used to support the tools, it appears that the effort required to create a large enough and representative enough set of training documents for them to produce adequate indexing might be prohibitive. Work in this area will continue.

In the meantime the project team is actively involved in configuring the Essex County Council's new content management system and seeking to minimize the amount of metadata that has to be input by individual content authors. We are doing this by keeping the number of mandatory and optional elements to the minimum required to support the functionality we require, by setting defaults wherever possible, by developing dropdown boxes for elements with a limited number of possible variables (for instance, audience) and linking it to the SeamlessUK thesaurus. The team is also interested in the potential of semantic web services to have a positive impact in this area and we are partners in a large consortium bidding for funding for a semantic web services project under the EU Sixth Framework Programme.

Appendix: current national information providers

General and active citizenship providers include:

- Age Concern, a charity that helps older people
- Common Purpose, an independent educational organization that encourages active citizenship through its website 'Justdosomething'
- the National Council for Voluntary Organisations, which provides information, advice and support for the voluntary sector
- UKONLINE, run by the e-Envoy's Office, the national portal for government information and services in the UK.

Education and lifelong learning providers include:

- the BBC (British Broadcasting Corporation), which makes available a vast amount of learning materials on its website
- Learndirect, which is the UK portal for distance learning and online courses as well as provider of information about part and full-time classroom courses throughout the UK
- the Department for Education and Skills, the Department for Work and Pensions and Jobcentre Plus, which have co-operated to create 'Worktrain', a website that provides information on job vacancies, training opportunities, childcare provision and voluntary work throughout the UK.

Government providers include:

- UKONLINE (see above)
- Her Majesty's Stationery Office, part of the Cabinet Office, which is responsible for access to and re-use of government information, particularly unpublished resources, held by the UK government.

Health providers include:

- nhs.uk, the official gateway to the National Health Service, which provides details of services and information on doctors, dentists, pharmacists, waiting lists, and so on
- NHS Direct Online, the 24-hour, nurse-led helpline that provides confidential healthcare information and advice.

Legal providers include:

- the Community Legal Service, a government agency whose website, 'Justask', provides legal information and guidance on where to get legal help
- the National Association of Citizen's Advice Bureaux, a charity that provides information and advice on subjects such as debt and consumer issues, benefits, housing, legal matters, employment and immigration.

Part 2

Software environments

Preface to Part 2

The theme of Part 2 is 'Moving from a print to IT-based environment: the need to understand the problem before plunging in to software solutions' and although the contents of this part may not reflect the theme specifically they do reflect our aspiration. Our experience shows that few if any implementers of an IA-type environment at an organizational level or even at a sub-level have the luxury of analysing the issues in detail before software is introduced to 'solve' the problem. Our writers recognize this and have attempted to provide cautionary tales of the pitfalls to be avoided.

A fundamental role of an IA designer is co-ordination. Content management systems have to be flexible to accommodate many input and output streams as well as the interface, which in today's environment is web based. In essence, the IA manager or information professional role is to identify content, to arrange its storage and to deliver it to the user who needs it. Simply stated, difficult to do.

Identification, or the organization of identification, was covered in Part 1. Storage and its associated indexing for retrieval is the main responsibility of information professionals and an area where there have been a lot of developments in the available software. There is a discussion about software for this area in Section 3, Managing Metadata, with case studies.

The wide application of IA in organizations, as opposed to its application to websites or intranets, means that all the hardware and software in place should become part of the IA. By implication this means IA managers must be involved in the decisions to purchase that hardware and software. This can immediately lead to conflict, a problem alluded to in Chapter 1, because in many cases not everybody concerned with IA is part of the IT planning and purchasing cycle.

In addition, wider considerations play a part. It is sometimes not reasonable or even desirable that the decisions about hardware and related software selection at the organization level should be predicated on IA. Specifically, if the organization is manufacturing goods then the IT decisions may well be prioritized according to the needs of the manufacturing plant, in areas such as process control or just-in-time raw material management. However, even in these cases an IA consideration might be how easy or difficult it will be to get data from the application. Can data be conveniently incorporated into a content management application, for example customer relationship management?. The issues here are not just software or hardware related but also data structure related, and therefore should be of interest to IA designers. This gives rise to another set of concerns: whether data structures should be proprietary or 'open' in the sense that they are known and accessible and can be incorporated into other applications locally. If they are proprietary then they may require either specific permissions to interface the data or that all related applications originate from the same vendor.

This brings up the most contentious question in software selection and use in IA: whether the organization has already committed to a single vendor software platform. More and more IT departments have moved to this environment, for very pressing reasons of cost control and/or training and management efficiency. There can be no doubt that such decisions can seriously limit the flexibility of IA designers. In an example in Chapter 4, Gregory indicates the primordial importance of the decision on the selection of a database application to information management and how that decision is often driven by operating system considerations. Even though it can be expected that the majority of installations will be based on Microsoft (MS) operating systems (OS) the decisions taken on the overlays on the OS such as the MS Information Server suite can have significant effects on interfacing, data formats, network applicability and other important elements of IA.

In a short white paper Trippe (n.d.) makes the following suggestions for requirements for software. It must:

- run on one of the dominant operating systems
- use industry-standard data access and storage mechanisms such as relational databases and XML
- have the kinds of application programming interfaces (APIs) that are commonly in use (COM, CORBA, Java, Web Services)
- be scalable, allowing organizations to add content sources without constant administration and tuning.

These may be realistic, almost trite, suggestions but they may be internally constraining as already pointed out. In addition, standards are not always what they seem; for example, MS has launched a 'version' of XML that works within their environment and while not necessarily restrictive, in that it provides most of the functionality of 'official' XML, it does illustrate how some basic decisions can influence applications.

We have included the paper by Kruse and Hauer not because it describes an example of best practice (though it undoubtedly reports an example of good, if relatively common practice), but because it serves to highlight some of the issues discussed elsewhere in this section. Nor, incidentally, have we picked out Lotus Notes as special software.

Apart from decisions on basic operating systems and services the more specific IA-related software issues concern software for content creation and management. Again, some of these decisions may be taken at a corporate level, for applications such as word-processing, e-mail and database software, but the content – including that originating outside the organization – needs to be organized; or at least the external content has to be identified and, as far as possible, integrated. However, Kruse and Hauer in their case study describe how they have used an existing Lotus Notes environment to extend the functionality of a routine library activity, journal subscription management, to become an intelligent news management and distribution activity. This illustrates how IA actions can and in many cases should be part of the existing environment.

The fundamental IA software tool is search software. In a seminal paper Collier and Arnold (2003) describe the process as 'looking for digital needles in digital haystacks' and, in their opinion, 'making software do what humans do when they understand language is hard'. They make the point that retrieval from a wide range of sources and media is the 'holy grail' of searching and refer to the need to deal with non-text sources. They also make the point that there are very few search software providers who are making a profit, an important point in software selection generally. It may be that a product has unique and interesting features but will it be successful? The decision to buy should be tempered, as Gregory and Wiggins advise, by questions concerning access to source code, to protect the investment and by allowing for innovative responses by not making specifications too prescriptive.

   This part of the book cannot do more than indicate the sort of thinking that IA developers need to apply to selecting and using software. For many the details of the whole software environment may prove to be beyond their technical capabilities and it may even be that too much emphasis on software can be unproductive. There is no 'one size fits all' solution to software in IA; each application requires specific thinking and planning. Knowing what is required is probably more important than knowing all the details of the capabilities of a particular set of software products. Best fit may be the basis of the ultimate decision on what to buy and install.

B. M.

A. G.

References

Collier, H. and Arnold, S. E. (2003) *Search Engines: evolution and diffusion*, Version 1.2 January 2003. Available at www.infornortics.com.

Trippe, B., *Delivering content that makes a difference*. Available at www.gilbane.com.

Chapter 4

Specifying and procuring software

BOB WIGGINS
Cura Consortium Ltd, UK

'Software is not the problem. Managing changes to organizational culture and day-to-day procedures generates 80% of the effort and heartache in the business,' said the manager of an electronic records management project two years down the line after the software had been selected. If that's the case, then specifying and procuring the software might not seem to pose much of a problem. But think again:

- Have organizations really understood why and for what purpose the software is being chosen?
- Have those involved ever sat down and thought clearly what benefits the adoption of the software might bring as against its costs and impact on the business?
- Do they know what resources in time, money and people skills are likely to be required to manage and run the project?
- Are organizations aware of all major information technology initiatives under way in their business that might have an impact on what they are planning?
- Have they a clear understanding of the procurement procedures?

Without properly addressing these types of issues it is likely that the project will fail and the business consequences will be severe.

The purpose of this chapter is to explain the main software specification and procurement stages and the consequences that can arise if attention to them is lacking. However, the effort and resources applied in undertaking these stages need to be tailored to the complexity of the requirement. Deciding which word-processing package to purchase is clearly a far simpler matter than choosing a content management system for a website. Nevertheless all these stages are still necessary and appropriate, despite some requiring only a matter of hours rather than weeks to complete.

The business case

A client needed guidance to build a business case to support a procurement decision. The client was asked if they would be content if the resulting business case determined that the decision that had been made was not the best way to proceed. Unfortunately the client was adamant that the business case had to support the decision. The obvious question then became, why bother preparing the business case?

A business case produced after a decision is made is less than fully objective and, although it may obtain funding, it is not the best way to make investment decisions. This can also happen when investment decisions are imposed, as exemplified by the UK Government's directive that all government records must be created electronically by 2004. In such cases it is reasonable to argue, why produce a business case when the decision has already been made?

An argument for exercising caution in reaching such a conclusion arises from investigations into why some information technology projects fail in UK government (National Audit Office, n.d.) These showed that *projects are often seen as IT projects, and not as part of a wider process to deliver business objectives. The end-goal is too distant with too few review points to confirm the business case.* The conclusion reached was that 'projects have little understanding of what they have to do to "succeed" and far too many stakeholders to satisfy. Without [a] clear definition of interim success or assessment of what is achievable, projects drift into long term activities which become uncontrolled and uncontrollable.'

Formulating a robust business case to justify an investment is therefore essential. From an organizational perspective, the main aim of an investment should be to effect some improvement in, or for, the business. If no improvement can be envisaged, then there is likely to be little justification for undertaking the work. A business case needs to address the sorts of questions listed in Table 5.1.

Table 5.1 Examples of questions addressed in compiling a business case

Questions to be addressed	Topics to be considered (examples only)
What is recommended?	• a description of what is proposed • references to business needs that are being addressed
Why should we do it?	• business rationale for the development (usually a qualitative focus) • business benefits (typically as cost-benefits – a quantitative focus) • consequences of not doing it • alternatives considered and why rejected
How much will it cost?	• total cost covering e.g. internal staff • cost of external contractors • cost of software licences or services • cost of hardware and equipment • training costs • support and maintenance costs
When will it be delivered?	• deliverables by date • money spent over time • benefit delivered as money over time
How will it be achieved?	• training or other purchased assistance that is required • technology • key risks and control measures • key dependencies, impacts and how to control them

Controlling the project

If the business case is approved then the various activities it outlines need to be managed by way of a formal project to get from 'Where we are now' to 'Where we want to be'.

Projects are engines of change, have certain attributes and need to be managed according to an agreed methodology (Office of Government Commerce, 2002). This will normally commence with some form of project brief or project initiation document that is approved by senior management to allow the project to proceed.

A suitable project organization structure needs to be established to manage and control the project involving representatives from users, solution suppliers and senior management from the business as shown in Figure 5.1. For a less complex software selection process, some of these roles may be combined, but one would always expect to have 'user', 'supplier' and 'approver' roles in some form.

The project board needs to approve all the project's major outputs and in particular the key documentation relating to the business case, requirements, procurement strategy and the process for evaluating tenders from prospective suppliers. It is vital that the evaluation process is approved before any request for information or invitation to tender is sent out as otherwise there could be accusations (even if unfounded) that the selection process is in some way suspect.

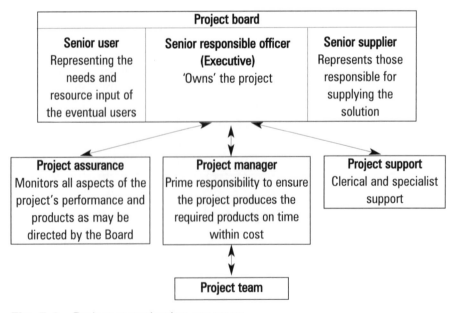

Fig. 5.1   Project organization structure

This is an example of a procurement schedule sanctioned by a project board:

- issue invitation to tender (maximum 12)
- give supplier briefing
- give deadline for written questions to be received
- despatch final answers to written questions
- give deadline for tenders (start of evaluation process and of contract clarification)
- inform shortlisted suppliers (maximum five) of decision
- visit to customer site by suppliers
- visit to reference site by suppliers
- supplier presentations
- identify two preferred suppliers
- supplier demonstrations
- identify single preferred supplier
- award contract.

These different stages are considered in more detail later in the chapter.

An important consideration is the relationship of the project with others that may be being undertaken in the organization. Ideally all projects should be managed coherently as a programme of projects, as what happens on one project may affect another. One example encountered with a client related to the database package that would be used to run the software application. Another project in the same organization chose a database package without consideration of what was required by the software application that would be using the same database server hardware. This meant that the desired performance in terms of speed and resilience (the ability to cope with system failure) could not be guaranteed.

Requirements specification

Having made the case for investment, there needs to be a clear vision and detailed exposition of what is required to be delivered by the project. This includes (Hall, 2002):

- user requirements (as expressed by the eventual user of the system or product)

- system or technical requirements (e.g. hardware, networks and required performance)
- functional requirements (the essential things the deliverables must do).

The review of project failure cited previously (Hall, 2002) noted that in such cases required outputs may not be described with sufficient clarity and there is no definition of project scope prior to authorization. Over-ambition can lead to sweeping into a single project all 'good ideas – all deliverable in one chunk'.

There is also the danger that too much reliance is placed on how others with similar needs have specified their requirements. For example the Public Record Office (called The National Archives since 1 April 2003) provided detailed requirements specifications for electronic records management to help government departments meet the 2004 deadline (Public Record Office, n.d.). Similarly the European Commission Enterprise DG's Interchange of Data between Administrations (IDA) programme commissioned model requirements for the management of electronic records (Information Society Promotion Office, n.d.).

Inevitably such documents present generic requirements, and too much reliance has, in some instances, been placed on them to the exclusion of the specific business needs of individual organizations, so that business benefits are not fully achieved. Poor definition of requirements may result in the delivery of a poor product despite the efficiency of the procurement process. It is therefore important to concentrate on those needs that are unique to the organization. Critically, make sure that users understand and agree each of the requirements and their prioritization as this will save time and avoid surprises later on.

Invitation to tender

The days of in-house development of large-scale, software-based systems are largely gone, because of the difficulties of finding and retaining suitably experienced staff and the fast-moving nature of the technological environment. The most common preferred route for acquiring new systems is the acquisition of standard 'commercially off the shelf' (COTS) packages through some form of managed tendering process.

The invitation to tender (ITT) needs to include:

- sufficient background concerning the requirement, the business context and the tender evaluation criteria so that intending suppliers are sufficiently informed to construct their response
- guidance to suppliers concerning the required content and format of response so that the 'customer' is provided with appropriate information on which to base evaluation.

Typical headings for an ITT will therefore be:

- executive summary
- introductory section (e.g. reason for request for tender, contact point and procurement process dates – when bids are due, when they will be evaluated and when product delivery will be required)
- business background and required scope of supply (e.g. is just software to be procured or is hardware and consultancy required?)
- statement of requirements (differentiating between mandatory and desirable items)
- procurement and evaluation process (e.g. need for presentations, demonstrations and reference site visits)
- instructions to suppliers (including form of proposal and conditions of contract).

While no important requirements should be left out of the document, it is advisable to limit their number as this will facilitate supplier responses, reduce the effort to evaluate the responses and make it easier to identify differences in the various suppliers' tenders. Furthermore it is sensible to avoid specifying the requirements to an extent that constrains the supplier from offering innovative solutions that might be equally or more acceptable in the business context.

Be sure to require or encourage explanatory text as it is not necessarily sufficient for a supplier to indicate compliance with a simple 'yes' answer. It is also important that the supplier indicates whether the required functions can be supplied 'out of the box' as standard, is a future development or requires specialized, 'bespoke' development.

The tender and evaluation process can be further eased by providing those tendering with an electronic copy of the ITT, and in particular the requirements section to which they should be asked to respond in a standardized way. The responses can then be incorporated into a spreadsheet or database with weightings applied to the different types of requirement to ease assessment and arrive at a shortlist of suppliers (as described later).

Identifying prospective suppliers

The ITT should be sent to a chosen list of suppliers, or advertised in some way to elicit response from the supplier community. In the former case there is a range of commercial directories and guides that can be consulted to identify prospective suppliers. It is wise to spread the net widely and not limit the search to one's own area of expertise. This increases the chances of finding an innovative solution better suited to meeting the project's requirements. On the other hand, the customer organization may have a preferred list of suppliers or a contract with an outsourcing firm that will act on their behalf in contacting the marketplace. For those working in the government or government-related sector within Europe there are special rules for procurement above a certain cost threshold (Système d'Information pour les Marchés Publics, n.d.).

To help ensure that the suppliers chosen to receive an ITT are most likely to offer solutions worthy of assessment, it is sensible to draw up a list of up to ten key functional requirements and contact candidate suppliers to see if they are likely to meet them. Also, confirm that their software will run on the required technical architecture (hardware, operating system and database) and obtain some cost estimates, for example based on a number of concurrent licences or the likely total number of users. The aim of this process is to arrive at a manageable number of prospective suppliers (say 12) who will receive the invitation to tender.

Assisting the suppliers

It is in the customer's interests to ensure that suppliers have all the information needed about the customer's business and requirements, in order to be able to tailor their responses accordingly. Nevertheless, there are always likely to be suppliers who wish to clarify aspects of the tender process or the content of the ITT itself. Where such questions are deemed appropriate, the questions (less their sources) and the answers should be circulated to all those who were invited to tender so as to ensure fairness to all.

Much of the need for such questions can be avoided by inviting the suppliers who have been approached to an open 'questions and answers' briefing meeting before the deadline for receiving their tenders.

Once a shortlist of suppliers has been established following detailed evaluation of the proposals (as described in the following section), it may be beneficial to provide a more structured and informative introduction to the customer's requirements and business background. This can help suppliers gain an understanding of the organization's information technology infrastructure, relevant systems and current activities. Sample data files and copies of internal procedures and policies can be provided as appropriate. This will assist the supplier in structuring their presentations and demonstrations if these are to form part of the remaining evaluation process.

Organizing the evaluation

The evaluation should be undertaken in line with an evaluation strategy and process approved before the ITT is distributed to prospective suppliers. This is the list of headings from a document detailing such a process:

* Introduction
* Objective
* Scope
* Evaluation strategy
* Assessment criteria
* Evaluation team
* Desk evaluation of tenders
* Reference site visits
* Supplier presentations
* Supplier demonstrations
* Contract clarification
* Report with procurement recommendations.

The evaluation process should be directed by some form of evaluation team involving representatives from all the stakeholders, for example:

* representatives from the internal project team
* user representatives from the various business sectors
* in-house information technology specialists

- in-house finance personnel (to assess solution costs)
- legal representation (to cover procurement and contractual matters).

Additional representatives can be co-opted, for example to undertake analysis of the financial aspects of the bidders as necessary.

Typical responsibilities of an evaluation team are to:

- develop the detailed evaluation process and scoring method
- identify and obtain additional assistance as needed for specific evaluation tasks
- report to the project board on the results of the evaluation and recommend the preferred supplier.

Evaluating the responses to the ITT

A typical tender evaluation process will comprise:

- assessment of suppliers
- initial filtering of proposals
- detailed evaluation of remaining proposals
- evaluation of shortlisted suppliers
- selection of supplier.

Initial filtering

The objective of the initial filtering process is to sift out those proposals that demonstrably fail the selection criteria, a key one of which is the ability of the proposed solution to meet mandatory requirements. The evaluation process should be able to cater for the possibility that none of the suppliers can meet these requirements. If such a situation arises, it may be necessary to revisit the prioritization applied when specifying the requirements and see if some of them truly justify the 'mandatory' tag.

This decision and the reasons for arriving at such a conclusion should be documented and approved, for example by the project board. This will provide part of the audit trail of the decision-making process.

The suppliers rejected at this stage should be told why they have not been chosen. Care should be taken to ensure that the reasons for rejection can be fully justified.

Detailed evaluation

Initially the detailed evaluation is a desk exercise examining the contents of the tender documents. For example the instructions to prospective suppliers for a document and records management system were to structure their tender document under the following headings:

- Executive summary
- Acceptance of ITT terms and conditions
- Proposed solution
- Project management and organization
- Supplier information
- Business details
- Customer base
- Reference sites of integrator and software supplier
- Compliance to detailed system requirements
- Cost breakdown.

The reason for requiring such a structure is that it eases the comparison of responses from the different suppliers.

Even where such strict guidance is not given, the ideal tender response should still be one that is readily comprehended and easy to navigate. It should be complete as regards conformance to the customer's instructions in the ITT and should present a solution that satisfies all those with a stake in the procurement process.

This is not always the case, and key information of interest to the customer may be buried in extensive promotional material and offerings from the supplier that are of little or no relevance to the requirements. For example one company bidding for a project was 'strong' in change management. It weighted its bid for consultancy input and cost in this direction even though the requirements and business actitivities of the department concerned did not merit such input. Largely as a result of this, the supplier lost out in the bidding process.

Where there is uncertainty in the submissions concerning key requirements it is sensible to seek clarification, although this approach is not appropriate where the submission is clearly defective. The detailed evaluation needs to focus on:

- the supplier that is proposing the solution
- the software solution (plus any technology and services that the customer has required to be delivered).

Evaluating the suppliers

While it is critical that the proposed software solution meets all the customer's requirements, the success of designing, constructing, implementing and supporting the solution will depend hugely on such factors as the quality and viability of the supplier. There are also more subjective elements to take into account. In reviewing the supplier's responses in the tender document, one will be seeking to satisfy oneself on all such matters, for example:

- *Does the supplier accept all contract terms and conditions outlined in the ITT?* It may raise concerns about working with those suppliers in the future if they raise extensive questions or objections at this stage.
- *Have they provided details of key names, addresses and contact points?* It is important to know who should be contacted if questions or clarifications need to be raised concerning the supplier's tender
- *Have they provided details of staff in key functions, site locations and years in operation?* Do they have adequate numbers of experienced staff in suitable locations dealing with such matters as software support and development and help desks? How long has the company been in operation?
- *What installed sites exist for their software?* It is important to have evidence that suppliers have existing customers running the type of software applications you are seeking.
- *Have they provided details of the support they will provide?* It is important that their proposed solution incorporates ongoing support.
- *Have they provided a full cost breakdown as requested?* If the customer has asked for concurrent or a specific number of licences, plus recommended hardware, suppliers should have structured their response accordingly
- *Have they provided evidence of sound project management approach and organization?* The ability of the supplier to manage its side of the project and interface with one's own organization's project team must be demonstrated. They must name their proposed project manager and supporting staff and provide evidence of their experience.

- *Have they outlined the total proposed solution to meet your requirements?* Simply indicating their compliance to specific functional requirements is an insufficient response. Suppliers should provide a narrative description of the proposed solution so that the customer can see how all the proposed elements interrelate.
- *Have they provided supporting information in addition to that specifically requested?* Such additional information may provide greater insight into the proposed solution, or offer innovative ways of satisfying requirements.
- *Have they provided relevant reference sites with contact and implementation details?* The 'proof of the pudding is in the eating' and a lack of relevant sites can indicate that the customer might be a guinea pig for the new software.
- *Are they ready and able to undertake the work?* Is the supplier over-committed with existing contracts?
- *Is the supplier response complete and does it provide the information requested?* This is a 'catch-all' assessment.

Over and above these more specific assessments there are more subjective questions to pose such as 'Could you do business with this supplier?' – the feel-good factor.

Assuming suppliers pass the detailed desk evaluation stage, they will be assessed further during any subsequent presentation and demonstration stages as covered later in this chapter.

Evaluating the proposed solution

This involves assessment of suppliers' responses to the detailed requirements in the ITT. As noted earlier, it is also helpful to list the requirements in spreadsheet form for completion by each supplier.

An evaluation spreadsheet can be built round the detailed requirements and other items to be assessed (excluding pricing), incorporating predefined weights for each assessment criteria. The weightings to be applied should be based on preferences expressed by the relevant stakeholders, for example user representatives attending requirements workshops.

With this approach the evaluation will involve copying the suppliers' response spreadsheets into the evaluation spreadsheet. The supplier responses to each requirement are then evaluated according to the criteria you have specified.

Each criterion is given a weighting to indicate its relative importance within each criteria set. A weighted score is calculated to provide results for individual criteria and for the response overall. To take an example in one project, the criteria comprised:

- compliance rating
- priority rating
- requirements category rating
- qualitative assessment.

For compliance, suppliers were requested to indicate their compliancy to each requirement by entering the appropriate letter as noted below:

S = Supported by standard feature of the product fully conforming at the proposal closing date.

C = Supported by configuring the standard package using in-built system features that enable end-users or in-house system administrators to configure the system readily.

B = Supported by using specially written bespoke software that does not form part of the standard product.

F = Supported by next or future release of software. The supplier must state the projected delivery date for items coded with an 'F' (future).

N = Not supported.

The priority rating was:

M = mandatory requirement
D = desirable requirement
I = request for information.

The last item related to requirements where suppliers were asked to provide additional information.

The requirements category enabled the relative importance of different types of requirements to be indicated. For example 'workflow' as a requirements category may be considered more important than 'searching and retrieval'.

Finally, the qualitative assessment was used to assess those responses where suppliers were not required to indicate compliancy; these included 'requests for information' and requirements concerning completeness of response and a 'feel-good' factor.

The weightings applied to these assessment criteria can be adjusted (if already agreed as part of the evaluation process) so that sensitivity analysis can be undertaken, for example to test the validity of the relative rankings of suppliers.

The pricing information in the tender cost breakdowns should be assessed separately by those evaluation team members concerned with financial aspects. At this stage pricing information should not be made known generally as the focus should be on satisfying the key requirements.

The detailed evaluation is typically undertaken independently by each of the assigned team members. The results from the evaluation are discussed and, as appropriate, agreed at a meeting of the full team who will agree any clarifications that may be required from individual suppliers. The results of the evaluation may be revised in the light of these responses with the final result being agreed at a meeting of the full team.

The foregoing process as described was employed on a real project and may appear to be largely mechanistic. However, the choice of supplier was and must not be based solely on the results of such a numerical calculation. The objective of the process is to rate the suppliers one against another so that a shortlist of two or three go forward to the final stages of the evaluation.

Supplier presentations and demonstrations

Shortlisted suppliers should be required to present their proposal highlighting its main features and benefits. The structure of the session should be predefined but allow some flexibility for the suppliers to structure their presentations. For this stage of the assessment, it is often useful to involve others and invite other staff from the organization to attend and provide their views in some structured form. The results of this assessment can be incorporated in the evaluation spreadsheet.

The elements of the presentation that might be assessed include the supplier's performance as regards general understanding, interpersonal skills, managing questions and their ability to work with the customer's personnel and culture. This session also provides the opportunity to learn about the supplier's proposed project plan and to question those staff, such as the supplier project manager, who will be involved in delivering the solution if their tender is successful.

More demanding is the requirement for suppliers to demonstrate their solution using real-world information and processes provided by the customer organization. The objectives of the demonstration are likely to include such factors as the system's ease of use and flexibility and the degree to which it provides the key functionality. For one customer this involved a whole day session for the two shortlisted suppliers covering key functionality and system administration according to predefined business scenarios. This enabled users to compare one supplier and its system with the other on the same day and reach a judgement over their relative merits.

Opening out these sessions to all prospective users also helps them feel part of the process and they may provide valuable feedback in addition to any formal assessment.

Reference site visits

Seeing the supplier's system operating in the way required and in a similar and real business environment is clearly highly desirable. Unfortunately it can be difficult for the supplier to find such a reference site. Even if one is found, the managers at that site may not wish to receive visitors because of the confidential nature of their operations, or because they have received too many such visits in the past and have had enough of them.

Where reference site visits are arranged, one should be aware that those visited may not readily admit their mistakes or the problems they encountered along the way. To help gather as much useful information as possible, prepare a list of questions for the reference site. Some may be specific to the software concerned, others will be of a general nature such as determining the quality of the supplier's support. The supplier may wish to be present at these visits. If this is agreed, ensure that there is an opportunity to question the site management on their own, out of earshot of the supplier.

As with the other assessment criteria, aim to come up with some scoring mechanism that helps provide a comparative rating of the suppliers.

Contractual negotiation and preferred supplier

Given that the evaluation process has resulted in the identification of preferred suppliers, the next stage is detailed contract negotiation. If it is a close call between two or more suppliers, it is sensible not to discard all but the one that came out on top. This provides a safeguard should contract negotiations fail with one's first choice. It is worth noting that the aim of the negotiating process is to arrive at an agreement satisfactory to both parties. If the customer causes the supplier to leave the completed negotiations dissatisfied in some way, then it is more likely that the supplier will stick strictly to the terms of the contract giving no latitude should the customer default from its obligations under that contract. This is not to say that one should avoid striking a hard bargain, but both parties should be able to leave the negotiations feeling that they have achieved their objectives.

In parallel with the negotiation stage, and before contract signing, it may be required to produce a supplier options paper for senior management. the paper should involve revising the business case with any cost–benefit appraisal that was undertaken then, and present an appraisal of the current situation with recommendations of the way forward with the preferred supplier.

In estimating the time that a procurement phase may take, it is often the case that the negotiation stage is allocated too little time. This is a critical stage of the procurement cycle and should not be skipped over lightly. Decisions made then become binding on contract signing and may be regretted later.

References

Hall, G. (2002) Requirements Management. In Association of Project Management, *Project Management Pathways*, High Wycombe, Association of Project Management.

Information Society Promotion Office. Available at http://europa.eu.int/ISPO/ida/jsps/index.jsp?fuseAction=showDocument&documentID=310&parent = chapter&preChapterID=0-17-49.

National Audit Office. Available at www.nao.gov.uk/intosai/edp/whyitprojectsfail.pdf.

Office of Government Commerce (2002) *Managing Successful Projects with PRINCE2*, London, The Stationery Office.

Public Record Office. Available at www.pro.gov.uk/recordsmanagement/erecords/2002reqs/default.htm.

Système d'Information pour les Marchés Publics. Available at http://simap.eu.int/EN/pub/src/welcome.htm.

Chapter 5

The care and feeding of software vendors for IA environments

JOHN GREGORY
United States Postal Service, USA

John Gregory provides a vivid example of the pitfalls in selecting a software supplier. His context was that he inherited a portal for which he needed to find some software that would improve the quality of the content management. John includes a wide-ranging analysis of the different influences on his selection, both internal and external to the organization. This paper is colloquial in style and many readers will identify with John's experience.

Five years ago I inherited an intranet information portal project. Content was loaded and delivered by a rudimentary, custom portal application. The search engine was delivered in a 6-inch square box containing disks and minimal documentation. Documents were manually, and inconsistently, indexed. Most documents lacked metadata. Nobody knew the system was broken until I started to play with it. The trade press was promising great things in portal, taxonomy and search technology. The train was leaving the station and I wanted to be on board.

You may find, or have found, one vendor that solves all your intranet presentation and administration issues. If so, don't stop reading yet. You may encounter problems you didn't know you had.

Just a few years ago, you could write a serviceable intranet portal program, which provided some information management functionality with a small team, in a few weeks. User expectations and baroque operating environments now make this neither practical nor desirable. Every software vendor in the IA space wants to sell you all-encompassing 'in a box' solutions. This ensures maximum revenue up front and places you at their mercy. The annual 'support' or 'maintenance' fee just gets you a registered licence. You'll be lucky to get a press release and a download URL for new versions. Some vendors are learning about customer relationship management; hopefully they will be the ones to survive.

Vendor choices may have been made long before your users' needs emerged. This may seem like an error, but is very common, mostly because decisions will have been taken on platforms, network topologies, and so on that will dictate future choices. Don't sacrifice your users to your (potential) vendor's business case. You, as an information manager, are in a war for attention. If you don't deliver the information critical to employees' success, they will be off surfing the net with one mouse click. Vendors will come and go, but the battle for attention has to be won every day. Workers in even the most hidebound bureaucracy confront new problems daily. If you're lucky, and prepared, you get the first shot at giving them answers.

Vendors want to nail your feet to the floor so you can never leave them. They are more likely to leave you. Most vendors wrestling for your cash today will not exist three years from now. That 'in a box' package could be your professional coffin. There isn't any insurance policy that will give you money to shop for replacement software. You want to pick winners, but you may have to settle for survivors.

This doesn't mean that you have to stick to the safe choices and stay off the bleeding edge. Today's experimental technology is tomorrow's commodity. Smaller vendors desperately need good customers. To the big guys you are revenue, to the small fish you could be the buzz that keeps them alive.

Enterprise management

Even US Government agencies, the largest collection of 'stovepipes' (an American expression for isolated inaccessible systems and information; the best example, 13 incompatible terrorist watch lists, inaccessible to all but a few people in each department) on the planet, now have to have an enterprise IT management plan. That doesn't mean somebody else makes all the decisions. It means you have to plan within some existing boundaries, if they make sense. For example, if all web servers are produced by Microsoft, it makes sense to stick to the standard. If an open source OS like LINUX is an option, you can save a lot in the purchase price; however, you have to factor in *much* higher administration costs, unless lots of folks are doing the same, when you can share experiences. Open source OS can run into real limitations on databases and search engines or taxonomy software may not work on the open source databases running under open source OSs. However, Microsoft SQL Server only looks at the world through Windows. Other high end databases, like Oracle, can run up the costs of a site very quickly. It is hardware hungry and requires a highly trained database administrator.

Mission creep

As IT budgets tighten, the bean counters are in search of return on investment (ROI) or enterprise-wide architecture as a way to pare down the number of programs running and 'align them with a business case'. While this is all positive up to a point, the risk is that innovation will be stifled. It will get harder to have best of breed, when there are only a couple of breeds. Beware the three letter acronyms (TLAs) as programs morph into 'Enterprise This or That' – see below for some examples. The word 'enterprise' should give you pause for thought. That's vendor-speak for 'You can never afford to leave us, we own you forever.' Accountants and IT careerists would love to get down to one vendor. They would never risk being fired and never have to make decisions.

A seemingly straightforward decision like selecting a database application software can have cosmic implications. In a network-centric environment, the database becomes the guiding reference or principle that all other software must navigate by. It can dictate operating systems, hardware vendors, even corporate culture. How did one program acquire such power?

First, it is the obvious repository for structured data. That means every time somebody takes the day off, buys new pencils or sells widgets to the waiting world, it goes into a database. All the basic functions of business would grind to a halt without a database interface. The post dot.com appetite for business intelligence deepens and narrows this relationship. The database can end up not only telling what you *do* know, but also dictating what you *can* know. The vendor's idea of data mining defines what is knowable.

With more content being accessed via an intranet, the database assumes a central role. Sites have few static HTML pages, they are dynamic sites, with pages and documents requested on the fly from a database. Migration to XML, with richer metadata, will increase the number of database transactions for any web display. Software agents on the horizon will autonomously and continually look for documents matching our profiles, or search for business conditions we must respond to. As web content marches towards enterprise content, server traffic will become dominated by agents, not employees. That's not as ominous as it sounds. If an agent worries about something 24/7, you don't have to. It offers the possibility of eliminating the search for information because your agent is examining the documents in your hard drive, trawling all changes to intranet and selected internet content and displaying summaries and links to new items. You don't have to open and close search programs or find bookmarks.

Portal software is already delivering some of these capabilities. The latest version of the product my portal uses has an option for a module displaying the user's e-mail inbox. You don't have to leave the portal to deal with people and information interactively. You can retrieve content, send it to colleagues and get their reactions. Imagine modules for agents, allowing more multitasking than your poor brain can handle.

Database-driven applications are proliferating. TLAs like customer relationship management (CRM) and enterprise resource planning (ERP) are all vying for your software dollars, and threaten to swallow your budget whole. It's like the early days of audio equipment, when manufacturers used proprietary connectors for components, or simply delivered a massive box with everything built in. When consumers demanded industry standards to use best of breed components, life got easier, and sound got better.

Unfortunately we're only just getting to the industry standards stage. The promise of Extensible Markup Language (XML) and web services have been delayed by three years of arm wrestling over the nuts and bolts that will make this a seamless architecture. The process of working out XML schemas and standards like Extensible Business Reporting Language (XBRL) will have to play itself out before we can discern the real significance of XML.

Crash test dummies

Microsoft set the crash test dummy standard for customer support and most vendors have sunk to this level. This is good for the bottom line, since they can sell you 'professional services' to make up for nonexistent documentation and technical support. As mentioned earlier, a few years ago a competent systems administrator could expect to be able to install an intranet program and get it to work. Today's programs call on so many system resources that even the developers can be stumped by some operating environments. Don't just ask the licence price, ask the rollout price. Assume that you are going to have to write a cheque to implement every new release. Your goal is to keep the cheque as small as possible, and have timely access to the people who can do the job. Being last in line to upgrade is not a good feeling. Get fixed, favourable support, maintenance and professional services rates as part of your contract.

Maintenance

Annual maintenance fees traditionally ran to 20% of the purchase price. That supposedly got you an upgrade path to new releases. Large corporations or government agencies can refuse to pay the 20% – the vendor will cave in to keep the revenue flow. The ploy today is to call a major release a new product and force customers to buy it all over again. This is risky. Maintenance is a routine expenditure, acquisition means a new contract negotiation and an opportunity for a hungry competitor to enter a low bid and steal the account. You can use a competitor's offer as a stick to beat your existing vendor down to a price you can live with.

Licences

One tactic of start-ups is the perpetual licence. They want your money *now*, and they will worry about getting more money later. You can build in an upgrade path, even specifying professional services rates for future rollouts. Vendors will give away a lot to get that initial contract. They will pay to get their foot in the door of a large organization, hoping for follow-on contracts or even an enterprise deal. They are staking out turf, battling for market share, and the perception of momentum in the marketplace.

Vendors are not above creative descriptions of contracts. A small implementation can be described in terms that might lead the unobservant to assume they were enterprise-wide. Another ploy is a schedule-like contract that guarantees departments a standard price and terms. This doesn't mean any department will actually purchase the software, but it can be hyped to resemble an enterprise contract. Competitors can be fooled into thinking they are locked out of an entire corporation or government agency, through issuing a 'creative' press release, fudging the terms of the contract.

Big institutions often sign deals for a proof of concept pilot project, followed by set rates for implementations. The implementations may never happen, but the vendor will beat the drum, claiming their software is vital to the operations of some global corporation. Claiming a company as a customer isn't really deceptive, the stuff is still running on some server somewhere, but nobody else wants to touch it. The 'customers' won't touch it because it doesn't fit the environment, or just doesn't work as advertised. Agencies involved in national security are often victims of this ploy. They test lots of technology. They cannot announce how well or badly it worked. It's a secret. The vendor could be claiming powerful installations, when in fact the agency has not purchased the complete rollout.

Pricing

The price is *never* the price. The sales person may need to meet a quota. Investors, venture capitalists or Wall Street analysts may have revenue or new account expectations, and sales executives need to meet them. They may be motivated by bonuses or live in fear of being fired. Either way, you can use it to your advantage. Getting a payment in by the end of a fiscal or calendar year or even a quarter can be worth dollars of discount.

Get a pricing structure that matches your use, not the vendor's revenue targets. Obviously, the easiest and best terms would be a perpetual enterprise licence, with no modification clause. Start-ups crave perpetual licences. You can take advantage of this addiction. As my portal vendor grew to become an industry leader, they dispatched a sales team to negotiate a licence renewal for a fabulous sum. Imagine their disappointment when I produced a signed contract with no changes foreseen. These are not impossible to get, but are becoming rare. A lot of vendors want to charge you for each processor running a product. For smaller installations, getting a second processor is a real advantage, so ask for a per server price, rather than paying double just for a two-processor box. The vendor is often willing to work out the combination of processors, servers and client seats that you really need and come in with the price it takes to make a sale.

Early adopters

Smaller vendors often don't have a quality control department. The developers that put something together are then asked to try to break it. They are unlikely to be able to switch gears and think like a user. They can't forget what they learned in the development process and they don't see the world from a user's perspective.

An example: a sales representative from a very hot start-up begged to run a web demo of their product for me, while having their chief technical officer (CTO) on a conference call. The CTO was explaining their program's document 'metadata repository'. I asked whether it was 'Dublin core' compatible. There was a long silence. The CTO had no idea what metadata meant to real users, and no customer had asked what elements could be included. The sales rep grabbed a piece of paper and printed in large letters, '*Just tell me what you want to pay.*' When you are the best (or only) customer, you get the best price. You are the vendor's market research department and quality control department. Just because that help is priceless doesn't mean you shouldn't expect to be rewarded. When you give something of value, they have to give you something in return.

Another example: when I was looking at portal technology, none of the offers ran on UNIX and nobody would talk about XML. Finding the guys who were writing a JAVA-based program and were serving on the OASIS standards committee was part luck and part persistence. Indexing or taxonomy software was limited to three choices. Two years later, some analysts put the number of taxonomy vendors as high as 70. Very few will survive the next two years, despite the rush to implement taxonomies.

Getting in on the ground floor of intranet portal and taxonomy technology allowed me to provide powerful online functionality at a fraction of the price others would pay. The good news is that this is not a one time deal. Vendors are rushing to add capabilities to gain competitive advantage. Each major release is a larger, more complex program. Being a beta tester for Version 4.0 may give you as much leverage as those that suffered with Version 1.0.

Source code

Companies are disappearing at an alarming rate. Any software contract should include the right to the source code if the company goes out of business or is acquired. With a viable vendor, the last thing you want to do is monkey with the code and make support impossible. If the company disappears, or the product is rolled into some buyer's gargantuan package, you want to have the option of managing your own upgrade path. It can be tricky, but it can be a lot better than starting over with a less desirable vendor, or watching the software grind to a halt with operating environment changes.

Being a reference account

All customers are not equal. The best customer is using every feature of a program and asking for more. If you are stress testing a program every day, the vendor needs you. If you are searching a database the size of Jupiter in nanoseconds, you are money in the bank to your vendor. If you are outside the US Federal Government, you may be able to discuss the performance of your contractor in sufficient detail to reassure nervous prospects. If you are not shy, and can speak in complete sentences, trade press writers will beat a path to your door. Analyst firms will ply you with free conference passes if you can pull together 45 minutes worth of shamelessly self-promoting PowerPoint slides. The wine, women and song incentives may be a thing of the past, but free food and drink and a few days away from the office are better than nothing. Besides, you cannot fail to learn something at a conference. If your employer has given in to the human resources fad of requiring so many hours of 'training' each year, while providing a laughable budget, the presentation-for-pass tradeoff can get you out of a jam. You're getting your ticket punched with a minimum of pain.

Good press can do a lot for budget-starved programs. Most geeks (computer specialists) toil in well deserved obscurity. Your vendor *lives* for the opportunity to get free publicity, and if it can make you look like a genius, well, who are you to hide from the spotlight? Geek envy is the greatest risk here. Some programmer may get his colon twisted because a 'know-nothing project manager' gets the attention, while he slaves away cranking out Geeks vs. Suits, the stuff of every 'Dilbert' cartoon.

In conclusion . . .

DO:

- evaluate your operating environment first
- seriously and formally examine user needs

- negotiate a licence best suited to your installation, not the vendor's business model
- get some kind of source code rights
- leverage your organization's buying power and prestige to minimize maintenance costs and exploit the vendor's need for a good reference.

DON'T:

- use what another department is using because somebody thinks it is a 'standard'
- pay list price
- forget to include services for installation, configuration, training and support.

Chapter 6: a case study

A flexible architecture for managing current awareness

SABINE KRUSE
Henkel KgaA, Germany

MANFRED HAUER
AGI-Information Management Consultants, Germany

Introduction

Henkel is a major global player in adhesives and surface technologies, established 126 years ago. It makes products in the fields of laundry and home care, cosmetics and toiletries, consumer and professional adhesives. There is a large consumer market with brand names like Persil, Pritt, Fa, Theramed, Vernel, Dixan, Schwarzkopf and many others, as well as industrial markets.

The strength in these markets is based on research and development, located in Germany. This internal knowledge community requires an 'enabling environment'. One part of this environment is the exchange of research results by asking, answering, listening and writing. For the 'written' part a library was installed with monographs, periodicals and patents. Much later a team of information professionals was installed around the managers – a business library. Today both science and business information are integrated in the Henkel InfoCenter using all kinds of media for storing knowledge and informing internal clients.

Periodicals remain a major channel for exchanging knowledge and keeping up to date in global scientific communities and most of our 5000 internal readers prefer printed publications to electronic versions. Only a small proportion of the periodicals currently in use at Henkel are online (120 titles). Henkel has signed contracts for access to all the e-journals that are available. Of course there is a move to e-journals, but the current role of paper versus online can be easily outlined by a comparison of the ratio of our total annual costs, which is 20:1.

Henkel uses Lotus Notes and Domino worldwide and has more than 30,000 Notes clients. As in most other global companies, other platforms are available and browser-oriented solutions are everywhere. Notes and Domino was already used in the InfoCenter by two programmers writing internal applications. The move from a mainframe-based circulation management system to a new one, based on Domino, was a difficult task. One of the very few German specialists in information centres as well as Domino technology was AGI – Information Management Consultants. The AGI model for circulation management was tested in pilot projects with a full data set and no performance problems occurred, but finishing the final version took several months. AGI has a modular approach and circulation management is just a part of their concept for information centres. The AGI Information Center runs with many more than 30 modules at different Domino clients. The application reported here has been running fully for two years. Figure 6.1 shows the home page for readers, which gives access to printed or online periodicals, loose-leaf material, yearbooks, software, patents and disclosures, as well as other information services.

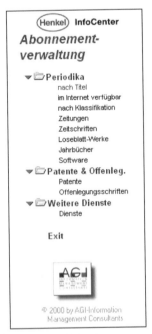

Fig. 6.1   The AGI Information Center
home page for readers

Benefits

Despite a tense worldwide economic situation, Henkel is a successful company with steadily increasing profits. Its success is a result of several factors. One of them is the fact that employees are always well informed in their professional fields thanks to the Henkel InfoCenter. Henkel's professional information department existed before the concept of knowledge management was invented.

Henkel's InfoCenter uses different tools and suppliers to organize the flow of information every day. One of the tools is the central access point available online for all Henkel InfoCenter clients for all periodical or annual subscription information products.

Reader's account – self-administration

Readers open their current accounts online (see Figure 6.2), whether they wish to order or to cancel new publications or services or simply require a summary of costs and services. Services are charged internally, and readers can manage their budgets via the system.

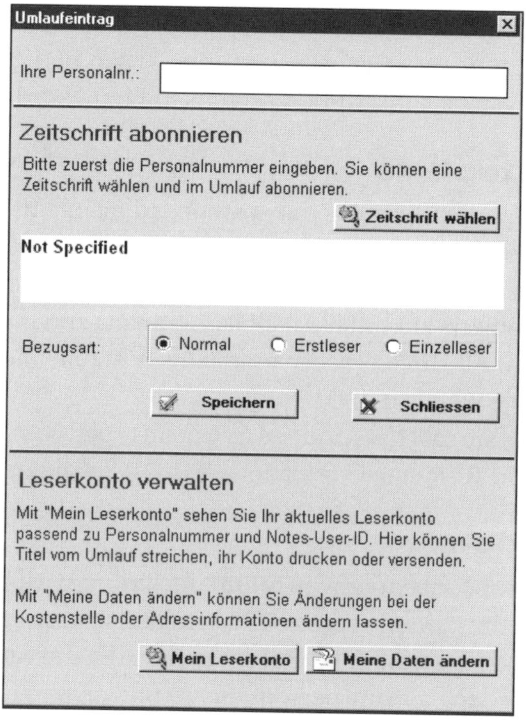

Fig. 6.2 The Henkel reader account

All users can personally manage their reader accounts by simply using the button that opens the 'self-administration' menu. At the top they can select a publication, below, the level of subscription, and save it. They can check the reader account below and send updates about personal data. The system also allows a third party to act on behalf of the reader, if they wish.

Originally, the application was conceived for journal circulation management. The periodical department at Henkel organizes the purchase and the distribution of almost 2500 newspapers and/or magazines as well as quite a number of loose-leaf publications, yearbooks and other periodicals. Altogether approximately 6700 copies have to be dispatched to readers and groups of readers, both within the factory premises in Düsseldorf and worldwide. The periodicals they read are managed centrally in the Düsseldorf headquarters, but all physical items are sent straight from publisher or bookseller to their home offices. The circulation of patent materials, specifications and disclosure documents are also managed by the periodicals department.

In addition, readers may purchase user IDs for various databases with this system. The same applies to GrapeVine, a kind of Spider (agent), which constantly scans the internal databases for appropriate topics and then sends links to relevant information directly to the mail-boxes of users. IntelligentNEWS, the new Henkel news portal, is part of the 'Other Services' offered (see magazine subscription screens in Figures 6.4 and 6.5).

The architecture

In order that the system remains transparent and maintains a high performance and stability under Lotus Notes and Domino it is best to divide the application into several Lotus Notes and Domino databases. In a first step, three database objects are sufficient: persons, media and links between persons and media. All three objects are relatively stable and not subject to continual change when so divided.

The databases are called IC Address & Contact (persons), IC Media Directory (media) and IC Media Circulation (links). (See Figure 6.3.)

Subscription

A person may subscribe to any medium, including periodicals, journals, patents, disclosures, online access, CD services, library access and news. A person can also subscribe to several types of media and each type of media can be subscribed to by many persons. So we find an n:m relation and each

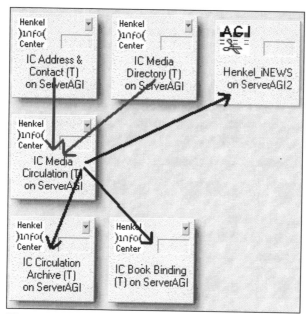

Fig. 6.3 IC Media Circulation links readers to
different media

link represents exactly one subscription or order – the connection between
person and medium. As mentioned earlier, a user can subscribe directly
online or ask a third person or the internal information centre to do so in
their name. The list of publications subscribed to by an employee can be
transferred to someone else without that person having to subscribe again.

Each person and each medium is controlled by a number of rules,
which means that the programming is complex. For example, for each type
of medium the maximum number of persons with access to a physical copy
is defined. While there is no specific rule in this case, the general principle that is applied is that every reader should be able to receive a copy on
time – the limits fixed depend on the experience of the internal employees, the publication interval and, of course, the budget available. These limits
can be changed dynamically.

Figures 6.4 and 6.5 show two parts of the magazine subscription screen.
The first screen (Figure 6.4) includes all the information that is needed to
manage a publication. The second screen (Figure 6.5) sets out the major
information elements for subscription management. All the programming
fields are set in English, but the user front end is German.

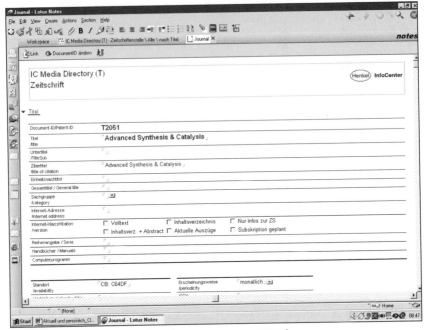

Fig. 6.4 Magazine subscription screen, part 1

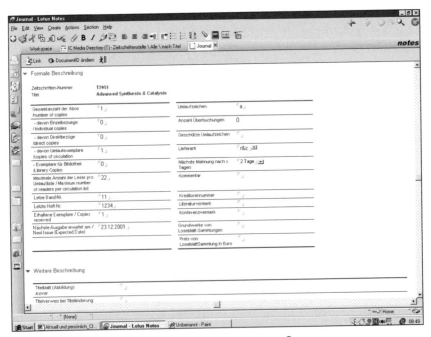

Fig. 6.5 Magazine subscription screen, part 2

Circulation management

Any number of readers may use one copy for any number of days. However, if somebody pays extra, that person can be registered as an 'Individual Reader' - as is frequently the case for daily newspapers - or as 'Number One' reader of a circulation list. The last reader on the circulation list will be the information centre, an internal library or a person who wishes to collect a back file of the publication.

The circulation lists are automatically sorted according to buildings, floors and room numbers. However, the information centre is able to adapt this automatic sorting by hierarchy and rank of employees. It is also often easier if external employees and other readers receive their copies directly, which means the information centre orders, pays for and cancels the publication, but it is always sent directly to the reader by the publisher or bookseller.

Paper can sometimes be lost, forgotten or damaged. Therefore, it is possible that a copy may go missing from the circulation list. The software is able to recognize this when the next issues are registered. A replacement is instantly ordered via e-mail and the new copy - easily recognized by its barcode - automatically dispatched to waiting readers if necessary.

As several hundred newspapers are treated every day there could be many entries in the system. However, the IC Media Circulation database does not register each issue individually, but considers the complete series. When all issues are present the series is complete. Consequently, only the exceptions have to be taken care of. Using the principle of the exception reduces overhead costs drastically. The typical cycle defines the time the next issue of a publication should arrive - if it doesn't, the journal's status is flagged as 'exceptional'. If the copy is then delivered, the 'exceptional' status no longer exists and the flagging disappears from the database.

Since one person cannot be expected to read a large amount of material every morning, each circulation list printout can show the order in which each copy is to be distributed.

The binding module and e-journals

A separate database manages binding. Any publication that is to be bound is taken out of circulation by the software when the issues are returned and 'lent' to bookbinding. The number of volumes to be bound per year can be fixed as desired. A reader can find out whether there is a bound copy of a publication by consulting the IC Media Directory. Only certain expensive, scientific magazines are bound. The number of bound volumes is being steadily reduced as e-journals are more commonly available.

There are 120 e-journals in the IC Media Directory and they include links to the full texts of the journals. Employees can open the IC Media Directory and read it online (see Figure 6.6). Library and other authorized staff have access to all the databases and use many very specific views.

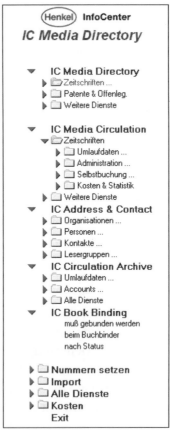

Fig. 6.6   Henkel's IC Media Directory

The accounting database

Cost centres are invoiced and each type of delivery (to a direct, single, first or circulation reader) has an internal price. An average price is fixed for most publications. However, if one of the magazines or one of the services is particularly expensive, the costs are allocated directly to the actual readers. This means that the price can vary from month to month, depending on the number of readers. Specimen copies are always free and some readers or units may receive certain publications free of charge. A complex set of rules is necessary in order to transmit the cost data to the internal SAP enterprise control application at the end of each month. However, more and more statistics are being directly implemented in Lotus Notes. All accounting data is automatically saved in the archive database when exported.

Configuration

The Henkel InfoCenter is designed for a distributed and decentralized environment with a variable number of modules. This means some modules can be run on one server only or on several servers as duplicate databases, or as separate modules related to one location only.

Henkel has a test environment and a production environment; AGI's German office also has a test environment and the AGI programmers based in India have their own development and testing environment.

The Henkel brands Cognis and Ecolab were sold to other owners and the system has been made available to them; only a few updates to the configuration were needed.

Setup defines the communication structure between databases' modules. It defines lists like taxonomy terms; administration team members; default fees; default addresses; default forms for Word 2000; printing features like circulation sheets, labels, and standard letters and faxes; and default text used for ordering or reminders sent to publishers, bookshops, booksellers or readers.

intelligentNEWS – an integrated news portal

Initially, in 2000, it was not planned to integrate several Henkel databases belonging to the news area into the central database. AGI's intelligentNEWS database was installed in 2002. Here data from Factiva (Reuters and Dow Jones), several Thomson Dialog databases, German Presse Monitor (PMG) and press clippings are integrated. More than 500 items are managed every day with push (automatic delivery through 'rules'), pull (retrieval by users) and powerful print facilities. Automatic indexing and machine translation is built in and a web interface is available. Personalization is possible via the built-in search engine GTR and other features. Portals to other

suppliers like Dialog NewsEdge or Deutsche Presseagentur (DPA, the leading German press agency) are built in, but not yet in use, until costs and
content have been agreed. This database can also be used to create an indi-
vidualized service like a printed newspaper.

Figure 6.7 shows a screen within intelligentNEWS that is only accessible to administrators. In this view the automatic indexing is visible in the
grey, green and golden columns. View is sorted by rubrics, defined by administrators and automatically merged with the rubrics of external sources. Some
titles have an attachment – a PDF image will start when opening automatically.

Figure 6.8 shows the templates behind the final design of intelligent-
NEWS. All the programming can be tested.

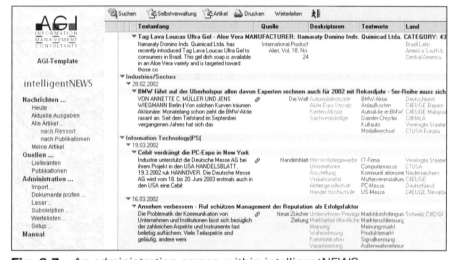

Fig. 6.7   An administration screen within intelligentNEWS

Advantages of Lotus Notes and Domino

'It is not possible to do that with Notes' is what the Henkel internal application designers thought when it was time to replace the mainframe-based
circulation application with a distributed environment. The application has
been running on Notes without problems for the last 18 months, so this
assumption was probably not quite correct. That it does work is probably
also a result of the data model and its application. The data model introduced here can almost certainly be implemented with a relational database,
but other factors defined the choice of Notes:

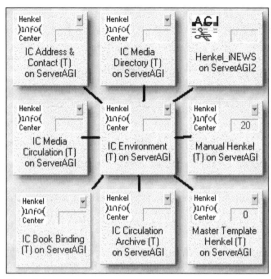

Fig. 6.8   The templates behind the final
design of intelligentNEWS

- Lotus Notes and Domino was already a Henkel group standard; the infrastructure was already available without additional costs for programs,
  installation or training.
- Notes Client was usually preferred to a browser, as observed for other
  applications. It is much cheaper to program a Notes interface because
  it takes less time than programming a web browser interface.
- Henkel InfoCenter had already programmed various associated applications under Notes, such as a metadata structure about all the activities
  of the department.
- Lotus Notes was ideal for an internationally distributed project team.
  The code was defined in India, the data model at AGI in Germany and
  the finer specifications and data came from Henkel. A distributed
  know-how and development environment has four people at the core
  of the project: two at AGI and two at Henkel.

It was possible to develop the complete application with the standard
tools of the Lotus Notes and Domino development environment, primarily Lotus Script. intelligentNEWS also uses Java and Javascript.

Project communication

Two-thirds of all IT projects fail is what we learn from general computer science experience. This did not happen in this project. Several easily measurable factors and 'soft' factors account for this:

- Aims were clearly defined during several meetings and through specifications.
- The costs were defined for the first operational version and the planned delivery date was respected.
- The core team, with four persons, was small.
- The staff of Henkel InfoCenter were integrated right from the beginning.

Problems were identified during the first tests that were carried out by the InfoCenter staff – at the time everything was completely new and not yet operating optimally. Despite all efforts made in the specifications, it was impossible to recognize and formulate all the necessary rules and exceptions. Tuning was still required because not all functions operated to the desired standard under normal working conditions (especially printing).

All tasks are documented in IC Task Management, a Lotus Notes database, which can be used by all AGI clients simultaneously. However, clients can only access their own data.

Henkel's opinion

Journal administration under Lotus Notes has brought many advantages to our company and is valued by the employees and the clients as a positive change. The system is very flexible and easy to handle for the user. People got used to the new system without difficulty and, more important, data import from previously available databases into the new system worked well. After overcoming a few start-up problems the program is now very stable.

Support to resolve problems and change or add programs is provided quickly and is straightforward as regards communication and application. Lotus Notes is a widely used tool at Henkel and therefore clients had no specific fears about using it, as might have been the case had another system been chosen.

The greatest advantage is the transparency of Lotus Notes for the clients. Every user has access to the actual list, status and monthly cost of any service (magazines, databases and other information services) subscribed to via the Henkel InfoCenter. Users are very happy to administer their reading material and do so effectively, which means that Henkel saves time and money.

Role of AGI as an external partner

There are organizational changes, new requirements and new ideas all the time, and AGI is being asked to make changes accordingly. Some are discussed face to face; all are also discussed via Lotus Sametime with the programmers in India in order to agree a detailed technical specification. A way that this information architecture might be developed in future might be by integrating library management. Some forms, views, agents and navigation are missing in the IC Media Directory. Ordering and lending modules have to be added – and a new library management system is ready. Another path of improvement could be the scanning, OCR and automatic indexing (based on CAI-Engine) of tables of contents of books. AGI's 'intelligentCAPTURE' would be suitable, and is already running in large public libraries. Tables of contents of periodicals are already integrated via SwetsScan and intelligentNEWS. In addition, automatic indexing of other internal or external documents could easily be added, as it is already running for press articles in intelligentNEWS. For improving the quality of human or automatic indexing, a Henkel-specific taxonomy or thesaurus and topic maps could be added, managed in IC INDEX. Another module that is available is IC Search Management, which supports information professionals in ad hoc search tasks: user data comes from IC Address & Content and some media information comes from IC Media Directory or the IC Media Directory guides the researcher to internal or external sources relevant for the research task. IC Search Management has documentation of research work – which is indexable with IC INDEX based taxonomies or thesauri – or automatically with the CAI engine. Additionally, authoring tools for managing contents have been operational with other clients for some years and could be added.

Finally, the role of AGI is to keep all these technical containers and workflow concepts up to date, which is a never-ending story. If the architecture is well designed and the platform powerful enough this is just additional work and there are no particular intellectual problems to be addressed.

Part 3
Managing metadata

Part 3

Preface to Part 3

The common definition of metadata – data about data – is deceptively cosy. It is also not true, as some seem to believe, that metadata refers only to those data that are captured automatically. In fact, metadata sets are as complex as may be needed or chosen, though it is a tenet of this preface that the information architect should strive for simplicity and an acceptable level of effectiveness. However, whether simple or complex, 'metadata management' may be considered to be at the heart of information architecture.

In principle, metadata can include any of the various attributes of an information object. Traditionally, in the LIS domain we have been used to dealing with two classes of metadata: cataloguing, the description of the physical aspects of a document; and indexing and classification, the description of the subject content or 'aboutness' of a document. Some of these metadata elements can be used as search keys, while some are purely descriptive. Over time, a range of *de facto* standards have been established to deal with such metadata in the library world, for example the MARC format for bibliographic records, the Anglo-American Cataloguing Rules for physical description and the Dewey Decimal Classification for subject description.

In the area of data processing, corresponding standards for record formats and description of data elements are commonplace, some of which such as the dd/mm/yy format for entering dates may be used in bibliographic work (though one should note the reverse order of the d and m elements in the USA). One could say, in passing, that the Y2K threat was essentially a failure to recognize that a specific item of standardized metadata might no longer behave properly at the onset of the new millennium. Standard forms of entries are features of data dictionaries and the authority files of libraries and information services, and the various professionals engaged in information processing all have access to a wide range of standards for such things as transliteration and country and language codes, but widespread standardization of subject description does not exist.

In the relatively new world of the enterprise-wide digital information space, the range of possible metadata types is wider and the metadata problem becomes correspondingly more complex. What the information object is (cf. cataloguing) may now include, for example, its purpose and intended audience. There is also a far wider range of document types to be dealt with, as internally and externally produced documents converge at the user interface; particularly if one considers the increasing ability to include multimedia in the information access and delivery process. What the information object is about (cf. indexing and classification) continues to be a central problem, exacerbated by the requirement to satisfy the search demands at individual workstations of a wide community of users, including the research, marketing, legal and financial functions, each of which might be looking for the same document for different reasons, and with different 'languages'. At least a third class of metadata has entered the scene, a class that might be called 'administrative'; this includes metadata relating to who owns (as opposed to who generated) a document, who has responsibility for updating that document (version control), security level information and data relating to digital rights management. (The design and use of metadata in film libraries and museums is even more complex, involving metadata such as camera angles, preservation of specific artefacts, and so on.)

There are two further complications to be considered in metadata management: the first is that the concept of a document is of a physical entity, but that content (which needs to be managed) consists of discrete parts of what may be printed out as a document. The second is that the value, status or meaning of metadata may change over time. Both of these factors can be exemplified in a potential problem in coping with the UK Freedom of Information Act, one that may turn out to be theoretical, but has been identified by at least one government department in the UK. The responsibility for claiming exemption lies with the author of the document, but exemption might be valid for only part of the document. Furthermore, after some initially indeterminate period of time the portion of the document not released might no longer qualify for exemption.

A guiding principle in information architecture is to appreciate its potential complexity, but to look for 'quick wins' in design and implementation. It is impossible to reinvent the organization or to clear the ground for a fresh start. As far as possible the architecture, and the supporting metadata management, should be kept simple while concentrating on priority issues. Leloup, in Chapter 2, has rightly drawn attention to the 'cut and paste' activity that results in the loss of agreement on what constitutes the reference document. The attendant risk, arising from poor design and control of metadata, when that document turns out to be a contract with a customer or a report to a government inspectorate should be a frightening thought. An adequate understanding of what is needed, which may be gained from information modelling, must then be turned into a sensible specification for software procurement, as Wiggins describes in Chapter 5. If the software is incapable of handling the metadata as intended, it is just as likely that there is something wrong with the specification as that the fault is with the metadata design.

Part 3.1 deals with the vehicles for carrying metadata, and Sturdy and Bater both draw attention to the critical necessity of metadata design and the proper and consistent labelling of concepts. (The < > tags of an XML construct constitute a 'floating' field, and controlling what is entered between the tags is no less important than it is with databases.) Underlying the concept of standards for carrying metadata is also the usual conflict between competing standards (as reported by Bater with reference to topic maps and the RDF), and the relationship between them. For example, the DOI *de facto* standard suggests using Dublin Core for carrying subject description, while Dublin Core suggests using DOI if unique identification is required. Both send the designer elsewhere for terminology standards of which, of course, there are many. Hence the need for flexibility and interoperability in metadata systems, and here Dextre Clarke discusses one particular and ambitious attempt to deal with the possibility of conducting searches across a range of repositories all using different indexing languages. Mapping continues to be a very real problem, and the Government Category List approach is just one of many. All the case studies point out that the compilation of structured vocabularies and mapping between them involves hard intellectual work, where computers may assist in the processes, but are not yet capable of replacing human interpretation. Dextre Clarke draws attention to the fact that most metadata must be assigned by humans, and that it is increasingly the author who is being asked to do that. This is causing a problem in many organizations, one that may be met to some extent by the provision of templates for metadata selection. Some of these are versions of the search taxonomy presented to the end user.

The concept of the semantic web has caught many people's attention, and anyone who has read anything concerning the detail will have noticed the vital part that will be played by metadata. If computers are going to be able to communicate intelligently and accurately with each other, then meaning and inference will be necessary, and both will be provided by ontologies whose terminological components will be supported by artificial intelligence. Until the time when the semantic web will become a reality, information architecture problems will continue to be solved by the establishment of increasingly powerful metadata management supported by 'enriched thesauri' and taxonomies that will contain more information about words and their meanings, and defined relationships between them. These will be used to enhance navigation and search and mapping between different systems.

B. M.
A. G.

Part 3.1

Managing interoperability

Chapter 7

Why and when would you use XML in text-based systems?

DEREK STURDY

Granite & Comfrey, UK

Introduction: from cult to working tool

Some years ago, a conference was held to discuss the handling of lots of text. The organization that called the conference was commercial, not academic, and there were serious issues to discuss. Several of those present wore badges, clearly labelled 'SGML or DIE!' During one of the discussions, a suggestion was made which was answered with chilling intensity by one of these badge wearers with the words:'But that would compromise the purity of the SGML [Standard Generalized Markup Language]'; (not 'If you do that, it won't work'; nor 'Here is an alternative way to accomplish what you want'). It seemed to me then, and it seems to me now, that those people, with their bizarre motto and their babble about purity, had lost the plot.

Elevating a mark-up language to cult status was very tempting, because all the right things were in place. The language was arcane – all that stuff about entities and elements. While the ordinary evangelists and practitioners were lowly souls, the high priests attained prestige and status. The ultimate purpose was impenetrable to the layman without long explanations. The rituals (document type definitions or DTDs) required long training, and the resulting sacred texts used secret punctuation of bitter complexity. Best of all, the marked-up documents were presented in different colours, with mystic headings, strongly reminding readers of the missals, prayer books and worship books of all kinds that they may have used in their youth (or still use).

All this did no favours to anyone. As the 'analysis' and 'DTD writing' phases extended for longer and longer periods of time, costs and managerial impatience rose in step. Except in the most rarefied circles, one question started to gain increasing urgency and frequency: 'What is all this work and expense actually doing for us?' The reaction against the high priests was in danger, at least in commercial circles, of killing off the concept of marking up anything except appearance (via Hypertext Markup Language or HTML). Systems loosely based on the artificial intelligence (AI) research of the late 1980s and early 1990s offered tempting alternatives, with the attractive proposition that everything that was needed could be done by amazingly clever software, and all those gurus and editors could be harmlessly sacked.

What saved the day for commonsense was the arrival of cheap relational database systems that could handle both text and metadata. Effectively this happened in 1999 with the commercial arrival of Microsoft's Structured Query Language (SQL) Server 7 (the 'October Revolution'). More or less simultaneously, XML took over from SGML as the practical approach for most people with text to manage. The costs of entry to managing text properly dropped substantially.

The argument of this chapter
Exchange

Extensible Markup Lange (XML) is above all the language of data exchange. You could argue that the X should stand for eXchange every bit as much as eXtensible, Where SGML describes (and prescribes the order of) content, and HTML describes form, XML provides the way to describe how content and form might be.

The key element of flexibility that XML provides is that it allows us to carry out a vital change in how we edit, handle, present and preserve text; we now have a way of marking up textual content in ways defined long after the content itself was loaded into any kind of database, for purposes that were undefined or even unguessed-at when the content was created or when it was initially processed.

It is not difficult to grasp the scale of the revolution in thinking that this makes possible. XML has the wonderful advantage that it simplifies and therefore reduces the cost of text processing, compared with working with SGML. But there are corollaries and inevitably disciplines attached to making the most of the opportunity.

Metadata

The flexibility that XML can be used to exploit requires the existence of properly constructed metadata. The metadata may be:

- *structural* the shape and hierarchy of content
- *administrative* the stuff about titles and authors and dates
- *referential* the references within text to people, organizations, other documents, websites and databases ('citation')
- *conceptual* what the content is about and what type of content it is ('subject indexing', 'classification', 'categorization')
- *processual* where the content fits in an ordered argument, in a work process, in a time sequence.

In order to be useful and flexible, the metadata must be standardized. Only in this way can the local idiosyncrasies of synonyms, the development of organizational names and their spawning of child organizations, and the all-important matching of like to like for updating and cross-reference, be handled.

Taxonomies and authority files

These are simply the way in which the metadata is standardized. Other advantages accrue from well organized taxonomies – hierarchies provide drill-down access for users. The opportunities of adding metadata to the taxonomies (it had to come) are discussed later in this chapter. For our purposes, the point is the standardization. It simply does not matter what the terms in the taxonomies are, so long as they are always related to the same thing (if you, the user or editor, don't like a particular term, that's what synonyms, obsolete terms and so on manage for you).

Relational databases

Again, there is no magic about these – almost all readers of this chapter will already be using relational databases. What relational databases do is to allow the storage of metadata elements, standardized against taxonomies and authority files, as 'IDs', and to relate the metadata to the correct positions in text and to other metadata. The databases themselves can thus grow and add vertical (time-based) and horizontal (cross-referenced) dimensions to the original text as more and more text is processed and the appropriate metadata is identified and entered into the database tables.

The key point for information architects is that this is how text content is made dynamic without endless back-editing. If you tag up content completely, you freeze it; if you just mark up the 'nodes', and use relational databases to store the metadata, you keep it live and active.

Relational databases drive mark-up, not vice-versa
The October Revolution in editing

The key rationale behind the 'October Revolution' was:

- Future proofing text was essential. Experience showed that publishing, storage and retrieval systems were all radically changing at increasingly short intervals. Each new 'system' therefore simply had to include a methodology for extracting the stored intellectual capital painlessly, ready for the next system.
- A strong element in future proofing was that the exact nature of the changes and upgrades was proven to be unpredictable. Therefore constraints applied to the management of the current text systems in the wrong way would inevitably create dinosaurs. Flexibility as well as ease were vital considerations. Solutions to this conundrum had to be cheap enough to be carried in the current work, and standardization of metadata rather than of document mark-up proved to be the way to go.
- Almost all text was destined for presentation to readers by way of more than one medium; conventional printing, printing via a word-processing package, editing and composing using specific computer applications and web browsing remain the most common. For some users, the ability to sell or exchange content was a core requirement – so it had to be easy for the recipient to acquire the content. Easy ways of making the text suitable for uses that had not yet been thought of, or defined, was essential.
- All text editors that involved the actual mark-up of text, completing the tags and checking the validity of the mark-up and text structures (parsing), imposed complex training needs on the users. Most authors were unlikely to submit to the training or apply it if they did.

The key points about the 'October Revolution' were:

- It became easy to identify metadata elements by reference to tax-onomies and authority files instead of typing the entries by hand into 'fields'.
- It became easy to relate like (text, graphics, etc.) to like, and later to ear-lier, without back-editing, because of the XML.
- Most of the actual mark-up of text could be stored in the database instead of in the actual text, so editing became hugely easier, and actual tag content became much shorter.
- The key mark-up job becomes simply indicating a place in a document, or some actual text, and identifying it against the content of the data-base tables.
- The mark-up language (XML) simply defined how to create the rules, not what the rules were – a vital advance.
- Tagging of text, when required, could therefore be completed automat-ically to a wide variety of different standards, including varying DTDs, by 'filling up' the tags from the database tables.
- As a corollary, the actual content of tags could be updated once in the database, instead of many times within the actual tags in all the text (for example, company names, which change with expensive fre-quency).
- BUT the data model of the database effectively controlled the range of variation possible in the schemas or DTDs that could be used to com-plete automated tagging from the content of the database.

Information nodes come into their own

We have all known for a long time that information nodes are the key to getting text 'right' where 'right' means 'usable and useful in its context' . The things that change, and the things that cross-refer, form the nodes; each can be the centre of a (usually temporary) web of information – as in 'What else do we know about this organization?', 'What else do we know about this subject?' or 'What else has this author written and who has written what about this author?' Identifying the node has always been the clever bit. Where rule-based systems and the artificial intelligence approach alike have bro-ken down is in coming up with a virtually fool-proof way of making sure that such identifications are comprehensive. This is where taxonomies and authority files have made their mark. These are the new rules:

1   Mark the fact of the information node in the text. Here are examples of how an author might be written in the text: 'John Doe'; 'Professor J A Doe'; 'John' (as in 'John's memo to the Faculty'); 'the Secretary of the Tiddlywinks Club' (who happens to be Prof. Doe this year). This can be as simple as inserting a bookmark round some text in Microsoft Word.

2   Look up the correct identification of the node – for instance an author, a company name, a journal citation, a subject term – in an independent list of the correct and detailed way to describe the particular person, organization, thing or concept. An example from an authority file of people might be 'Doe, Professor John Aloysius, born 1947' and link tables might relate Prof. Doe to skills (e.g. heuristics, semantics, tiddlywinks), roles (e.g. Dean of Faculty, Club Secretary, Morals Mentor), organizations (Mid-Southern Faculty of Semantics, Abilene Tiddlywinks Club), dates when affiliations were true, and so on.

3   Confirm the relationship of the piece of text marked to the identification. What this does in fact is to make an entry in a table in a relational database, relating the text to the identification, in both cases using the identification references rather than the actual words. So our document might be doc #12345, and Prof. Doe's authorship might be the third node we have identified; he is himself listed as person #492 in our authority file 14 (people). So we have simply identified doc #12345, reference 3, as authority file #14, unique entry #492.

Now consider how you could create XML tagging for this entry, for various DTDs or resource description frameworks (RDFs), and bearing in mind future developments. Suppose that one organization to whom you supply data requires personal tags to be in this format:

```
'by <person personname='Doe, J' personorg='Mid-Southern
Faculty of Semantics' persontitle='Professor' orgtype='University'
orgaffil='May 2004 – June 2009' personrole='author'>John
Doe</person>':
```

Well, no problem, just use the rule book for creating personal tags for that organization, collect the data from the relationship database and populate the tags. The next organization – or the future development of your own database – might have different formatting rules:

```
'by <author authorname_id='14/492' role_id='17'>John
Doe</author>'
```

where 'role' means something quite different from the first example: it refers to the job the author was doing, not to his role as an author, and so on. This is equally no problem. The XML has been formatted by using the data in the database to populate tags, after the event, according to the rules defined by the DTD, schema, RDF, etc. This is illustrated schematically in Figure 7.1.

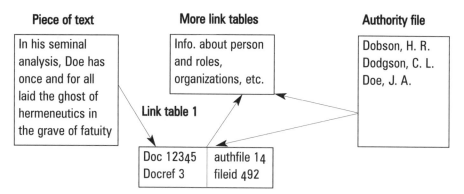

Fig. 7.1 An XML schema

Obviously, the same thing has been done with the citation ('in his seminal analysis'). This will have been linked to an authority file of bibliographic citations; each entry in that file will in turn be linked to one or more people in their role as authors. Those familiar with data models will have done this kind of thing many times before; those who are not so familiar, yet have read this far in this chapter, will be able to set down on a piece of paper the kind of authority file and link tables that would be required, in simplified terms, to accomplish this.

Using taxonomies and authority files to enrich the metadata

Taxonomies are treated elsewhere in this volume and there is no need to recapitulate how they are constructed, nor to discuss their wider roles within information management and architecture. We have already touched on their cardinal importance to the population of tags and the definition of data. We need to note how the three corners of the metadata – relational database – taxonomy triangle can interact after the original content has been processed, in order to provide a much enriched later mark-up of the material.

Taxonomies and authority files can be quite extensive in the metadata that they carry attached to terms, bibliographical references, or whatever else it is they cover. There is then an additional advantage in being able to add detail and depth to the subsequent population of tags of text, based on the metadata that is added one single time to the taxonomies themselves.

An example of how this enrichment takes place can be given from the citations of learned papers. Rather than simply list the correct citations by reference to the journal, volume and pagination, taxonomy and database constructors can get together and create a link table that refers learned citations to each other – together with a way in which they refer to each other. In this way, for example, one reference may relate to another by amplifying it, superseding it, correcting it . . . the possibilities will be constrained only by the database purpose.

Consider our example piece of text:

> 'In his seminal analysis, Doe has once and for all laid the ghost of hermeneutics in the grave of fatuity.'

Suppose that this piece of text is correctly related to the bibliographical citation in which Professor Doe sets out his argument. Suppose further that two years later his argument is refuted by another paper. When the original content comes to be output again for some future purpose, it would be perfectly possible to include in the DTD or other tagging definition the facility to note subsequent citations and thus to highlight potentially contentious paragraphs – completely automatically. Nobody has to do anything more than they would do anyway. But subsequent users have greatly enriched content – updated on the fly. Note that there is no need for publishers to standardize their linking and citation methodologies: using the metadata stored in the authority files, the individual linking or citation recognition for particular publishers can be formatted on the fly. (The baseline standard of citation content exists, avoiding having a very large set of routines to look up.)

Worked example

Figure 7.2 illustrates the concept outlined above. Although inevitably this is a simplification of the actual model and data tables, the way in which this can be done practically can be followed.

The original paper that cites Professor Doe's paper has the document number 12345 in the table of titles, and two information nodes within its text have been identified: the first is Doe himself and the second is the paper cited, which has the ID 10762 in the table of titles. Link table 1 records the relationship between the information nodes in the paper's text to Prof. Doe, and link table 2 records the relationship to the title of Doe's paper. The title table relates the title of the paper cited to the authority file of authors (authority file 14 in the figure, i.e. back to Doe) and the authority file of journals (authority file 3 in the figure). In the figure we show the citation information for illustration purposes only in a column (or 'field'); of course in reality the citation information would be kept in a standardized form, with columns for year, month, issue number, volume number, pagination and so on, in order to provide a means of formatting citations in different ways, to suit particular bibliographic conventions and linking rules used by different publishers. Similarly the entries in authority file 3 would have the abbreviations listed, and so on, which are not shown.

The second paper that cites Professor Doe's paper has the document number 14803, and again the two information nodes, to Doe and to the paper, will be identified. If we look at the diagram, we will see that the editor has used the editorial system to make a further entry in both instances. As well as identifying the actual information nodes – the author and the paper citation – the relationship between these nodes and the text in which they are found is summarized in link table 3. A standard list of ways in which people cite papers is illustrated by authority file 7. So we know from the entries in link table 3, which are created only during the original editing of the documents to which they refer, that Prof. Doe's paper has been cited twice: once positively and once negatively. The identifiers point to the piece of text   more link tables   authority files

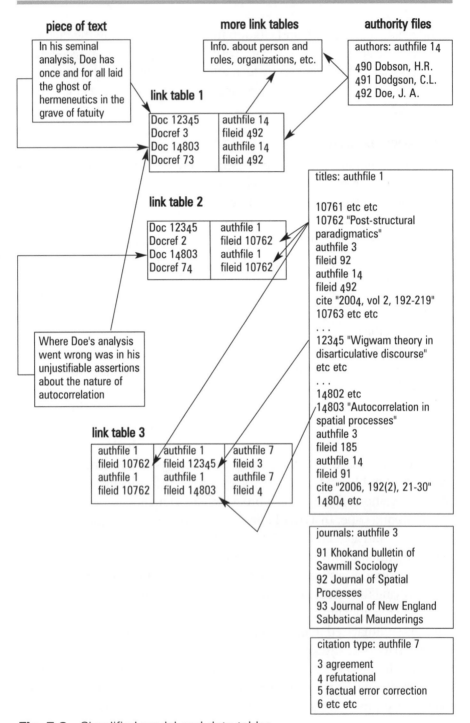

Fig. 7.2 Simplified model and data tables

right sources of other information – for instance, that the negative reference, the one where the author disagrees with poor old Doe, is later in date than the positive reference. This is easy to do at the time, especially if the database designers and architects have kept the entries in authority file 7 simple and unambiguous, and have resisted the temptation to add complex shades of meaning, which leave the poor editors puzzled when they come to do the actual work.

Let us now consider how the original piece of text, at the top left of Figure 7.2, could be output from the original text mark-up and the metadata. Note that at no time will there be any back-editing: nobody revisits this text after the original mark-up. This is simply a way in which a request for text to be output in XML incorporating subsequent references can be handled automatically.

The original mark-up shows, in effect, this information (the actual mechanism will be familiar to those who edit Word documents for this sort of purpose: this would normally not be done in XML!):

```
'In his <docref docid='12345' refid='2'>seminal analysis</docref>,
<docref docid='12345' refid='3'>Doe </docref> has once and for
all laid the ghost of hermeneutics in the grave of fatuity.'
```

When it is output two years later, the XML can be fully populated from the metadata. No human intervention will be needed: merely the rule books (DTD and so on) and the content of the tables. So, then, the text could look like this:

```
'In his <citation cite_title='Post-structural paradigmatics' cite_cita-
tion='J. Spatial Proc. 2004, 2, 192-219'
cite_category='agreement' cite_crossref_title='Autocorrelation in
spatial processes' cite_crossref_auth='Rosenkrantz, Henry J'
cite_crossref_citation='Khokand Bull. Sawmill Soc. 2006, 192(2),
21-30' cite_crossref_category='refutational'>seminal analysis</cita-
tion>,      Doe<person       personname='Doe,      J'
personorg='Mid-Southern Faculty of Semantics' persontitle='Pro-
fessor' orgtype='University' orgaffil='May 2004 – June 2009'
personrole='author'>John Doe</person>'
```

Readers will be able to construct their own examples from the figure, using more or less sophisticated ways to reformat citations, refer to people, and so on. The key point remains: with this example, the automatic incorporation of later references in XML output of documents, without back-editing, simply as the direct result of well designed data models and simple editorial systems, is not only possible, but easy.

Worked example: conclusion

The essential point for information architecture is this: database designers and taxonomy and authority file definers and creators need to work together to consider how much, and what kind of, additional metadata should be attached to each taxonomy or authority file element to increase their usefulness. But this does not have to be done once and for all before the database is populated. This kind of additional facility can be added in when its importance is recognized. This is not true of text that has been fully marked up and then 'frozen' but it is true of text that has simply been identified against taxonomy nodes, and which is then fully marked up by populating tags at the point of reuse from the content of the database tables.

Rules of engagement

The corollary of all this is that the XML is the servant not the controller, the passenger not the driver, in the process. Provided that the database design – the data model of your relational database – is sufficiently wide-ranging to cover the information elements recorded in your authority files and taxonomies, then you can create XML effectively on the fly for the purpose defined long after the database entries were made and the text stored.

There are those who find this anathema. The long-drawn-out analysis of textual minutiae is replaced by the relatively straightforward analysis of information nodes, which can play havoc with consultancy fees. But consider the advantages:

- Data models can be expanded (it is much more difficult to change them, but good modellers create a core on which you can build).
- Since XML tag content is a product of the text 'bookmarks' and the database content, a data model that has subsequently been expanded or enriched can instantly provide more tagging options.

- Instead of a static SGML or XML document, the document can be dynamically re-created as needed for specific purposes. The text – the bit the author wrote and editors edit – is the only constant. This has the flavour of common sense.

Using XML
XML editing

Great strides have been made in the last few years with editors. It would be invidious to single out any particular vendors and their products. All sorts of features and wizardry are available. But the fact is that all XML editing, just like SGML editing, is *complicated*. It's very much a job for trained people who do little else – or they forget how to do it. To do the job well, they often need to know a good deal about the context of the material and not simply how to edit in XML. (Fine, but as an aside I did wonder whether your average editor would want to decide what was negative and what was positive in the citations!!) The screens are often counter-intuitive and full of tags and structural markings, which make the text almost unreadable in itself. Only very strange(?) or serious(?) people can actually compose text using an editor designed for a mark-up language.

This brings us back to a simple set of propositions:

- Authoring and editing of the content and format of documents will be carried out using the current word-processing packages.
- Tagging of such content will be at the 'bookmarking' or 'place marking' level, consonant with identifying structural and information notes, and will always be kept as simple as possible.
- The 'tag content' will be dynamic; it will reflect what is stored against the 'bookmarks' in the database at any time, and not necessarily what was stored against those same bookmarks at the time that the content was processed.
- 'Tag population' is done by removing the formatting and other junk specific to the word processing package, and using the bookmarks to add in tags to the resulting raw text and to populate those tags according to the rules required for the purpose of the tag population from the metadata stored in the database.
- The processing of content is checked by using a set of rules that apply the most complex available tagging and structural mark-up available

from the current state of the database and metadata, populating the raw text and parsing the result. This allows the power of XML parsing to be deployed without freezing the tag content. Obviously, content checkers will use the XML editorial systems for this purpose. [See above].

Application of XML

We have seen, therefore, that XML is ideally suited to being the end-product, rather than always the starting point, of text mark-up. Of course, this makes the 'XML database' valuable much less frequently. Instead, many of our databases will have 'XML potential'. Information architects may find this reassuring, or disturbing. To assist in clarifying thinking on this, here are some typical answers to the question 'But what is it all *for*?' with a classification into whether or not the text marked up in XML is likely to form an 'XML database' or not.

Exchange

Usually the requirements of text exchange mean that the recipient wants certain sorts of information marked up in the text. Whether the recipient simply gets a data feed of new material, or a completely updated archive of a set of content, does not really matter. Provided that the metadata that the recipient needs adding to the content is available from the database, formatting content to suit these requirements is a one-off exercise in writing the appropriate script or application, which can then be used as needed. For this purpose, an 'XML potential' database is ideal – especially if there is reason to believe that recipients may change their requirements, be prepared to pay extra for updates to content, and so on.

Future-proofing

XML's neutrality and flexibility make it the perfect – possibly the only – way to plan for future changes in systems and content management. Separating as far as possible the original output of the author of the content from the metadata means that enhanced, revised and updated metadata and additional enrichment can be added to the original text at the time that systems are replaced and the content is output for inclusion in the replacement system. For this purpose, an 'XML potential database' rather than the marked-up documents as originally processed is, to all intents and purposes, essential. The amount of intellectual capital in the form of corrections, updating, cross-referencing and enhancement that is otherwise thrown away is too great to contemplate.

One-off archiving

The time scale here is the critical factor. When we are planning for system replacement, we don't know exactly what system will replace the current one. But we do know one thing – that the old system will still work up to the moment that we transfer to the new one. We don't know this at all with archiving for the future. If we reflect for a moment on our abilities to recover text we wrote ten years ago – stored perhaps on 5¼in. floppy disks or in an Amstrad's word-processing package that was popular 12 years ago – we ask who can read such documents today without colossal effort?

Once again, XML's neutrality and flexibility mean that future generations would need only to recapture the written text of XML documents to recover the content. Printed paper has survived remarkably well as the long-term medium and can be stored in multiple copies to guard against vandalism, accident and violent acts. By outputting a one-off content set onto printed paper of the right quality, with XML mark-up and explanations of the mark-up (as with DTDs and RDFs), future generations can be assured of a means of accessing a given state of knowledge from our times. For certain archiving purposes this is much the safest route and remains, perhaps, the only justifiable example of the 'XML database' proper.

Chapter 8

Topic maps

Indexing in 3-D

BOB BATER

Infoplex Associates, UK

Introduction

An information architecture (IA) is not designed as an *objet d'art* in itself. It has a very practical purpose to serve as a way of organizing and relating the knowledge and information resources in some domain in order to facilitate their management and use. Any work of architecture requires some kind of gateway if effective use is to be made of it, and for an IA that equates to suitably sophisticated means of knowledge and information discovery and retrieval.

In most organizations, IAs deal with a range of heterogeneous resources: digital documents of various formats, databases, news feeds and so on, as well as paper. To provide access to these, the only recourse in the past has been to provide individual browsing or searching interfaces for each proprietary system or format – a multiplicity of porticos rather than a single gateway – with the complexity and expense which that entails. Where the tendency has been for increasing numbers of resources to migrate into one or other of the standard web formats, the response of web technologists to their discovery and retrieval has been the web search engine – a technology for which we must surely be thankful.

However, the search engine is a solution designed for 'blanket' retrieval from a massive, and in certain respects relatively homogeneous, resource collection – the web – and web search engines are therefore resource-dependent. They expect resources to comprise text files that they can read and index. Search engines therefore cannot help us when it comes to information held in databases or other non-text proprietary formats and structures. Nor are they aware of those fundamental parameters of effective retrieval, *precision* and *recall*. If we wish to transcend these limitations, we must look elsewhere.

In corporate environments, portals, often combined with search engine technology, have achieved some degree of success. However, another solution is now emerging in the form of topic maps. Topic maps are a web technology employing Extensible Markup Language (XML), whose specification is permanently licensed to the public. Topic maps can therefore offer a less complex, cheaper and more interoperable means of providing access to a collection of heterogeneous information resources. Moreover, they have the additional advantage of being firmly based upon the principles of classification, as well as embracing the semantic signposting of the thesaurus.

While the term 'topic map' may be unfamiliar to many, the functionality to which it refers is not. A topic map is essentially an index to the content of some collection of information resources, usually but not necessarily digital in form. But because the topic map itself is computer-based, it exhibits a number of useful characteristics that distinguish it from the paper-based index to which we are accustomed. These distinctive characteristics derive from differences in the dimensionality of the information spaces addressed by topic maps and by paper-based indexes respectively.

Print-based media have served us well and will no doubt continue to do so. But just as language can often prove inadequate to express the finer points of our understanding, so print-based media have inadvertently trapped us into a two-dimensional (2D) perspective onto the world of information – a world, in truth, every bit as three-dimensional (3D) as the real world it describes.

Nowhere is this more pointedly demonstrated than in the world wide web (the web), where the linear, page-by-page model of the printed word has largely been abandoned in favour of a network of associations. Yet long before the advent of the web, efforts were being made in a number of diverse fields to escape the restricted dimensionality of print. Among the earliest to tackle this problem were the pioneers of artificial intelligence (AI) and the cognitive psychology theorists whose multi-dimensional models of cognition the former sought to reproduce in machines. Closer to home, there was an equally heroic and prescient example in the form of PRECIS – the PREserved Context Index System – developed by Derek Austin (1921–2001) and his team (Austin, 1974).

PRECIS applied the immense power of computer processing to the production of a sophisticated form of permuted index that preserved the semantic and syntactic context of the key term or phrase. It was first used in the British National Bibliography in 1971 but, despite being superseded by the simplified COMPASS, it was eventually dropped in 1996 because it was considered over-complex for the job at hand. However, it may be argued that the problem lay not with PRECIS, but with the application of computer power to an inherently limited 'information space' – the 2D printed page. It was a bit like taking a high-fidelity sound system and playing it in a potting shed.

The problem with the 2D information space, as PRECIS recognized, was that it didn't allow the effective preservation of *context*. This problem had not gone unnoticed elsewhere in the information profession. Ellis (1989) had argued that information retrieval (IR) systems should 'provide more navigational routes' and Belkin, Marchetti et al. (1993) went even further to advocate that IR systems should be designed using a network of associations between items as a means of filling the knowledge gap. What these researchers were saying is that by changing the question from 'What is the information need?' to 'Why does the information need exist?', the crucial notion of *context* could be addressed.

The aim of topic maps

Topic maps are about modelling real-world relationships, among objects, people or concepts – anything, in fact, can be a topic. Human consciousness is endowed with a unique awareness of situation and context that governs how we interpret and interact with our environment. This applies equally to what might be termed the 'geophysical space', as to the 'social space' and – particular to our context – the 'information space'. With this in mind, we can define the primary purpose of a topic map as to provide a context-rich environment in which the topical landscape of a collection of information resources may be interpreted and navigated. For information professionals, a topic map is therefore first and foremost a browsing tool. That it is also a means of representing, organizing and exchanging knowledge is a matter for discussion on another occasion.

Traditionally, browsing has been very much a haphazard affair, a matter of wandering along pre-set paths, with no real indication of whether one was going in the right direction and few degrees of freedom to change course if not. Where pathways from one topic hierarchy to another were provided, the different topic structures and their interconnections were 'flattened' into 2D, obscuring each other. Browsing in this sense is more a guided tour than an expedition of discovery.

With topic maps, the magic of the hyperlink combines with a systematically articulated structure of interconnected, navigable topics, and a flexible user interface, to make it much easier to provide the rich contextual feedback required for truly explorative browsing. The more a browsing tool is able to indicate the *context* of where one is – by indicating relationships with other, superordinate, subordinate and lateral terms and concepts – the more it allows one to keep one's bearings, to ward off uncertainty and to make a sensible decision on which direction to take. And as in real-world navigation, success often depends upon strategically placed signposts and short-cuts, which bridge the gap between where one is and where one wants to be.

The 'navigation layer' of a topic map, however, is only the top-most of three. Underlying the navigation layer is what might be called the 'resources layer'. Linking resources to appropriate topics can effectively co-locate them irrespective of where they might actually reside within the IA (rather like a library catalogue), making them accessible at the click of a mouse, so that the topic map serves both as index and gateway. Note, however, that a topic map need not reference any resources at all, in which case it can serve as an ideal framework for the construction of a taxonomy or a thesaurus showing the relationships among concepts or terms respectively.

The third level of the topic map paradigm is concerned with subject identity. 'Topic' and 'subject' are often used interchangeably in casual speech, but it is not always the case that the term chosen to name a topic identifies its subject unequivocally. The published subject identifier (PSI) provides a means for agreeing and publishing precise definitions of subjects, and for relating topics to those subjects. There are a number of introductions to topic maps available, on and off the web. For an excellent overview, see Pepper (2002), or for an exhaustive treatment, see Park and Hunting (2002).

Topic map key concepts

Topic maps are the subject of the international standard ISO/IEC 13250:2003 (ISO/IEC, 2003). This describes the use of two alternative 'languages' for the construction of topic maps. HyTime is a Standard Generalized Markup Language (SGML) vocabulary intended for general use, while XML topic maps (XTMs), are XML-based so as to enable their use with the other web technologies. The XTM section of ISO/IEC 13250 lists some 19 XML element types, which among them allow the formulation of the four key concepts of the XTM model: topics, associations, roles and occurrences. A topic is merely any word or phrase chosen to represent a subject. The declaration of a topic in the topic map syntax permits characteristics to be assigned to it so that its relationships to other topics and to resources may be established.

For instance, in a topic map about the ISO/IEC 13250 topic map standard, the document itself would obviously be represented as the topic 'ISO/IEC 13250'. One would want to include information about the provenance of the standard, so the parent organization itself, the Joint Technical Committee responsible and the subcommittee that actually wrote the standard, would also be represented as the topics 'ISO/IEC', 'JTC1' and 'SC34' respectively.

One might then consider how to characterize the associations among these topics, and this is where topic maps break free of the conventional 2D constraints by allowing associations to be *typed*, that is, given a type. Neither conventional data modelling methods (with the notable exception of entity–relationship modelling) nor conventional semantic modelling methods for information retrieval such as taxonomies and thesauri have employed the typing of associations to any significant degree.

Returning to our example, the association between Topic 'ISO/IEC' and Topic 'ISO/IEC 13250' may be called 'publishing' – 'ISO/IEC' is associated through 'publishing' with 'ISO/IEC 13250'. Similarly, the association between 'SC34' and 'ISO/IEC 13250' may be called 'authorship', and that between 'JTC1' and 'SC34' may be called 'partitive' since SC34 is a part of JTC1. The terms are deliberately chosen so as to be directionless, since in the XTM model basic associations are unitary – a single label suffices for both topics' points-of-view (PoV).

However, XTM provides a device for distinguishing each topic's individual PoV in the form of that topic's *role*. Each topic involved in an association may be said to play a role, so that in the example above, in the association 'authorship', 'SC34' plays the role 'author' and 'ISO/IEC 13250' plays the role 'work' (in the sense of 'opus'). Similarly, in the association 'partitive', 'JTC1' has the role 'whole', while 'SC34' has the role 'part'.

In some contexts, it may be preferable to choose different terms. Thus, in the case just cited, the association might be called 'subsidiarity', when 'JTC1' might play the role 'super-body' with 'SC34' playing the role 'sub-body'. This open-ended structure of XTM has advantages and disadvantages. But should we decide to extend our topic map further, we could simply add a further topic 'standard', denoting a *type* of publication, with a view to relating ISO standards to the rest of the world of 'publications'.

To do this, we could define the association 'is a' as existing between the topic 'standard' and the topic 'ISO/IEC 13250'. This would then read 'ISO/IEC 13250 *is a* standard'. we could then characterize the role of the topic 'standard' as being 'regulatory/advisory publication' and the role of 'ISO/IEC 13250' as being 'instance'. For the sake of completeness, we would also wish to name the association between the topic 'ISO/IEC' and the topic 'standard' as 'sponsorship', with topic 'ISO/IEC' having the role 'sponsor' and topic 'standard' acquiring the role 'regulatory/advisory publication'. The resulting topic map is shown in Figure 8.1.

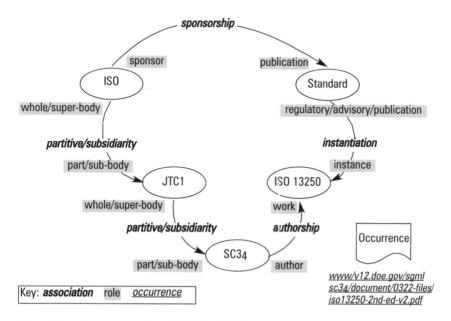

Fig. 8.1 Topic map for ISO/IEC 13250

This topic(role)>association<(role)topic mechanism provides tremendous scope for precision in browsing or searching, since any of its elements may be employed in either of those processes. However, it must be said that for the less experienced constructor it can take a substantial effort of semantic analysis and linguistic contrivance to derive effective terms.

Topics have other characteristics besides associations and roles. They may also have *occurrences*. Occurrences are discrete information resources, which relate to a topic. An obvious case of an occurrence in our example is the ISO/IEC 13250 document itself. Figure 8.1 shows an iconic hyperlink to a location on the web from which an Acrobat PDF version of ISO/IEC 13250:2002 may be retrieved. Occurrences may be of any format. Digital resources – text files, HTML pages, XML documents, databases, images and 'office' formats (Word, Excel, PowerPoint, and so on) – are therefore accessible at a click of the mouse. Non-digital resources may of course be identified through bibliographic references in the conventional way.

As well as these four key concepts, XTMs includes two further vital characteristics of topics (and associations): the published subject identifier, mentioned earlier, and scope. PSIs are formally adopted 'definitions' of a subject that uniquely identify that subject across different topic maps, which may be using different terms to refer to the same subject. The form of definition of a subject and its immediate super-ordinate and sub-ordinate concepts is ideally a taxonomy. Scope is used to indicate the specific context within which an association is valid. Both PSIs and scope can be useful to humans and computers alike. For human navigators of a topic map, an interface could be designed to display a definition to indicate the exact identity of a topic. For computers, these characteristics can be used when merging topic maps, so that the machine can know from the PSI that differently named topics actually refer to the same subject, and in which circumstance (scope) each synonym is used.

Thus for instance, a topic map may include a topic indicating that a resource has content relating to the language 'Ladino'. Inclusion in the topic map of the relevant PSI (http://psi.oasis-open.org/geolang/iso639/#lad) would unambiguously identify that the language referred to is the dialect of Spanish spoken by the Sephardic Jews and represented in ISO 639 by the code 'lad'. On the other hand, a resource in French covered by the same topic map would use the French name for the language, 'judéo-espagnol'. Associations using this French term and those using the English equivalent could be shown to be referring to the same language by linking each to the same PSI, and separate scopes on each association could indicate that one was the English term and the other the French term. Using scope, topic and association names can be duplicated in different languages, allowing topic maps to be converted from one language to another at the click of a button.

Making and using topic maps

Using the key concepts in XTMs, it is possible to build one or several topic maps to provide ready access to resources in any information architecture. Different points-of-view of the same architecture may be represented by separate topic maps, which can be employed separately or merged when required. Usually, anything but the very simplest topic map will contain a number of hierarchies semantically cross-linked to produce a rich, three-dimensional (and more) navigational network.

In such a network, it is possible to navigate to an occurrence via one topic, then from that occurrence, to navigate via any of the further topics associated with it to other occurrences that have some kind of association with the first, and so on. Because the user can be provided with contextual information, signposts and shortcuts at each point on the journey, the browsing experience is so much richer and provides a far more comprehensive purview of the resource collection content.

Topic maps may be created in a number of ways, including hand-coding the XTM itself (not recommended!), hand-coding in a linear topic map language provided by some vendors, conversion from structured source data in databases or XML documents, or from scratch using a topic map designer/editor tool. However, starting from existing source data will often present the choice of either compromising on the quality of the end product, or investing further time in refining the result.

In order to use a topic map, a browser-based topic map viewer application such as Omnigator® from the Oslo-based Ontopia (Ontopia), or k42® from the UK–German company Empolis (Empolis K42) is required. Omnigator is a component of Ontopia's Ontopia Knowledge Suite (OKS). Like k42®, its numerous modules combine to form a fully comprehensive development and deployment environment for topic maps, including authoring and editing, ontology generation and editing, application development and querying.

The best topic maps are achieved by applying a mix of human taxonomic and semantic analysis skills combined with a certain linguistic agility. Thus, topic maps represent perhaps the best type of human–machine co-operation, where human cognition provides the substance and technology the vehicle. For many of us, that is just as it should be. However, it does mean that quality topic maps are often time-consuming and therefore expensive to produce, although this should ease in time as the technology becomes established and 'libraries' of basic topic map building blocks become available.

Uses of topic map technology

Because topic map technology is designed specifically to support an infor-mation architecture and to provide structured access to its resources, it may be applied in a wide variety of different environments where such a facil-ity is desirable. One of its most common uses is to form the underlying structure for portals, catalogues, web 'site maps' and even the website itself. Interest is also being shown at the time of writing in using the tech-nology to provide a classification-driven environment for content management systems (CMSs), where the integration of information from diverse sources is often a major problem, and for B2B (business-to-business) exchange (de Graauw, n.d.). A further possible application is their employ-ment as the underlying engine and user interface for expert systems. As previously noted, topic maps are also ideal for the articulation and presen-tation of taxonomies and thesauri.

All of these possible applications are arguably aspects of knowledge man-agement (KM), although they deal ostensibly with information resources. However, as has already been suggested above, the fundamental distinguish-ing feature of topic map technology is its ability to preserve the *context* of the topics, associations and occurrences with which it is concerned. There is a growing body of discourse that places this notion of *context* right at the heart of a mature vision of KM, and it is fitting therefore to consider whether the topic map paradigm might actually provide the hitherto elu-sive bridge between technology and human organizational, cultural and cognitive structures.

Many authors and researchers have observed the uncertainty in organ-izations that arises from the dynamics of individual versus organizational meaning and purpose. Simply because people are people, they introduce personal, social and political dimensions that modulate manager and managed, peer and professional relationships in unpredictable and context-sensitive ways. It was Karl Weick, Rensis Likert College Professor of Organizational Behavior and Psychology, who wrote: 'To reduce equivocality, people do not need larger quantities of information. Instead, they need richer qualitative information' (Weick, 2001).

Equally, Michael Lissack, one-time Research Associate at the UK's Henley Management College, and now director of the (US) Institute for the Study of Coherence and Emergence (ISCE), has written extensively on the application of complexity theory to management, where *context* and *situated action* are central concepts (Lissack, n.d.). Others, notably Nidumolu et al. (2001), have described a similar scenario, which they term the 'Situated Knowledge Web'.

Topic maps have the ability to create information spaces that provide a rich awareness of situation and context, including signposts and shortcuts to alternative but allied pathways, together with one-click access to resource occurrences. It is not unreasonable therefore to speculate that topic map technology could support, better than ever before, the broader set of knowledge-seeking behaviours including searching, browsing, touring, sensemaking and personal interaction. In other words, an opportunity to explore an information space in much the same way as we explore the world around us.

Topic maps and the semantic web

One information space crying out for the sort of context-preserving knowledge representation, navigation and retrieval facilities that topic maps can provide, is the world wide web. If it were possible to indicate the subject of each resource on the web and also the semantics among related resources, then manual retrieval would not only be easier and yield higher precision, but the lion's share of the work involved could be passed to the computer. It is this vision that is behind the concept of the 'semantic web', as conceived by Tim Berners-Lee and his colleagues at the World Wide Web Consortium (W3C).

The cornerstone technology chosen for the Semantic Web is the XML-based resource description framework (RDF). RDF has its origins largely in predicate logic, mathematical theory and object-oriented database concepts. Thus, the basic model for an RDF statement is subject–predicate–object (termed a 'triple'), where either the subject or the object – or both – may be resources. The RDF model (RDFM) was conceived essentially as a carrier mechanism for fine-grained metadata. Because RDFM's syntax is written in XML, an XML schema can be constructed that allows for control of metadata structure and validation of metadata values in specific applications.

So far, so good. But from a topic map perspective, RDF harbours a number of problems. For a start, the structures and superstructures of XTM and RDF are inverted with respect to each other. Topic maps start by building a semantic framework from topics and their associations, then 'attach' resources to that framework at appropriate points. RDF starts with the resources themselves, then applies 'identities' and 'types' to indicate semantic relationships. This difference arises simply from the fact that the semantic landscape of a topic map is aimed primarily at humans, while the landscape of the RDF is intended primarily for computer manipulation. As a result, XTM is able to offer a rather more sophisticated semantic environment.

RDF's basic building block – the triple – may be seen essentially as a binary or 2D concept, extendable only by linking it end-to-end with other triples to form a semantic chain. In contrast, XTM's topics and associations are 'n-ary' and may be cross-linked in three dimensions to form a semantic network. Add roles and scopes, and you can have multiple, superimposed networks.

The topic map community however, reserve their most vitriolic indictment of the RDF model for what they call the 'identity crisis' of the web – its inability to distinguish between a *resource about a subject* and a *subject itself*. In other words, it cannot distinguish between a surrogate for a subject (such as a document *about* Fred Smith), which is *addressable* and therefore retrievable in cyberspace, and Fred Smith himself, who is unlikely to be found in cyberspace (unless there's been some astounding bio-digital research we've not been told about). The distinction is hairbreadth in magnitude, but can nevertheless be crucial.

This issue of disambiguation is viewed by the topic map community as central, not only to the topic map model, but to the semantic web itself. As one of the founders of topic maps, Steve Pepper, comments:

Why is this important? Because without clarity on this issue, it is impossible to solve the challenge of the Semantic Web, and it is impossible to implement scaleable Web Services. It is impossible to achieve the goals of 'global knowledge federation' and impossible even to begin to enable the aggregation of information and knowledge by human and software agents on a scale large enough to control infoglut.

Ontologies and taxonomies will not be reusable unless they are based on a reliable and unambiguous identification mechanism for the things about which they speak. The same applies to classifications, thesauri, registries, catalogues, and directories. Applications (including agents) that capture, collate or aggregate information and knowledge will not scale beyond a closely controlled environment unless the identification problem is solved.

(Pepper and Schwab, n.d.)

While both the topic map and RDF communities agree that there is little prospect of unification, there is a consensus that there is considerable synergy between the two models and that interoperability is both desirable and possible. To their credit, they have established an ongoing dialogue in order to try to resolve the problems. A number of possibilities exist; one school of thought suggests minor changes to the topic map model, while another recommends modification of the RDF model to allow the distinction between *subject* and *surrogate*. In either case, the aim is to allow the mapping of one model onto the other. The problems, potential solutions and efforts towards reconciliation are charted eloquently by Garshol (n.d.). Watch this space!

Further reading

For an introduction to, and more advanced information on, topic maps, see TopicMaps.Org (n.d.). Excellent examples of the topic map paradigm may be navigated at Mondeca Publishing and Ontopia. For PSIs related to modelling thesauri, other hierarchies, subject classification and facteted classification, see Techquila. For a case study integrating topic maps and the semantic web with 3G mobile phone technology see Shark.

Austin, D. (1974) *PRECIS: a manual of concept analysis and subject indexing*, London, Council of the British National Bibliography.

Belkin, N. J., Marchetti, P. et al. (1993) BRAQUE: design of an interface to support user interaction in information retrieval, *Information Processing and Management*, **29** (3), 325–44.

de Graauw, M. (n.d.) *Business Maps: topic maps go B2B!*, Amsterdam. Available at www.marcdegraauw.com/itm/businessmaps.htm.

Ellis, D. (1989) A Behavioural Approach to Information Retrieval Design, *Journal of Documentation*, **45** (3), 171–212.

Empolis K42. Available at http://62.231.133.220/empolisDemo/tmv/tmv.html.2.

Garshol, L. M. (n.d.) *Topic Maps, RDF, DAML, OIL – A Comparison*, Oslo, Ontopia. Available at www.ontopia.net/topicmaps/materials/tmrdfoildaml.html.

ISO/IEC 13250:2003 *Topic Maps*, International Standards Organization.

Lissack, M. R. (n.d.) *Sensemaking Conflicts Among Organizational Levels: an exploratory hypothesis*. Available at http://lissack.com/writings/senseconflict.htm.

Mondeca Publishing. Available at http://mondeca-publishing.com/s/anonymous/title10013.html.

Nidumolu, S. R. et al. (2001) Situated Learning and the Situated Knowledge Web: exploring the ground beneath knowledge management, *Journal of Management Information Systems*, **18** (1), 115–50.

Ontopia. Available at www.ontopia.net/omnigator/models/index.jsp.

Park, J. and Hunting, S. (eds) (2002) *XML Topic Maps: creating and using topic maps for the web*, Boston, Addison Wesley.

Pepper, S. (2002) *The TAO of Topic Maps*, Oslo, Ontopia AS. Available at www.ontopia.net/topicmaps/materials/tao.html.

Pepper, S. and Schwab, S. (n.d.) *Curing the Web's Identity Crisis: subject indicators for RDF*, Oslo, Ontopia. Available at www.ontopia.net/topicmaps/materials/identitycrisis.html.

Shark. Available at http://ivs.tu-berlin.de/Projekte/Shark/index_en.html.

Techquila. Available at www.techquila.com/.

TopicMaps.Org. Available at www.topicmaps.org/.

Weick, K. E. (2001) *Making Sense of the Organization*, Oxford, Blackwell.

Wilson, T. (1999) Models in Information Behaviour Research, *Journal of Documentation*, **55** (3), 249–70.

Chapter 9

A devolved architecture for public sector interoperability

STELLA G. DEXTRE CLARKE
Independent consultant, UK

Introduction and summary

This chapter will describe developments in the UK designed to promote easy access to public sector information. Rather than developing a centralized database or system, the aim is to enable seamless flows of information from one system to another. This is to be achieved by means of standards for interoperability, including a standard for metadata and a simple controlled vocabulary.

Devolution of responsibility is a key feature of the emerging scene. While the standards set minimum requirements, information producers and aggregators have the opportunity to build on this platform. Many players are already seeking to extend the subject vocabulary, linking it with specialized thesauri for particular sectors. Mapping from one vocabulary to another, as a potential aid to semantic interoperability, is discussed later.

The aim

A very important strand of the UK's 'Modernizing Government' agenda is to make information and services more available to the people. Whether a service is provided by a local authority, a government department, a regulatory watchdog, a quango or an executive agency, everyone should be able to find out about it and even apply for it through a personal computer (PC) near at hand. The vision is of easy universal access to everything produced by the public sector.

In 2000 the Office of the e-Envoy was charged with developing policies and standards for achieving interoperability and information systems coherence across the public sector. Throughout central and local government, senior officials were appointed as 'e-champions'. They formed an Interoperability Working Group, and reporting to that a Metadata Working Group (MWG). Each of these bodies has a wide membership, and welcomes participation from private sector organizations too. Thus the policies and other products stand a good chance of reflecting the needs and the opportunities.

Existing models

The vision of making everything available to everybody is not new. Useful comparisons can be drawn with at least one widely used model – the collaborative bibliographic databases of AGRIS and INIS, aiming to cover the world's research literature in their respective fields, agriculture and nuclear energy.

In the case of AGRIS, the idea is that each country appoints a national representative, who inputs bibliographical records for the country's entire agricultural literature and in return gets free access to the database of combined inputs from the whole world. The database is maintained centrally and its outputs may be delivered in print (the most popular medium a long time ago), on CD-ROM, or via the internet. The operating costs at the centre are offset by sales of the products to other parties. The system is underpinned by standards, covering the field structure of the database, the style of entry required in each field, and the controlled vocabulary of subject descriptors.

One key characteristic of the AGRIS model is centralized assembly of the final product. Central co-ordination enables maintenance of the standards, a degree of quality control over input, and selection and design of the retrieval interfaces. The result is a good strong working model. After 30 years the system is still widely used. But it has limitations if the attempt is made to apply it to organizing public sector resources in today's context.

First, a comprehensive national database maintained centrally is an expensive undertaking, needing a strong commercial driver. Not many Western governments can be relied on for the necessary financial backing over years and decades.

Second, bibliographic records are only one step along the path to full content (not just text but graphics, maybe audio and video transmissions, and so on) and interactive services such as filing a tax return. Some electronic services from government organizations need leading-edge security protection.

Third, the user population may not want access via one website or portal dedicated to public sector content. Some users may want to go to their favourite health-related portal, and find there National Health Service or Department of Health guidelines, along with alternative medicine sources, news about HIV in South Africa, and so on. Today a centralized operation just does not seem the way to go.

Emerging needs and opportunities

The first complication now is the wide variety of content to be accommodated. Among the items are mixtures of text and graphics, spreadsheets, databases, video clips, interactive application forms for a passport or a vehicle licence or a claim for compensation.

Second, today's electronic resources are not so neatly and irrevocably organized in discrete packages. A document that starts as a draft on a PC may be completed by a colleague and released on an intranet website. From there it may pass into an electronic records management system, it may be published on the internet, it may be cited in copious reference lists. People may find it by searching on *Google* or *Yahoo!* or *UK Online*, and when they actually get to the text, they could have navigated there from anywhere and be unaware what system they are 'in'. Somehow, the little items of information need to be wrapped up and labelled so they can swim about in an ocean of resources, retrievable and still intelligible from almost any fishing vessel.

Third, who does the wrapping and labelling? In the old days, publishing was the responsibility of a select band of trained people. Nowadays the task may be devolved to almost anyone with a PC on their desk. Tools must be provided so that authors can assign the 'labels' with a minimum of effort, without the need to look up manuals, and still achieve acceptable indexing.

The bibliographic model described above, although not the only option to consider, helps bring out a key contrast with the context now to be addressed, namely the absence of centralized control. How can we encourage the free and universally intelligible flow of information, if we do not control its production or its point of access?

The UK government is by no means the only one addressing this question (Hudon and Hjartarson, 2002). Strategies and solutions are well advanced in countries such as Australia, Canada, Denmark, Ireland and New Zealand. In the present chapter there is room to describe only the UK approach, but the references at the end of this chapter include pointers to some of these comparable initiatives.

Standards are the key

If control is not an option, an alternative strategy is to enable and empower. In a world brimming with PCs and networks, one may develop the standards and protocols that support the seamless flow of information, and leave it to the supply and demand chain to do the rest. That is one way of describing the strategy adopted by the Office of the e-Envoy. The key guidance issued by its working groups is contained in the e-GIF, the e-GMS and the GCL, all to be described below.

The e-GIF

The e-GIF (e-Government Interoperability Framework) sets out the policy statements, implementation and compliance regimes for achieving joined-up government in the UK. It is really an assembly of standards, overseen by the Interoperability Working Group.

Overall, the e-GIF addresses interconnectivity, data integration, information access and content management. The standards are aligned with those commonly used on the internet and world wide web. EXtensible Markup Language (XML) is the primary standard for data integration and presentation tools. Browser based technology is stipulated for public access interfaces. For content management, electronic resources must conform to the e-Government Metadata Standard (e-GMS). These basic standards are complemented by others, for example for secure data transfer, for interactive services and for particular access channels such as mobile phones.

The e-GMS

A Metadata Working Group (MWG) was established to thrash out the details of the e-GMS, and ensure that it covers the needs of central and local government as well as other public sector bodies. The e-GMS is derived from, and compatible with, the Dublin Core set of elements, which are well known and widely applied all over the world. Only a few of the e-GMS elements (date, title, creator and subject) are essential to all items. The other 21 elements can be thought of as optional extras for special situations. For example, several of the elements are relevant only to records management systems. See full details in the standard itself at www.govtalk.gov.uk/schemasstandards/ metadata_document.asp?docnum=763.

The subject element generated more debate and development work than any of the others. Probably this reflects the importance of accessing information by subject, and also the intrinsic difficulty of consistent subject description. The MWG took the view that a controlled vocabulary is needed if subjects are to be described systematically. But deciding what sort of controlled vocabulary was not straightforward.

Initially, in 2000, the MWG had considered developing a 'pan-government thesaurus'. This would comprise perhaps 7000 terms to cover the whole span of government interests, to be used both in indexing (or meta-tagging, as it is often called in the web environment) and searching. But then the practical implications were considered. If the people preparing metadata are not information professionals trained in thesaurus use, indexing will seem an unnecessary chore. Most authors find a thesaurus complicated as well as time-consuming. The absence of a mechanism for quality control across the public sector could lead to inconsistent indexing. And even supposing this hurdle were overcome and the resources all adequately indexed, it seemed doubtful that end-user citizens of all ages and persuasions would use the thesaurus effectively for searching.

So, despite the potential of a thesaurus to standardize search terms, the project to build and implement one was judged unrealistic. Several other types of vocabulary were considered (Dextre Clarke, 2002). In the end it was decided to go for a simple browsing tool rather than a search vocabulary. It should look something like the *Yahoo!* directory, offering users a hierarchical set of headings to choose from. This would make it more feasible for the indexers and searchers to apply. Thus began development of the Government Category List (GCL), which was issued in January 2002. It forms part of the e-GMS and is mandatory for application throughout the public sector. By 2005 every electronic document, web page and so on to emerge from a public body in the UK should have at least one GCL term present in its subject metadata.

The GCL

The GCL is a polyhierarchical, high-level taxonomy of about 375 preferred terms and over 1200 additional lead-in entries, expressed in layman's language and covering the broad range of subjects on which the citizen might expect government sources to provide information and/or services. It is neither a traditional classification scheme nor a thesaurus, but a hybrid of the two, designed to support browsing rather than searching.

The GCL is an electronic creature, not a printed reference work. To get a feel for it, the best way is to look online, at www.govtalk.gov.uk/schemas-standards/gcl.asp on the *GovTalk* website. Alternatively, download it from the same site, in the GCL documents area, as a set of HTML files for easy navigation on your own PC. Portable data format (PDF) versions are also available, but much more cumbersome to use. A plain text version is there too, for direct implementation by computers. XML is coming shortly.

Also on the *GovTalk* website are various guidance materials. See Table 9.1.

Table 9.1   GCL guidance materials available on GovTalk

Guidance material	What it covers
FAQs about the GCL	FAQs: the easiest place to start
Guide to meta-tagging with the GCL	Advice for webmasters and authors of electronic resources when entering metadata
Specialized vocabularies and the GCL	Guidance for organizations using their own taxonomy or thesaurus as well as the GCL
Implementing the GCL	Notes for system administrators, especially when using the plain text version to integrate GCL data into in-house systems
GCL Maintenance Guide	Maintenance information, useful for the GCL editor and for developers of other category lists, thesauri, etc.

The GCL represents a compromise between keeping things simple and providing enough specificity – the capability to discriminate between similar subjects. Although it lacks the potential of a full thesaurus, implementation should be feasible for most organizations and users. It is frequently updated, and anyone can submit suggestions for change.

More than one controlled vocabulary?

The MWG decision in favour of a simple taxonomy was unanimous, but not the end of the story. For the subject element of the e-GMS, two refinements were approved: subject.category and subject.keyword. The standard indicates that the metadata of every electronic resource must include at least one GCL term as a subject.category value, and preferably also should include several terms as subject.keyword values. The keywords should reflect the level of specificity of the resource, and they should ideally be drawn from some other controlled vocabulary. The choice of vocabulary for the keywords is left open, since no one thesaurus is likely to suit the needs of all sectors. Uncontrolled keywords may also be applied, using the element without refinements.

In theory at least, this approach satisfies all the main needs for subject retrieval. High-level browsing via the GCL can be complemented by precision searching with thesaurus terms, and free text searching will typically be available too. But in practice, the open-endedness of the choice presents challenges for system implementers and managers. There are design choices at both the input stage and the retrieval interface.

At the input stage, indexing with any controlled vocabulary has always been an issue – it consumes time and/or expense, and quality control is not easy. The problem is multiplied if two controlled vocabularies are to be used. Confronted with this choice, many organizations will do the minimum to comply with the standard, that is to say, ensure there is one GCL term on every item. But for others the GCL is inadequate, especially for their internal needs. Having taken the trouble to apply metadata to all their resources, they want to reap the benefits for their intranets, corporate portals and electronic document and records management (EDRM) systems. They want search access via a thesaurus tailored to their own subject interests. But immediately this raises the question of how to index efficiently and effectively with two separate controlled vocabularies.

At the retrieval stage, manipulation of one browsing vocabulary and one search vocabulary is not such an issue. Assuming the basic functionality for browsing and searching is in place, the two tools can be set up in complementary fashion. This takes care of the internal needs of most organizations. A problem arises only when there are more vocabularies, which could be the case for a public access portal. For example, a portal focusing on the environment might want to integrate resources culled from several different government departments, local authorities, executive agencies and other public bodies. At least half a dozen different thesauri and other controlled vocabularies are already in use among these organizations. If the terms from them are mixed indiscriminately, then the benefits of a controlled vocabulary are lost. The design challenge is to help searchers make use of the indexing, without having to phrase search statements in six or more different indexing languages.

Mappings

Faced with multiple vocabularies, many organizations are devising automatic processes to map terms from one to another. Mapping can be done either at input or at the retrieval stage or at both, so we shall consider these situations separately.

Metadata mapping at input

As anyone who has tried it will testify, mapping from one vocabulary to another is difficult. Terms that are synonymous in one context may take different meanings in another, and this may invalidate the mapping. However, mapping from the specific to the more general is much easier than the reverse process. Since the GCL is a high-level vocabulary, mappings are usually feasible from departmental thesauri, which typically cover one sector in much more detail.

In developing a mappings capability, step one is to assign to each term in the source vocabulary a corresponding GCL heading. Occasionally it may be appropriate to assign more than one GCL heading. Effectively this builds a one-way correspondence table between the vocabularies. Step two is to build the table into the indexing system, in such a way as to minimize the effort for the indexer. The way this is done varies tremendously because of the variety of content management systems (CMS), web publishing platforms, EDRM systems, etc.

Some simple cases will illustrate how a few organizations are tackling the challenge of efficient indexing with two vocabularies.

Case 1: Drugs action team website

For this website (www.drugs.gov.uk), operated by the Home Office, all documents are required to have a subject keyword chosen from a list of about 40. To comply with the e-GIF, they must also have a subject category chosen from the GCL. Since the scope of the site is subject specific to drugs, there are only four GCL headings commonly applicable to all the resources on the site. So applying GCL headings is not very onerous.

The Home Office has implemented a CMS that supports authors in entering resources using a template (see Figure 9.1). Just like most CMS templates, it prompts for entry of title, description, and so on. For the subject element, it requires both a keyword and a category to be entered. When the template is in live use and the author reaches the keyword line, a page appears with the entire list of keywords. The author ticks all the appropriate ones, and these are added to the resource metadata. Selection of GCL headings is even easier, from the short drop-down list shown fully extended in Figure 9.1.

In this case, the vocabularies are so small that double indexing is feasible without any need for mapping.

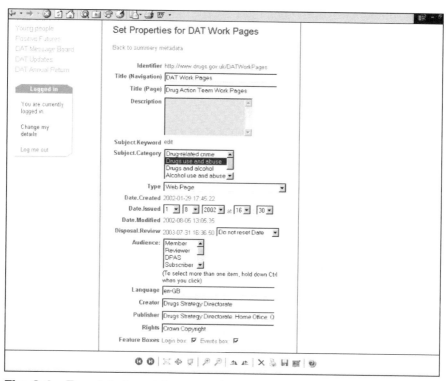

Fig. 9.1 Template for adding metadata to DAT resources

Case 2: Other Home Office applications

Other applications have a much wider scope, as reflected in the Home Office thesaurus of around 2000 preferred terms and 1000 non-preferred terms. This vocabulary is likely to be applied to a range of situations, such as the intranet, internet, electronic document and records management system (EDRMS) and others. And in each application GCL indexing may be needed. To provide for all of them, mappings have been developed within the thesaurus database.

Figure 9.2 shows a typical record in the thesaurus, with broader, narrower and related terms in the conventional style. In addition to the usual elements, the last line of the record shows a mapping to the nearest GCL term. Every descriptor in the thesaurus has one. With this in place, it should be straightforward in future to organize double indexing, without the indexer being aware of it. So if an author adds a keyword such as 'Animal welfare' to a metadata record, the system should look it up in the thesaurus and provide the corresponding GCL term, to be added automatically behind the scenes as a subject category. The author may have to be trained and/or motivated to use the thesaurus, but will not even need to know the GCL exists.

Animal welfare	
SN:	Responsibility for animal welfare and hunting passed to the Department for Environment, Food and Rural Affairs in June 2001.
BT:	Animals
NT:	Protection of Animals Act 1976
	Royal Society for the Prevention of Cruelty to Animals
RT:	Constitutional and Community Policy Directorate
	Department for the Environment Food and Rural Affairs
GCL:	Animal rights and welfare

Fig. 9.2   A typical record from the Home Office thesaurus

Case 3: Policy Hub website

Policy Hub is a web-based resource (www.policyhub.gov.uk) developed by the Policy Studies Directorate (now part of the Cabinet Office Strategy Unit) designed to be the first port of call for promoting improvements in policy-making and delivery. It uses a controlled vocabulary called the Policy Category List (PCL), having around 300 preferred terms. Some of the PCL terms are identical to GCL headings, but others are more specialized, and the orientation throughout is towards the interests of policy-makers.

Figure 9.3 shows the start of the meta-tagging template for entering new items to the Policy Hub. In Figure 9.4 the template has been scrolled down to show the portion where subject metadata are added.

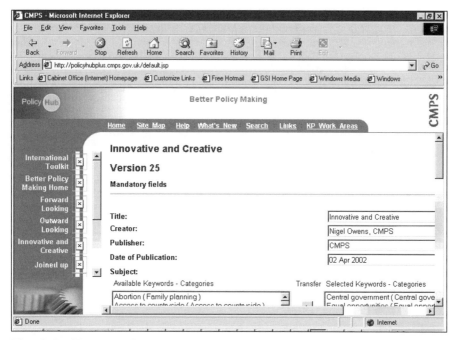

Fig. 9.3 Template for meta-tagging Policy Hub resources – view 1

The left-hand box in Figure 9.4 shows a scrollable list of all the PCL key-words. In parentheses after each one is the corresponding GCL category. The author scrolls down the list, selects the term(s) wanted, and transfers the keyword–category pairs to the right-hand box by clicking on the right-pointing arrow in between. The right-hand box now displays all the subject keywords and categories selected. If the author has a change of mind, the procedure can be reversed by clicking on the left-pointing arrow.

The author continues scrolling down the template adding the rest of the metadata. When finished, the final metadata properties can be inspected as shown in Figure 9.5.

Case 3 illustrates another simple way of managing the indexing process so that the job has to be done only once, but two controlled vocabularies are simultaneously applied. Of course, for both Case 2 and Case 3, somebody in the backroom had to work out a suitable mapping for every term in the specialized vocabulary. This can seem like a long job, but it is very much more efficient than compelling every author to index twice.

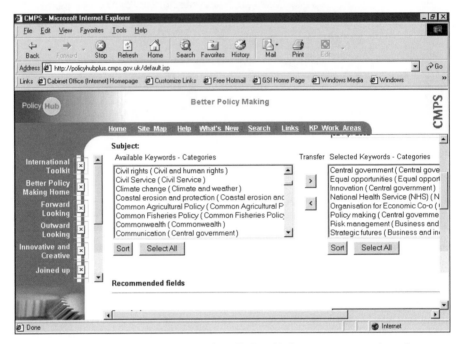

Fig. 9.4 Template for meta-tagging Policy Hub resources – view 2

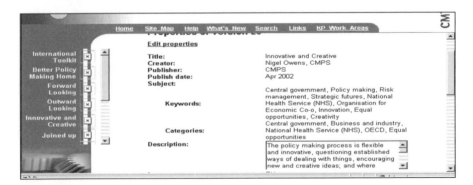

Fig. 9.5 View of properties in Policy Hub when meta-tagging is complete

Other cases

The three cases above were selected because they are simple to explain. But some situations are more complicated. In one government department, the prospect of examining each of the 15,000 descriptors in the thesaurus seemed so daunting that the decision was made to map only from the terms at the top of hierarchies. All the other mappings are derived indirectly through the hierarchical structure.

In other cases, automatic categorization is employed. This technology, if effective, lets the computer take over all the subject indexing. Work is still needed to build a rule-base or train the categorization software but, again, this is a small investment compared with indexing all documents individually. The fully automatic solution has not yet been widely implemented. We can only speculate that in time it could supplant mapping as the more cost-effective solution.

Mapping at the retrieval stage

If the collections to be searched have been indexed with several different vocabularies, then one option is to map the user's search terms to the corresponding ones in each of the vocabularies. The situation is much more complex than that of mapping at input, because there are many more variables. The user's query, even if it contains keywords present in one or more of the vocabularies, may have been prepared without reference to any of them. So one could choose to convert the query directly into each one of the vocabularies; or to convert into just one and thence map to the others; or to ignore the vocabularies and simply search the full text of the resources instead of the metadata.

If we put the other approaches to one side and focus only on mapping between vocabularies, then we still have to consider conversion from any one of the vocabularies to any or all of the others. This time we may not be going from the particular to the general but the other way round, or perhaps from one very detailed vocabulary to another with a different scope, slant and structure. In practice the developer may be wise to limit the options so that all queries are expressed in just one of the vocabularies, and from there mapped wherever possible to the others.

Care must be taken with level of specificity, because mapping from the particular to the general may now broaden the search unacceptably. For example, the term 'Arthritis' in a health thesaurus might map to the GCL heading 'Diseases'. This is fully acceptable as metadata input, because the objective is to add a broad subject category while retaining the original more detailed term as a keyword. But the same solution cannot be applied to convert search statements. If a search for arthritis retrieves hits for all kinds of diseases, the result is probably unacceptable.

Plainly any attempt to exploit a mix of controlled vocabularies by mapping at the search stage must be carefully crafted if it is not to confuse users and/or cause unwelcome noise.

Discussion

To summarize the developments so far, the e-GIF does not claim to be an architecture. It does, however, provide a framework of standards and protocols on which architectures can be built.

The GCL is an umbrella structure. It does not have *centrally managed* links to the many thesauri, classification schemes and taxonomies used in the public sector. But *devolved* links are already there and more are being built. As public bodies strive to meet the 2005 deadline to comply with the e-GMS, many of them are building the GCL into their data input tools, together with mappings from their own vocabularies. The sum of them may be viewed as a virtual, devolved architecture for semantic interoperability.

Devolution of the bridge-building may look like a smart way of avoiding the cost and complication of a centralized system. The cost of developing the mappings (usually an intellect-intensive process) is still there, but it has become much less of an obstacle because it has been farmed out to many hands. Furthermore, devolution gives the mapping job to people who know the nuances of their own vocabularies. Compared with a central team, they should be more competent to understand their specialized terminology and map it correctly. And the responsibility for getting the right metadata on to each electronic item remains with its originating body rather than being passed to a centralized management unit.

Of course there are disadvantages too. Thesauri are not well understood outside a specialized band of information professionals. Even they do not all have the skills to build the mappings. Software tools for integrating controlled vocabularies with off-the-shelf search systems, EDRM systems and CMSs are often rudimentary, and almost never include a mapping capability. Farming out the responsibility to individual organizations obliges each of them to scale a steep learning curve. It has to select, or sometimes commission the tools, for the job. That said, some of the software vendors are noticing the demand for vocabulary tools, and supporting products are beginning to come on to the market.

To help with the learning curve a MWG subcommittee called the Thesaurus Working Group has been formed. In this forum ideas on vocabulary development are shared and the word is spread throughout the public sector. At the time of writing the Group has recently published a survey of controlled vocabularies (see www.govtalk.gov.uk/schemasstandards/metadata_ document.asp?docnum=770) and its next project is to develop guidance on mappings.

Take-up of the devolved model is now steadily expanding. The signs are that the GCL will soon be widely implemented, and this will enable public sector portals to exploit its structure as a high-level directory for users to browse.

Less well developed is the complementary exploitation of thesauri. Internally, many organizations will implement them and will reap the benefits. The same organizations may also enable thesaurus searching on their own internet websites. But for portals and search engines presenting resources indexed with a mix of vocabularies, solutions have still to be developed.

If the mapping tables developed for metadata input make up a virtual semantic architecture, it is tempting to speculate that the same structure in reverse could be used at the retrieval stage, to overcome incompatibilities between thesauri. But this is too simplistic. The mappings work only at a broad level, as demonstrated by the 'Arthritis' example above. To map between thesauri with deep specificity, it is no good using a high-level vocabulary as mediator. An ingenious mapping solution may emerge, but it will probably demand considerable intellectual effort and will certainly face competition from all the other search technologies.

Conclusion

The benefits of standardization flow from constraining everyone to do the same thing the same way. The e-GIF is an assembly of standards, so there are a great many such constraints. But also there are degrees of freedom, particularly in the application of additional controlled vocabularies. This freedom is very helpful in enabling individual organizations to meet the needs and expectations of target audiences in their own sector. At the same time it presents implementation challenges. The input challenges are well on the way to finding solutions. At the search interface, however, there is still huge scope for improving interoperability.

References

Aagard, P. (2001) OIO: Open Public Information Online – in Denmark. In *Online Information 2001*, London, Learned Information, 75-8.

Australian Governments' Interactive Functions Thesaurus (AGIFT). Available at www.naa.gov.au/recordkeeping/gov_online/agift/extract.html.

Dextre Clarke, S. G. (2002) Planning Controlled Vocabularies for the UK Public Sector. In López-Huertas, M. J. and Muñoz-Fernández, F. J. (eds), *Challenges in Knowledge Representation and Organization for the 21st Century: integration of knowledge across boundaries. Proceedings of the Seventh International ISKO Conference; Jul 10-13 2002; Granada, Spain*, Wurzburg, Germany, Ergon Verlag, 142-8.

e-Government Metadata Standard (e-GMS). Available at www.govtalk.gov.uk/schemasstandards/metadata_document.asp?docnum=768.

Google. Available at www.google.com/.

Government Category List (GCL). Available at www.govtalk.gov.uk/schemasstandards/gcl.asp. Links on the same page lead to downloadable versions in several different formats, as well as to related guidance documents.

Government of Canada Core Subject Thesaurus. Available at http://dsp-psd. communication.gc.ca/Thesaurus/index-e.html.

GovTalk. Available at www.govtalk.gov.uk.

Hudon, M. and Hjartarson, F. (2002) Governments Meet People: developing metathesauri in the framework of government online initiatives. In Howarth, L. C., Cronin, C. and Slawek, A. T. (eds), *Advancing Knowledge: expanding horizons for information science. Proceedings of the 30th Annual Conference of the Canadian Association for Information Science; 30 May–1 Jun 2002; Toronto, Canada*. Toronto, Canadian Association for Information Science, 46-60.

Irish Public Service Thesaurus. Available at www.gov.ie/webstandards/metastandards/pst/.

NZGLS thesauri. Available at www.e-government.govt.nz/nzgls/thesauri/.

Policy Hub. Available at www.policyhub.gov.uk See also its sister site, the Strategy Unit, at www.strategy.gov.uk/.

Thesaurus of Australian government subjects. Available at www.govonline.gov.au/projects/standards/TAGS/TAGS.htm.

UK Online. Available at www.ukonline.gov.uk/.

Yahoo! Available at www.yahoo.com/.

Chapter 10

Identifiers and interoperability

ELIZABETH SCOTT-WILSON
The Stationery Office, UK

What are identifiers?

Identification is a fundamental concept in computing. Operating systems and programming languages have to keep track of data and objects resident in memory or in file systems. They do this by being able to point to the thing that they are interested in – a database key being one such example. These private identifiers are maintained within self-contained systems. Often they are not even exposed to programmers – such private identifiers exist to allow access to resources within an encapsulated environment and are designed to work without human intervention. The degree to which resources are accessible in more open computing environments is very different.

A resource in the context of content identification is anything that is a component of some content or document. A resource may be considered to be a distributable item or a content item that exists for some specific purpose, predetermined or not. In this respect, the resource is analogous to an object in computer science. Resources will generally exist within a collection or content package and any particular resource may be used in multiple content packages, each one representing a meaningful view of the data set.

An identifier is a name for something that is believed to be unique within a particular context. As with names, identifiers can be constructed in a variety of ways, including using properties of the resource itself or some random or arbitrary mechanism. Any identifier can only be unique within its intended scope of use. Public identifiers need to be constructed using mechanisms to ensure their uniqueness within a very large domain (all possible public uses).

Identifiers exist separately from the particular resources they identify. The identifier is a referrer to the resource (which is the referent). This means that the entity itself does not need to be digital, but can exist as a digital or physical manifestation, or as an abstraction. The identifier itself is thus an object in its own right with associated properties and processes, and the ability to articulate relationships with other identifiers. Identifiers can be applied to anything that can be described and classified; hence the object being identified can be digital, physical or abstract.

In a digital environment, identifier capabilities can serve to create a separate application layer enabling access to services and the discovery of relationships pertaining to a particular resource.

The most common use of an identifier for an object is to locate it, but there are many other applications that an identifier can enable. Services, such as being able to access a unique description of a resource, are key to interoperable digital systems.

The identifier landscape
Uniform resource identifiers

The uniform resource identifier (URI) is the *de facto* standard for identifying resources on the world wide web. It consists of names and addresses – the union of uniform resource names (URNs) and uniform resource locators (URLs) – and can be references to resources, to people – or, indirectly, to anything.

URNs and URLs are subsets of URIs. They are all supposed to work together in a general scheme for naming, describing and retrieving resources on the internet.

Example URIs include the HTTP scheme for Hypertext Transfer Protocol services, the FTP scheme for File Transfer Protocol services, the Gopher scheme for Gopher and Gopher+ Protocol services and the mailto scheme for electronic mail addresses.

Uniform resource locators

A URL describes a resource in terms of its location – the domain, directory path and file name of the resource. Otherwise described as the global address of that resource on the world wide web, a URL can point to any document, file or directory in any machine on the network. URLs 'break' because information is moved or deleted, networks are busy, sites go out of service or are revised, or computers change addresses. As the world wide web grows, the problem of 'Error 404 Document Not Found' and 'time-out' responses increase. They arise because URLs confuse the name of a resource with its location (Daniel, n.d.).

The widespread use of persistent URLs (PURLs) can help to alleviate this problem.

Persistent URLs

Functionally, a PURL is a URL. A PURL acts as an intermediary for a real URL of a web resource. When a PURL is entered into a browser, the browser sends the page request to a PURL server, which then returns the real URL of the page. This is known as a standard HTTP 'redirect'. PURLs are persistent because once a PURL is established it never needs to change. The real address of the web page may change but the PURL remains the same.

There is a one-to-one relationship between PURL and URL. A PURL cannot point to two different copies of the same resource (Werf-Davelaar, 1999). Developed by OCLC Inc. (US), PURLs were intended to be an interim solution to the uniform resource name problem. A PURL service is being run and maintained at OCLC, though other organizations and individuals are able to register as 'owners'. The success of PURLs is reliant upon the commitment of the owners and service providers in maintaining the PURL–URL relationship (Kuny, 1996).

Uniform resource names

The uniform resource name is a name that identifies a resource or unit of information independently of its location. URN refers to the subset of URI that is required to remain globally unique and persistent even when the resource ceases to exist or becomes unavailable. A URN differs from a URL in that its primary purpose is persistent labelling of a resource with an identifier. URNs are the precursor of Digital Object Identifiers (DOIs).

National bibliographic numbers

The national bibliographic number (NBN) is a URN namespace identifier (NID) used by the national libraries (and only by them) for the identification of deposited publications without an existing identifier (Hakala, 2001), for instance an ISBN, or for descriptive metadata (used in cataloguing entries in national bibliographic databases). Traditionally the assignment of an NBN has been to print-based resources but they are now also being allocated to digital resources.

Some identifiers are not designed for online resources or supported by a resolution system. They include:

- Serial Item and Contribution Identifiers (SICIs)
- Book Item and Component Identifiers (BICIs)
- Publisher Item Identifiers (PIIs)
- Common Information Systems (CISs)
- the Compositeur, Auteur, Editeur code (CAE)
- the International Standard Work Code (ISWC).

Business and technical drivers for the use of identifiers

New capabilities increase interoperability across systems, and promote integration both within and between organizations, by binding identifiers and the functionalities that they allow access to.

If something can be uniquely named within a context, then it can be identified and hence managed. But, just because it is possible to create an identifier does not mean that it always makes sense to do so. As there is a cost associated with the storage and maintenance of identifiers, it is not always pragmatic to identify everything explicitly. The divining rod of what is worth managing and what can be left unmanaged is known as the principle of functional granularity. This can be stated as: 'it should be possible to identify an entity whenever it needs to be distinguished in order for it to perform some function'. Once resources attain a certain significance they demand management.

In an age when content can be broken down into smaller and smaller components, it is less clear at what level they need to be managed. However, organizations must know where they can move their assets so that they can apply policies accordingly. Business factors affect functional granularity such as the need to keep track of rights and permissions related to items within an information source. Such drivers can determine the functional granularity at which components need to be managed and hence identified.

The applications that identifiers support are numerous. Everything from file sharing to tracking use is managed around the application of identifiers. Although it is not always necessary to use an infrastructure to manage these identifiers, when they become public and are used in multiple contexts a new responsibility emerges to maintain those access points to content services.

Some commonly accepted features of identifier-centred solutions include:

- *unambiguous identifiers:* reliable addressing enables supporting and related processes to be automated
- *standard identifiers:* future-proofed for incorporating into other domains
- *rationalized information sets:* reduction in document replication with acceptance of centralized, accessible and controlled sets of information
- *integrated information sets:* linking of multiple versions of the same document giving confidence in the status of the current version
- *confidence in information integrity:* a controlled, current set of information saves much chasing of missing information and checking which version is the latest
- *information conformance:* the new information disciplines and metadata standards conform to accepted standards.

Common benefits sought by using an identifier-centred solution include:

- *information tracking:* maintaining access to information and developing audit trails of the publication life cycle across departments, even post-departmental reorganizations, and across document management, content management and records management IT applications
- *cost reduction:* users no longer waste time following broken links and using out of date information; collaborative workflow is enabled through complete auditing and versioning capability
- *interoperability and permissions:* enabling organizations to manage access permissions to information within, across and outside the

organization; for example, DOI enables conformance with the e-government interoperability framework

- *multiple resolution:* advanced DOI technology empowers users to select the most appropriate form of information, the up to date (or a previous) version, the appropriate language and the most useful format
- *adding value:* building links to related legislation and other relevant information, even to the sub-document level, increases value to the citizen or customer
- *compliance:* with regulation and legislation such as the Freedom of Information Act, the Data Protection Act and the Information Asset Register.

Interoperability

The namespace within which an identifier is created will typically have scheme semantics associated with it. These semantics allow the expression of common approaches to de-referencing (see glossary) any identifier within the scheme. Such scheme level commonality allows for interoperability at the level of technology deployment since this is the means by which the scheme semantics are interpreted.

It has been observed that there are common content types to which a particular resource may be associated. This level of classification allows for the discovery of particular semantics below that of the scheme. These content types are typically developed across organizations as community initiatives by those who recognize that they have a common interest in self-organizing for the good of the community.

Since the identifier exists externally separate from the resources and systems that it is associated with, there is no need to modify data storage systems significantly so they can use the identifiers. The externalization of the identification infrastructure layer means that the distribution of resources across existing repositories and systems, and management of them, is immediately accommodated.

Indeed, identifier management provides a new layer of available services that can be used to address issues of reliability and tracking across existing deployments.

The ability to delegate responsibility for management to an appropriate organization level is another important requirement for identification systems. Many content management systems focus on allowing those who are responsible for content to maintain the resource – yet they often have no means of maintaining identity-related data.

Metadata

In considering how identifier systems enable interoperability, it is important to consider the role of metadata. Different content communities have developed their own metadata element sets. These sets meet specific requirements but are restricted in terms of interoperability. However, by mapping metadata sets into a common format using the identifier as the connecting key, many data sources can be brought together to allow the construction of services that work across their schemas. This process is known as normalization and allows different metadata sets to be used to generate the data that a resolution service requires to build services.

Identifiers have a unique relationship with any item of content, but without metadata it is difficult to understand what has been identified and what the relationship of the identifier to the resource is. Within a resolution system, metadata and identifiers are intricately related (indeed an identifier is itself a piece of metadata). Metadata provides information needed to make use of identifier-based services. The relationship is deeper than the simple ability to construct identifiers to ensure uniqueness within a particular domain, since metadata is often used to build the services that are available when a resource is dereferenced.

In the case of identification, the basic actionability requires the availability of metadata to access services. These elements can contain descriptive, administrative, classification and service information. Metadata serves to characterize the identified resource and can be used to build various applications and services including the administrative controls on the metadata itself.

The simplest application of identifiers is to provide a persistent means to access a resource – at a location that may change. The information associated with the identifier in this system is simply a URL and relevant administrative information for managing this data. From this very basic metadata a persistent service can be provided via a resolution system.

Metadata also supports different functions outside the identifier system. One primary use for metadata is resource discovery – finding a particular resource based upon some characteristics it possesses. In building identification services, it is also useful to think of associated services that may use metadata – such as resource discovery. It can thus be seen that meta-data and services are complementary and both benefit from residing in an identified environment.

The Digital Object Identifier System

The Digital Object Identifier (DOI) System gives persistent identification and interoperable access to intellectual property on digital networks. It provides a framework for managing intellectual content, for linking customers with content suppliers, for facilitating electronic commerce, and enabling automated copyright management for all types of media. In addition, the DOI provides an extensible framework for managing content in any form and at any level of granularity in a digital environment. A DOI is a globally unique and persistent alphanumeric string assigned to an information resource. The information resource or object can be digital, physical or abstract in nature. The information resource is typically, but not limited to, a piece of content such as a document or web page. Every DOI has an optional set of metadata that describes the object referred to by the DOI (title, creator, date, and so on). Thus a DOI provides a means of persistently identifying a piece of intellectual property on a digital network and associating it with a description of that piece of property. DOIs are implemented using Handle System technology and governed by the International DOI Foundation (IDF, www.doi.org), which appoints registration agencies to deal with specific client communities.

DOI was developed by the American Association of Publishers (AAP) in response to the issue of rights management in a distributed network environment and had its official launch at the Frankfurt Book Fair in 1997. Responsibility for the DOI is allocated to the International DOI Foundation, a non-profit organization founded by the AAP. Membership of the IDF includes major publishers and software companies.

DOI has been registered as American National Standard ANSI/NISO Z39.84-2000. DOI resolution is the action of looking up the object(s) associated with a DOI. Both single resolution and multiple resolution are supported using DOIs; single resolution causes a single object to be returned, for example a web page. Multiple resolution allows richer functionality (also called services) to be delivered via the DOI. This might include a choice of multiple formats (HTML, Word, PDF, and so on), multiple languages, multiple versions (draft 1, draft 2, release 1, and so on). The precise kinds of multiple resolution possible and how they are visually represented can be determined by the content owner.

The Handle System

The Handle System is a defined collection of internet protocols and software libraries that are used to implement Handle System functionality. The System was developed and is maintained by the Corporation for National Research Initiatives (CNRI) as part of the Computer Science Technical Reports project, and is funded by the Defense Advanced Projects Agency. CNRI's founder Dr Bob Kahn, co-inventor of TCP/IP, recognized the need for a name management technology as part of a digital object architecture. The Handle System was conceived and developed under the auspices of Dr Kahn.

The Handle System manages handles, which are persistent and unique names for digital objects regardless of where and how they are stored. Each handle consists of a naming authority joined with a unique local name through the use of a forward slash character. A handle us an 'actionable' or 'resolvable' object. It has an associated resolution mechanism that allows the content object associated with the handle to be looked-up over a network (internet) environment.

DOIs have a specific but flexible format that consists of a prefix that identifies a content owner (the naming authority), and a 12-digit alphanumeric suffix that identifies a content component local to the naming authority. The prefix and suffix are separated by the forward slash (see Figure 10.1). The Handle System was designed to have:

Prefix/Suffix
DOI. Naming Authority/Unique Local Name
10.1786/H14N6H2Y50SP

Fig. 10.1 Anatomy of a handle showing the prefix and suffix syntax with a DOI instance given as an example

- *Persistence* Data associated with an identifier can be changed. This allows updating of associated information without the need to alter the identifier associated with a resource. Persistence then becomes a function of administrative care – allowing the same identifier to persist over changes of location, ownership and other state conditions. The Handle System's design allows persistence to be maintained at the level of each identifier so that management of resources can be genuinely delegated.

- *Multiple associations* A single handle can refer to multiple data items within its data structure. Applications can take advantage of this to store a variety of state and service information related to a resource.

- *Flexible syntax* Existing local identifiers may join the handle namespace by acquiring a unique handle naming authority. This allows local namespaces to be introduced into a global context while avoiding conflict with existing namespaces.

- *Distributed architecture* Within The Handle System flexible management configurations are possible allowing management of any given service at multiple sites where each site may distribute its service into a cluster of individual servers. Each handle may also define its own administrator or administrator group, which defines the ownership of each handle. This allows any handle to be managed securely over the internet by its administrator from any network location.

- *Efficient resolution* The Handle System protocol allows highly efficient resolution performance. Separate service interfaces for handle resolution and administration may be defined by any handle service to avoid resolution being affected by computationally costly administration services.

Resolution requests are routed from a high level service to a particular site (which may itself be distributed), which takes responsibility for locating the particular record requested.

Handle-associated data values can be changed as needed to reflect the current state of the identified resource without changing the basic value of the handle itself. This allows handles to be used as identifiers that persist over changes of location, particular implementation and ownership. The Handle System data model allows access control to be defined for each handle, allowing administration that is independent of network architecture.

The Handle System has been designed to accommodate very large numbers of resources and to allow distributed administration over the internet. It supports secured handle resolution and security services such as data confidentiality, service integrity and non-repudiation that are provided upon request.

The International DOI Foundation

Managed by the International DOI Foundation, a member-driven organization, issues of development, policy and licensing of the DOI System to registration agencies are centrally co-ordinated. The IDF is gradually changing its membership basis to an operating federation model to support the growth of and interoperability between appointed registration agencies.

Registration agencies are appointed by the IDF to allow the deposit of DOIs into the Handle System. They operate registration (data deposit) and can build other value-added services based upon metadata supplied by registrants or third parties. This registration creates a record for the DOI in the Handle System and populates that record with associated data. This data can support applications that use the relationships defined in a particular record, and the DOI can then be used in other systems that interact with the Handle System.

The IDF defines policies that apply to all DOIs. These policies are intended to ensure quality in the identifiers created in the system and relate to issues of persistence and interoperability. In addition, since the IDF co-ordinates the system across all registration agencies, there are mechanisms in place to ensure the continued operation of DOIs should any particular agency cease to exist.

In September 2000 the IDF announced the appointment of The Stationery Office as a DOI registration agency.

CrossRef, the first major DOI implementation

CrossRef is a not-for-profit network founded on publisher collaboration, with a mandate to make reference linking throughout online scholarly literature efficient and reliable. It is an infrastructure for linking citations across publishers, and the only full-scale implementation of the Digital Object Identifier System to date.

It holds no full text content, but rather effects links through DOIs, which are tagged to article metadata supplied by the participating publishers. The end result is an efficient, scalable linking system through which a researcher can click on a reference citation in a journal and access a cited article.

Recognizing that a lookup system based on the DOI held the key to a broad-based and efficient journal reference linking system, at the beginning of 2000, the world's leading scholarly publishers joined to form the non-profit, independent organization, Publishers International Linking Association, Inc. (PILA), which operates CrossRef. The board of directors comprises representatives from AAAS (Science), ACM, AIP, APA, Blackwell Publishers, Elsevier Science, IEEE, Kluwer, Nature, OUP, Sage, Springer and Wiley.

The DOI is undergoing registration as a URI scheme in a request for comments, where the DOI semantics are defined such as to ensure that DOIs are resolved using the Handle System and the returned records can be understood. DOIs thus operate in a particular way and this predictability can be used in the construction of applications and systems integration.

Conclusion

Persistence of identifiers is as much a social problem as a technical one. The principle of functional granularity helps organizations select what is worth assigning public identifiers to – and the process of selection is a step forward in the proper management of intellectual property portfolios. But it is not sufficient to create identifiers and to leave them without maintenance. Active management is required to ensure that optimal benefit is gained from the assignment of the identifier. So, there is an ongoing responsibility associated with creating a DOI to ensure that its state is maintained either by the creator or by some delegated third party. The Handle System provides the technical infrastructure by which identifiers may be easily maintained, but maintenance is ultimately an act of administrative diligence, although the availability of tools, made possible by using DOIs, significantly helps.

Glossary

Dereferencing: To access that thing to which an identifier can be resolved. Can also be considered as a look-up operation.

Digital identifier: An identifier that is intended for use in a networked (digital) environment, possibly via a particular scheme.

DOI (Digital Object Identifier) System: A system for registering and resolving identifiers.

Handle System: A system for dereferencing identifiers to a data structure used to store information about a resource.

Metadata: Information about a resource, which may be used in conjunction with an identifier to facilitate the provision of services.

Registration agency: Agent responsible for the deposit of DOIs and registration of data in the DOI System.

Resolution: Mechanism by which data about an identifier is made available to a computer program (also known as dereferencing). Also implies presentation of the resource or service/s back to the requesting user.

Resource: Anything that may be identified, in particular intellectual property in the form of content that might be subject to copyright. May also include physical assets and conceptual or abstract entities.

Scheme: A namespace for identifiers, the name of the class to which something belongs.

Service: A process accessed through the dereferencing of an identifier.

References

Daniel, R. (n.d.) *Uniform Resource Identifiers (URIs)*. Available at www.acl.lanl.gov/URI/uri.html.

Hakala, J. (2001) *Using National Bibliography Numbers as Uniform Resource Names*. Available at www.ietf.org/rfc/rfc3188.txt?number=3188.

Kuny, T. (1996) *Persistent Uniform Resource Locators (PURLs)*. Available at www.nlc-bnc.ca/9/1/p1-224-e.html.

Werf-Davelaar, T. van der (1999) *Identification, Location and Versioning of Web-resources*. Available at www.kb.nl/coop/donor/rapporten/URI.htm#8.3.

Part 3.2
Terminology tools

Chapter 11

Information architecture and vocabularies for browse and search

AMY J. WARNER
Lexonomy, USA

Introduction

As websites have become increasingly large, complex and database-driven, the information architecture that underlies them has become more sophisticated. During the last several years, as it has become more and more difficult to find information on many sites using only natural language, the interest in using controlled vocabularies has grown. It is now possible in many cases to search databases on the web, in addition to the navigation devices that have always existed. However, navigation has also become more complex, as it can now also be database-driven.

This paper discusses the vocabularies that are used in browse and search on the web. It investigates the definitions of these vocabularies, their similarities and differences, and how they are a product of the diverse information architecture that employs them. The paper discusses:

- the basic modes of accessing information on the web: browse and search
- the types of vocabularies that are used on the web and their definitions, similarities and differences
- the basic architectures that employ these vocabularies
- how practical issues affect the choice of the best approach to vocabulary implementation on the web.

There are several excellent publications that discuss the principles of vocabulary development and use on websites, including Rosenfeld and Morville (2002), Reiss (2000) and Wodtke (2002). Specific issues associated with building, using and managing taxonomies within an organization are covered by Becker (2002), Bryar (2001) and Trippe (2001). There are also many publications that address vocabulary construction based on existing standards for their development, the most recent one being Aitchison, Gilchrist and Bawden (2000).

Two modes of finding information
Browsing
Rosenfeld and Morville (2002) describe browsing as both an information-seeking behaviour and a component of the information architecture of a system. Users who browse are sometimes looking for information on a specific topic or even a specific item, but they are also simply exploring the information space of a website to see if it satisfies their information need. Information needs are often amorphous and not defined well enough to be articulated in words that can be formulated into queries. In the information architecture of a website, browsing is accomplished through navigation systems. The basic elements of navigation systems are called labels.

Searching
Searching is a complementary way of finding information. It is more often the case that users know what they want and can therefore formulate a request to the system for the information, although in many cases it is also possible to browse the search terminology to find the exact terms needed. Searching is facilitated in the information architecture through search engines. Search engines tend to fall into two different categories. One category, exemplified by a search engine like Altavista or Lycos, mainly indexes each word in the content object, and then supports natural language searching of the index. Other search engines, such as Verity, used in combination with a content management system, allow for tagging of content objects with terms from a vocabulary, and provide an interface that supports a more structured search. There are many different words to describe the basic elements of search vocabularies, including keywords, keyterms, search terms, terms, index terms and descriptors, among others.

Although natural language indexing and retrieval are important areas, this chapter focuses mainly on systems that employ some type of 'control' over their vocabularies, whether they are labels or search terms.

This chapter covers a few aspects of natural language indexing and search, mainly as a mechanism to show some of the advantages and disadvantages of controlled vocabularies.

A continuum of vocabularies

Vocabulary design and development can be seen as being part of a number of choices along a continuum. Vocabularies may be anywhere on this continuum, which shows how their design can become increasingly complex. This continuum ranges from least to most complex as follows.

Simple lists

These are straightforward lists of terms, which are sometimes controlled and sometimes are not. In many cases, organizations have specific lists of terms for things like format (for example text, image or sound) and target audience (for example students, educators or administrators), to name a few. The major characteristic of simple lists is that they are short enough for the user to grasp them without requiring further organization other than alphabetical.

Synonym rings

These are sets of terms that are considered to be equivalent for the purposes of retrieval. An example of a synonym ring for stars (in the sense of astronomy) might be:

    Stars
    Constellations
    Galaxies
    etc.

In the case of synonym rings, these terms are used to expand queries for content objects. If a user enters any one of these terms as a query to the system, all items are retrieved that contain any of the terms in the cluster. Synonym rings are often used in systems where the underlying content objects are left in their unstructured natural language format, and the control is achieved through the interface by drawing together similar terms into these clusters.

Taxonomies

Taxonomies are systems of labels that form a hierarchical navigation scheme. It is important to note that the term 'taxonomy' is much broader within the information architecture community than it is within the scientific community. This term originally began within the scientific community; for example in biology it would be used to describe hierarchies of families of plants and animals that are increasingly more inclusive as one moves up the hierarchy.

In contrast, in the information architecture community, taxonomies can mean anything from simple lists to navigation hierarchies to true thesauri, depending on who you are talking to. In this paper, taxonomy will be restricted in meaning to navigation hierarchies only, for example:

> Planting implements
>> Hoes
>> Spades
>> Trowels
>> etc.

Thesauri

Thesauri are the most complex of the controlled vocabularies covered in this paper. Thesauri are usually restricted to a particular subject domain (for example medicine or horticulture) and usually consist of a large number of terms, sometimes numbering in the thousands. Thesauri currently organize terms in three ways: as equivalent, hierarchical or related terms.

Equivalent terms

These are sets of terms in which one is the preferred term for the purposes of tagging and searching. Terms that are equivalent for the purposes of retrieval are mapped to the preferred term, as in:

> Eye doctor
>> USE **OPTOMETRIST**

> **OPTOMETRIST**
>> Used for Eye doctor

Optometrist is the preferred term, the term that is used in tagging items in the collection. Eye doctor is called an entry term or a non-preferred term. This term is not used in indexing but can be used in searching, in which case the system will automatically retrieve all the items tagged with optometrist.

The equivalence relationship in thesauri differs from synonym rings in the sense that synonym rings are used to provide control over similar terms in a collection that is not tagged; that is, there is no control at input (tagging) but there is control at output (searching). On the other hand, thesauri provide control at both input and at output.

Hierarchical terms

Once equivalent terms are identified, all the preferred terms are sorted into broad categories called facets (as described in the next section). These terms are then organized into hierarchies of increasingly specific terms. For example:

    Pet birds
        NT Canaries
            Parakeets
            Parrots

The hierarchical relationship can aid users in finding the most specific term they are looking for in a search.

Related terms

These are terms that are related in a way other than hierarchally. In general, these are terms from different facets or categories that are related. For example:

    Canaries
        RT Canary seed
            Canary breeders
            Canary cages

These vocabulary options are shown here in a continuum because, in fact, all of these vocabularies are related in some way and because one can stop anywhere in this continuum. Where one stops depends on the money avail-able to devote to vocabulary control, the characteristics of the collection, and the technical infrastructure in place to implement it.

Another point is that these vocabularies relate in different ways to the basics of browse and search. Simple lists can be used either as labels in a navigation system or as search terms in the search engine. Synonym rings are exclusively related to searching and can be generated either manually or automatically, through a statistical analysis of the collection. Taxonomies are defined here as being restricted exclusively to the navigation system, and differ from simple lists in that the number of labels to be organized is much larger and therefore a hierarchical scheme is used. Finally, thesauri are used strictly in search operations. However, they do have a relationship to browsing, as in many systems the taggers and searchers can browse the thesaurus to pick out tagging or search terms.

Facets of content objects and facets of vocabularies

Content objects and, in many cases, vocabularies need to be organized. A principle known as faceting is basic to organization of this sort. Facets in information architecture are described by Fast, Leise and Steckel (2002). However there is a basic distinction in how the term 'facet' relates to these two.

Facets of content objects are really attributes that need to be described (indexed) so that they can be found later in searching or browsing. Con-sider the following example:

> A written content object describes methods for cultivating roses. It is written in a very basic style, appropriate to someone who is a beginner in this area. The website that provides access to this content object also has an educational mission and wants to help people who teach horticulture find basic material for their students.

This is only one of several hundred items in the collection that are about specific flowers or plants.

To retrieve this item it is necessary to set up a structure that separates the distinct aspects of items that appear consistently throughout the col-lection. These aspects, or facets, in this case might be:

- *topic* What the item is about, in this case, cultivation (as distinct from eliminating pests, flower arranging, or any of many other topics)
- *content type* How the item treats the material, in this case whether it is text, image, sound file or another format.
- *plant type* The kind of plant described, such as flower, tree, shrub, and so on.
- *intellectual level* How scholarly the item is (at basic, intermediate or advanced level)
- *target audience* Who would be most interested in retrieving this item (beginners, greenhouse owners, educators, and so on).

In a search system, these facets become the structure of the underlying database that is searched, in other words the fields that can be searched. This can be thought of as structural metadata, since it describes the structure of the items in the collection. It is this type of metadata that is implemented in schemes like XML and to which the many technical metadata standards refer. Having separate fields in a database-driven website enables the user to make clear distinctions between elements that need to be searched.

In the case of a browsing system, the different elements that need to be highlighted might be set up in the interface as separate hierarchies that could be navigated. In a navigation system having separate hierarchies, it helps the user clearly identify the basic organization of the collection. In more advanced systems that have navigation systems associated with databases, it allows for postcoordination through the navigation system, which will be described later.

It is important to distinguish between the fields or aspects of items that are to be described (the structural metadata) and the actual elements that are put into those fields. In the context of this paper, these are the actual terms or labels that come from controlled vocabularies or labelling schemes.

In the case of these elements, whether or not they are divided into facets depends on how many of them there are. Sometimes these are short lists of terms, such as for a target audience. So, for example, if the choices for target audience consist of only the three terms (basic, intermediate and advanced), a simple list will certainly be enough. They can be implemented as lists of links or pull-down menus in the interface.

However, if there are hundreds or thousands of elements, it is important that some organization be applied. This organization is called facet analysis. In this case, there is a significant amount of intellectual effort during the design phase of the website that consists of identifying the basic categories of the vocabulary and sorting these terms into those categories. For example, in a medical system that implements a large medical vocabulary, the facets might be:

Diseases
Disease-causing Agents
Surgical Procedures
Treatments and Interventions
Medical Personnel
etc.

Facet analysis was introduced in the previous section and is one of the first steps in organizing a vocabulary with a large number of terms or labels.

In search systems that use thesauri, a similar methodology is employed. Again, terms are collected and sorted into facets. The medical example just presented could just as easily be used for terms in a thesaurus as for a navigation scheme.

There are different methods for obtaining the terms for taxonomies and thesauri. In many organizations there are lists or partial lists of terms floating around that can be quite useful as a starting point. Users can also be asked to supply lists of terms that they frequently encounter in their work, although it is generally more successful to generate candidate lists and have them react to these. Another useful way, if the organization has a search engine, is to analyse search logs for candidate terms. Finally, the actual content can be analysed to determine the most useful terms.

Precoordination, postcoordination and specificity

The notion of specificity and how it relates to precoordination and postcoordination is central to understanding controlled vocabularies on websites. This is because hierarchies are basic to browsing and searching and they tend to arrange terms in order of their increasing specificity.

In its most straightforward application, specificity is relevant to simple lists as described above. As stated here, these are aspects of items such as target audience or format. These are usually fairly short lists for two reasons:

- There simply aren't very many of them.
- Users don't search a collection for items on these aspects alone. They combine them with other facets, such as topic. In information retrieval, this is referred to as limiting a search. It is useful to determine which aspects of the collection are limiters and which are primary search terms, because very often limiters have fewer terms with simple organization schemes.

Recall and precision

In order to understand how specificity relates to primary search terms such as topic, it is necessary to understand the notions of recall and precision. In any given retrieval system, including those on the web, when content objects are tagged, they are essentially being put into the same set as other items tagged with the same term. The goal here is to maximize the number of relevant items in the set that are considered to be about the same topic without overwhelming the user with peripheral or completely irrelevant content. Precision relates to the number of retrieved items that the user deems relevant to his or her search; it is a measure of accuracy. Recall is the number of relevant documents retrieved as a proportion of the total number of (hypothetically) relevant items in the collection; it is a measure of comprehensiveness. The goal in topical retrieval is not to get one item (unless the user wants a specific item, in which case he or she would probably use another approach) and also not to get thousands, but to aim for a number that can be evaluated thoroughly.

Recall has had a controversial history in information retrieval and is probably not a very useful measure for the web. In static databases the situation is bad enough – imagine trying to determine the total number of relevant items in a database of thousands of items for any given search. In the web environment, this is even more problematic given its dynamic nature.

Precision is another matter, however. Precision has become an increasingly big problem as the web has grown in size and users frequently complain of retrieving thousands of items when they try to use many of the search engines. Hence the introduction of metadata and the notion of adding more structure to content objects and searches.

So the notion of specificity as applied to primary search elements such as topic involves mainly the notion of maximizing precision. One way this was done on the web initially was to add ranking into search engine algorithms. In the more structured environment discussed here, achieving optimal specificity involves considering additional variables in designing vocabularies.

The first of these is the size of the collection. Assume, for example, that there is a collection of 6000 items in a given subject area. Contrast that with a collection in the same subject area of 60,000 items. In this case, the number of terms that would need to be created to cover the subject domain exhaustively would be the same. However, one of the common misconceptions about search and retrieval is that tagging languages have to be exhaustive in the same way that the definitive dictionary would. This is not the case because, as stated differently above, the goal is to produce useful sets of items rather than a complete inventory of the language of a subject domain. Thus the collection with 6000 items would require a smaller number of useful sets and the collection of 60,000 items would require more. To achieve this, the vocabulary for the smaller collection would in general have fewer and more general terms, while the larger collection would work with a larger number of more specific terms.

One way to increase the specificity of a vocabulary is to increase the number of semantically complex phrases. Consider a situation where there are items that discuss information architecture software. There are three ways to accomplish this through the design and implementation of a vocabulary.

- create a vocabulary with three terms
  - information
  - architecture
  - software
- create a vocabulary with two terms
  - information architecture
  - software
- create a vocabulary with one term
  - information architecture software

The first two options would be considered for small collections, while the third would be considered for larger ones. In other words, there are specificity choices that take the individual words in a subject domain and either leave them as single words or combine them into more complex topics.

The advantage of achieving the right level of specificity for a given vocabulary is that the sets that are retrieved are maximized for precision. The disadvantage of having terms that are too general is that they tend to combine in unpredictable ways. Consider the example above. Suppose a user combines 'software AND architecture' in a search of the system that has been tagged with the three individual terms. This will retrieve items that are about software for architects along with the items about software for information architects. The disadvantage of having terms that are very specific is that the vocabulary quickly becomes very large, since in most cases the terms 'software' and 'information architecture' would also exist as useful terms.

Precoordination and postcoordination

The notions of precoordination and postcoordination relate directly to this notion of specificity. Precoordination and postcoordination systems combine terms from the semantic space of a subject domain to form more semantically complex terms. In precoordinate systems, many of these combinations are made at the time the vocabulary is designed, as exemplified by option three above. In postcoordinate systems, the semantic space is broken up into simpler, more basic terms, with the assumption that users will make more complex topics by dynamically combining the basic terms at the time of searching. The first option above is the best example of this. The second option is a compromise and often a good one in vocabulary design.

In general, search systems can rely more on postcoordination than precoordination, assuming the availability of appropriate technology and the ability of users to use postcoordination. Browsable, navigation systems, by their nature, are more limited in their ability to allow users to combine terms, and therefore their labels tend to be longer and more specific.

Another important point that the information architect should take into account is that in systems with both a taxonomy and a thesaurus, the terms in both may not be in one-to-one correspondence because of the issues just discussed.

The point of this discussion has been to emphasize how semantically complex information architecture can be. The best design often comes from a combination of past experience and trial and error.

Vocabulary implementation and information architecture

So far, this discussion has focused on different types of vocabularies, their characteristics and basic issues in their design. The two main types of vocabulary are those for searching (mainly thesauri) and those for browsing (mainly taxonomies). There are four options for implementation based on the technologies that currently exist on the web:

- browsing taxonomies that cannot combine labels
- browsing taxonomies that can combine labels (facet combination through the interface)
- searching systems that cannot combine search terms
- searching systems that can combine search terms.

Browsing taxonomies that cannot combine labels

The first option, browsing without facets, is the oldest one in existence on the web. It involves a system of discrete HTML files, many of which contain hyperlinks. The challenge of the designers of this system is to determine what hyperlinks to choose for each file and how to 'hard code' these into a network or web. This option is mainly adopted by organizations that have small websites and/or limited resources. It is technologically the simplest of the four options, but it does not scale. There are numerous cases where sites that have grown organically in this way have simply become uncontrollable, as the organization and its collection have grown. This has been aggravated by the fact that in many of these situations organizations have moved from a centralized method of design and maintenance to a decentralized one. Often communication in these situations breaks down, as does any consistency in the design of the website. Examples of organizations that continue to use this option well are those that are small enough to remain centralized in design and maintenance.

Browsing taxonomies that can combine labels through the interface

The second option, creating a browse structure that supports a combination of labels through the interface, is an interesting one. In this case a centralized database is created. Items are tagged with labels from each facet in the taxonomy and the database contains these labels along with the URL pointing back to the HTML file. The advantage of this system is that changes are made through a centralized database rather than a collection of possibly decentralized HTML files. A good example of an implementation of this is Epicurious.com. Recipes are tagged for their ingredients, cuisine, special occasions, ethnic origin and other useful aspects of these items. Instead of requiring users to choose aspects of items through a search interface, the system allows them to click on links they are interested in iteratively and progressively narrow their searches. Underlying this interface is a system that formulates a search and passes it to the database. The advantage of this type of system is that it feels very comfortable to users, and in fact is transparent to them. The disadvantage is that it only works well for systems that are not too complex, like recipes or greeting cards. When this approach is scaled to larger, more complex collections, the number of facets involved frequently becomes too numerous and there is a danger that users may get lost.

Searching systems that cannot combine search terms

The third option refers mainly to sites where the statistical indexing algorithms are performed on unstructured items. This is the second oldest type of system on the web, and is exemplified by most of the publicly available search engines, such as Lycos, AltaVista and many others. Many organizations take this option for their intranets, as some of this software is relatively inexpensive and does not involve setting up and maintaining a structured database.

Searching systems that can combine search terms

The final option is the most recent. It involves the most expense and technical sophistication, as the organization must invest in a content management system to house their metadata, some kind of tagging infrastructure and a search engine that will handle the structured nature of their data. Organizations must also be able to rely on their users to understand the system and how to maximize its benefit. The advantage is that through this structure and high quality tagging, searches are often more targeted and produce better results. Because of the expense and time taken to set up these systems they are considered or implemented mostly by larger organizations.

Putting it all together

The discussion here has focused on the range of options in controlled vocabularies, their advantages and disadvantages, and how they might fit into a basic information architecture. There are many options and variables to compare and contrast, and no definitive answers to the many questions that arise when considering this subject. Factors to consider include the size and subject domain of the collection, the size and resource base of the organization, the availability of necessary technology and the level of sophistication of end-users.

In information architecture there are no laws or definite answers about vocabularies. However, there are some trends and tendencies that are worth pointing out. One is that browsing and searching satisfy different information needs and therefore they are both now available in more and more sites, especially the larger ones.

Another tendency is for sites to create 'hybrid' systems; this happens especially with the larger sites. This involves thinking about the collection to be tagged and searched in terms of its characteristics and value to the organization. For example, there has been a tendency to decide only to apply more expensive, labour intensive manual tagging to those parts of the collection that are deemed more valuable to the organization and to use other, less expensive and less labour intensive methods to sections of the collection that are deemed either too peripheral or ephemeral to deserve the investment of a manual approach. Often these are automatic approaches.

In the end, any organization must evaluate the utility of designing and implementing controlled vocabularies and taxonomies against the internal needs of their employees and the outside needs of their customers. This paper has shown that these decisions rest on many factors, dealing with business context, system issues like amount of content and technology, and the characteristics and sophistication of end-users. The answers to the complex questions of controlled vocabularies will differ for each organization because each one is unique in its resources and orientation to staff and users.

References

Aitchison, J., Gilchrist, A. and Bawden, D. (2000) *Thesaurus Construction: a practical manual,* 4th edn, Chicago, Fitzroy Dearborn.

Becker, L. (2002) *Taxonomic Distress: the challenge of developing effective taxonomies for web-facing businesses.* Available at www.adaptivepath.com/publications/essays/archives/000032.php.

Bryar, J. V. (2001) *Taxonomies: the value of organized business knowledge.* Available at www.newsedge.com/materials/whitepapers/taxonomies.pdf.

Fast, K., Leise, F. and Steckel, M. (2002) *All About Facets and Controlled Vocabularies.* Available at www.boxesandarrows.com/archives/large/003137.php.

Reiss, E. (2000) *Practical Information Architecture: a hands-on approach to structuring successful websites,* New York, Addison-Wesley.

Rosenfeld, L. and Morville, P. (2002) *Information Architecture for the World Wide Web,* 2nd edn, Cambridge, O'Reilly.

Trippe, B. (2001) *Taxonomies and Topic Maps: categorization steps forward.* Available at www.econtentmag.com/r21/2001/trippe8_01.html.

Wodtke, C. (2002) *Information Architecture: blueprint for the web,* Indianapolis, New Riders.

Chapter 12

The taxonomy

A mechanism, rather than a tool, that needs a strategy for development and application

ALAN GILCHRIST
TFPL Ltd, UK

Introduction

'Taxonomies are chic,' said Thomas Koulopoulos somewhat alarmingly at one of TFPL's annual EBIC meetings. But Koulopoulos, as CEO of the Delphi Consulting Group, also knows that developing and applying a taxonomy is hard work and requires a lot of effort. The Delphi Group and others, such as PDR (the 'club' of pharmaceutical industry documentalists), have all produced figures charting the rise in the number of enterprises embarking on the taxonomy trail – typically, for corporate enterprises, the figure has grown from 20% two or three years ago to around 80% in 2003. A great deal of activity, then, acknowledging the need for hard work and exhibiting a wide range of approaches and techniques, indicating evidence of the importance of human intervention. It is not surprising in these relatively early days to find a lack of case study material, particularly success stories with encouraging pictures of good practice. (On the other hand, the honest account of building a taxonomy by McLaughlin and Greenwood described in Chapter 14 should not be regarded so much as discouraging as a useful indication of the pitfalls that many must be experiencing.)

Drivers

The obvious generic driver is, of course, information overload; this phrase has become a cliché, while the problem continues to get worse. The prime example of unorganized information glut may be the internet, but many large organizations are facing similar problems on their intranets. Three or four hundred servers publishing material with little more standardization imposed than the look-and-feel aspects of web pages is not unusual, resulting in silos of information that are virtually inaccessible by anyone other than the originators. Companies like Microsoft and BT estimate the number of documents on their intranets to be between two and three million, tending to grow exponentially; the situation is further exacerbated by the availability of gateways from the intranet to the internet. A second driver, widely reported and acknowledged, is that many people are unable to conduct effective searches, either through lack of expertise, interest or time, or indeed all three. The most common search uses either one word or a phrase with no Boolean operators. Even the most sophisticated search engines using combinations of complex mathematical algorithms, a sprinkling of linguistic analysis and relevance ranking will often produce thousands of hits (a search on 'information architecture' using Google produced 'about 4,570,000 hits', while combining the two words into a phrase produced 'about 245,000'). The hapless user skims through the first couple of pages, picking out the references most likely to be useful and moves on to the next task. A third problem is that of the variety of functional and organizational languages, which are often so mysterious to outsiders as to limit, or even prevent, communication between functions within organizations or between similar functions in different organizations. A figure often quoted is that some 80% of the information stored by an organization has been created within that organization. This communication problem can become particularly acute following mergers and acquisitions, or with the establishment of extranets linking organizations with their suppliers or clients.

Consequently, many enterprises are discovering that when installing second-generation intranets and/or portals it becomes necessary to provide more effective navigational aids to repositories, documents, content and people. This will often become entwined with a new or revised content management system (CMS), or electronic records and document management system (ERDMS), which will lead to an examination of metadata and metadata standards and so to the question of navigation and search, and the supporting role of the taxonomy.

External drivers will include the Freedom of Information Act in the UK, and the Sarbanes-Oxley legislation in the USA, following the Enron scandal. It is a truism to say that senior management is constantly seeking ways in which individual employees and groups can improve their efficiency and effectiveness, while at the same time avoiding such risks as loss of trade and customers and of litigation caused by negligence. A taxonomy is not going to solve these problems by itself, but it is a key component of information architecture. This is not yet widely appreciated by senior management, IT specialists or users, so that many information architects may be found working quietly in the background with limited resources.

What is a taxonomy?

Several authors in this book have mentioned taxonomies, and Amy Warner has described it well as one of the techniques in the armoury that includes the classification and the thesaurus. Unfortunately, the word is used in different ways by different people. Briefly, a taxonomy can be a humanly produced algorithm to support automatic indexing where huge inputs militate against the employment of indexers; it can be a categorization automatically produced by specialist software (though human intervention is usually found to be necessary); it can be a tool used at the search interface to aid query formulation by, typically, the provision of synonym clusters and search term disambiguation; it can, most commonly, be seen as a front-end navigation tool where the user is presented with a series of interlinking menus allowing the searcher to 'drill down' to required content – the most widely known examples being provided by the manually produced Yahoo! and the Open Directory Project, and the automatic categorization tools mentioned above.

TFPL takes the view that a 'corporate taxonomy' can be viewed as an enterprise-wide master file of the vocabularies and their structures, used or for use, across the enterprise, and from which specific tools may be derived for various purposes, of which navigation and search support are the most prominent. This master file can encompass terminology that relates not only to information objects or content, but to people and their expertise, and to the organization itself – its functions, processes, rules and regulations, procedures and forms. Such a taxonomy would support a system capable of providing answers, or routes to answers, to a continuum of questions that might be asked by any employee, including:

- What rights do I have as an employee?
- What training is available, and how can I prepare for performance assessment?
- What are the procedures for applying for an upgrade of my PC?
- What patents have been applied for recently relating to the project on which I am working?
- Who in the company has information on some aspect of my research?
- Does the company support any communities of interest in my area of concern?

This wider view of taxonomy building can have interesting consequences. One UK government agency has built a taxonomy that focuses on its own functions, its 'clients' and their activities, and document types. While actual subject content does not currently feature as a search option, the ability to navigate to content indirectly, via a function or a client activity, has been found to be effective.

It should, by now, be clear that the word 'taxonomy' represents a complex of considerations revolving around words and their meanings, and their relationships; it is located in the space previously occupied by classification and the thesaurus, both of which continue to be vital ingredients in the present electronic environment.

A taxonomy strategy

TFPL's eight-step process takes clients through the stages of taxonomy construction and implementation. The exact process will vary for different clients, but the process can be useful in helping organizations determine their starting point and the essential stages to follow.

1   *Creating the foundation* Organizations approach taxonomies from a variety of directions and often have little practical experience of their creation and use. It can be vital to hold an initial orientation workshop as a foundation for subsequent work. The purpose of such workshops is to build consensus on project objectives among key stakeholders and to raise awareness of the kind of issues involved in introducing a corporate taxonomy.

2   *Environmental assessment* The purpose of the environmental assessment is to gain an understanding of the organization's existing information

policies, systems and behaviour so that a clear business case can be made for the creation and use of a taxonomy and a realistic project plan drafted.

3   *Developing the business case* This step includes estimating the scope and resource requirements of the project as well as assessing the likely benefits of the working taxonomy. Although it is notoriously difficult to quantify the costs and benefits of information management activities, a project of this sort requires a sound business argument to justify the likely investment in time and resources. Reducing search time and frustration, enhancing knowledge sharing are goals whose performance can be measured. Reducing the risk of litigation or of losing customers may also be used as sound arguments.

4   *Establishing the management framework* The exact management framework for the project will depend on the nature of the particular enterprise. It is important the project is owned by the business and has a suitably senior sponsor or high level steering group behind the project manager and team.

5   *Planning the project* A sound plan is essential for the success of any taxonomy project. Detailed consideration should be given to objectives and priorities; targets, schedules, and key milestones for review; implementation planning and interaction with other activities; estimate of required resources; identification of constraints and risks; and assessment of skills required and their availability in-house.

6   *Project implementation* This will vary from organization to organization depending on the size and complexity of project and existing systems with which the project must interface. Consideration should be given to all aspects of the launch. Proper documentation should be available to ensure that the system's administrators and users are aware of the innovation, and are prepared to run and use it effectively. Orientation workshops may be useful.

7   *Monitoring and feedback* A taxonomy is an organic thing, constantly subject to changing requirements. Some of these changes will be demanded by the system itself, others by organizational growth and shifting user requirements. Continuous monitoring and feedback are therefore necessary to make sure the taxonomy evolves in harmony with user demands and corporate requirements. This may be monitored automatically through logging software, although one-off evaluation exercises

should also be considered and the taxonomy team should be alert at all times to user feedback through formal and informal channels.

8 *Maintenance* Monitoring will be unproductive if user opinion is not acted upon. This requires formal mechanisms for validating changes to the system and a system manager who has the authority to revise the taxonomy following consultation with users.

The eight steps in practice

Many organizations, if not actually falling at the first fence, find it difficult to reach that critical mass which sets the project on its way. On one occasion, an initial orientation meeting was attended by the principal stakeholders of a multinational manufacturing firm. Round the table were individuals in charge of the company's internet website, the corporate intranet and an e-commerce initiative; representatives of the corporate communications function and marketing; and webmasters from two of the business divisions. There was also someone who had been responsible for the procurement of a search engine for use on the corporate intranet and on offer to the intranets of the business divisions, and who took the view from the start that a taxonomy was not therefore needed. Nevertheless, the meeting concluded that a new meeting should be convened with representatives of the corporate function and webmasters from all the business divisions. At this second meeting it was agreed that navigation between business divisions could be greatly improved by the building and implementation of a common taxonomy, and even that in certain cases control of electronic publishing in the company was getting out of hand. The participants departed, charged with the task of gathering data on the situations prevalent in their areas prior to a meeting for them to discuss the way forward: in essence to agree a project plan. That meeting never took place when it was discovered that the costs of the project were to be borne by the business divisions, and not by the corporate centre.

Some managers in corporate enterprises opt for the less visible approach, hoping to be able to construct a proof of concept in one area, in the hope that the idea will spread. One project manager, who was trying to facilitate the start-up of a number of communities of interest (CoIs), became hooked on the importance of the taxonomic approach and was looking for ways of establishing some corporate commonality of language between the CoIs, while encouraging them to grow their own specialist vocabularies.

The final hope was that if enough CoIs made advances in this area the whole organization might become 'infected'. These two cases point to one of the debates in taxonomy building: whether it is better to work top down, or bottom up. In practice, it is probably best to attempt both at the same time, where the top down concentrates on functions and business processes, and so on, and the bottom up focuses on content. Eventually, the question of the optimal level of descriptive detail needed will arise, and hence the optimal use of a search engine, or other supporting software, in conjunction with the taxonomy.

There is a danger in bypassing the early stages of foundation building and holistic planning, which was highlighted in a project to conduct a 'health check' on taxonomy work in progress. This international consultancy was on the point of rolling out a content management system to support a new intranet, accompanied at a very late stage by a taxonomy hurriedly put together by the company librarian in bilateral consultation with subject experts in the various business centres. The health check consisted of a greatly cut down environmental assessment, which identified a number of failings and potential risks that could have been avoided had proper consultation been instigated earlier, particularly between the Librarian and the CMS developers; and multilaterally between the Librarian and a number of information professionals in different parts of the company. Another international consultancy developed an 'enterprise-wide' taxonomy in one Anglophone country, only to have it totally rejected by another.

This chapter has not touched on the basic techniques of taxonomy building, techniques that have adapted the older ones of classification and facet analysis, and the construction of thesauri. What has been proposed is that the building of a corporate-wide taxonomy involves considerable intellectual effort and consultation over a significant period of time, not including the resource needed for continuous maintenance. It therefore seems ridiculous not to plan and resource a taxonomy project properly when one reflects that it is often designed to support a corporate intranet and/or portal – installations costing orders of magnitude more than the cost of building a taxonomy.

Chapter 13: a case study

From architecture to construction

The electronic records management programme at the DTI

LIZ MACLACHLAN
Department of Trade and Industry, UK

Introduction

The Department of Trade and Industry (DTI), with around 5000 staff in HQ and a further 6000 in executive agencies, is one of the major UK departments of state. Its overall aim is to generate wealth for everyone in the UK by helping people and businesses to become more productive and more successful through innovation, creativity and enterprise. It promotes UK business at home and overseas, invests in the UK science and technology base, protects the rights of working people and consumers, and works for fair markets in the UK and internationally. As an organization it is heavily dependent on good information, both to enable it to function and also as a product – the DTI produces a very large number of reports, advice and guidance in support of its various activities. But DTI's history of over 200 years of mergers and de-mergers with other bits of government – and the wide variation of its activities, from promotion and support to business at one end and regulation at the other – has resulted in a highly federal, independent culture. Until recently information has tended to be held and managed locally, with little encouragement for sharing or the adoption of common standards. However, a number of factors, one of which is the DTI's own championing of the knowledge economy, have combined in recent years to promote a more 'joined-up' department. This case study describes how this new approach is being supported by the development, through practical projects, of an information architecture.

Information management – early days

DTI's formal interest in information management dates back to the late 1980s, when two separate drivers, one negative and one positive, came together to raise awareness.

The positive driver was a seminal Cabinet Office study into managing information as a resource (Cabinet Office, 1989), which recommended a number of practical steps for departments to take, including a formal information policy and an audit of information resources. DTI was an active participant in the study, adopted its first information management policy in 1993 and undertook a series of audits into both resources and IM practice between 1993 and 1997.

The negative driver was senior embarrassment when, on several occasions, files could not be produced when needed. This was the consequence of decisions taken in 1982, when an internal review had recommended that business units should take responsibility for the management of their records, that local administration staff should be trained as records managers and, crucially, that a central IT system should manage the files. The reasoning behind this was sound – records should be close to the people who needed to use them, so speeding up decision-making – and at first all went well. People still worked mainly in paper off the file, and most staff were familiar with good record-keeping practices. But, over time, those staff left or retired, records management was not included on induction courses and gradually the organization forgot how things used to be done. The status of record managers declined, and 'filing' was often given to the newest, most junior recruit with little or no training. And, because of cost and complexity, the unifying IT system was not developed.

The aim of the Records Management Initiative, launched in 1990, was to raise the standard of record keeping across the Department through improved training of staff and records managers, and through audits of existing practice. It was not a moment too soon. In 1993 the Department implemented its first cross-department office system, Office Systems in Protected Environment (OSPREY), including e-mail, spreadsheets, word-processing, electronic bulletin boards and a basic document management system. While many parts of the Department had had computers for some time OSPREY put a computer on everyone's desk and allowed them to create and store information locally much more easily than before. An outline policy on the handling of electronic records, which became one of the source documents for the first Public Records Office (now renamed the National Archive (NA)) standard, was developed that same year. And, in 1996, a project to put in place the computerized system to manage the Department's files, the departmental records management system (DRMS), was finally begun.

But by the late 1990s existing paper and electronic systems were under considerable strain. Internal information could be stored in multiple locations; some were official, such as the paper registered files managed through the file management system DRMS, or the OSPREY document management system used by some but not all units. However, there were many more unofficial storage locations such as unregistered paper folders or multiple local electronic stores. Some of these stores were shared, but most (personal drives or e-mail folders) were not. The intranet, launched in 1996, had become very popular, with many local sites springing up. But there was no overall editorial control and information was often duplicated or out of date. External sources were increasingly available through the intranet, as were the staff directory, the DTI version of the knowledge network and the finance and personnel systems. In short, it was difficult and confusing for anyone seeking to find relevant information quickly.

There was also external pressure to improve information management in the shape of the Modernizing Government initiative driven from the Cabinet Office, one of whose key themes was sharing information and knowledge, and which set all government departments the target of 1 January 2004 for their records to be available electronically. DTI initiated a major programme towards the end of 1999 to meet this target. The electronic records and document management (ERDM) programme, designed and delivered in conjunction with the Department's strategic IT partners Unitas, itself a partnership between Fujitsu and LogicaCMG, included major streams to address information and change management as well as system design and development. But a major question was what the information management stream should comprise. To help answer that question a working group on information architecture was set up.

Information architecture – theoretical model

The working group comprised around 25 people drawn from operational units as well as information professionals. Its remit was to design the Department's information space to meet business needs, both now and to support changing needs in the future. It was clear that we needed a flexible approach, to have access to a wide range of sources, and to improve our ability and willingness to share information with others both within and outside HQ. Over a series of meetings the working group came up with a model architecture, which comprised three main elements: structure, navigation and content.

1   *Structure* The function of structure is to support the architecture. It therefore needs to be reliable, capable of being managed and follow well-understood standards. It is central to the discipline of information science and encompasses metadata, taxonomy and classification.

2   *Navigation* The function of navigation is to guide the user to the information. It therefore needs to be simple and easy to use. On a technical level it will be concerned with search engines supported by a controlled language through a lexicon or thesaurus and hyperlinks. But there are other less tangible aspects that need to be considered. Not all information can be made available to everyone. Information on individuals needs to be protected to comply with the Data Protection Act, and all organizations will hold some sensitive information, which would cause harm if shared indiscriminately. So the architecture needs to consider how access to the different sets of information should be managed. And however self-evident a system sets out to be, users need to understand how to find it. That means they need to share a common understanding about how it is managed, and have a level of skill to be able to find what they are looking for.

3   *Content* It might seem obvious that the architecture should contain all necessary information, either within itself or by linking to other sources. But this in itself is a complex issue. First it requires us to identify all the information needed by the Department to support its business. Then, having built this map we need continually to renew and refresh it as business changes. Information is not just what we create internally or buy in from external sources, but also the information that exists in people and communities, and which is knowledge created by their interactions. To be useful for decision-making, information needs to be of a known quality so the user can judge how far it can be relied upon. Again there is a skills issue – the extent to which the user is able to determine whether the available information is fit for the intended purpose.

The working group also looked at the relationships between these three elements, as shown in Figure 13.1.

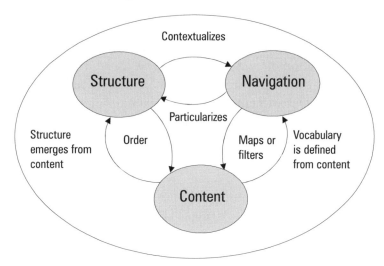

Fig. 13.1 The relationship between structure, navigation and content

Having developed the model this far we decided to focus next on developing the tools and processes it described for real, through the ERDM project. The information management stream would develop the metadata, taxonomy and thesaurus to form the bones of the structure of the information architecture. It would also review and revise the information management policy and the roles and responsibilities for individuals in managing information. The change management stream would embed awareness of the policy and roles, and develop skills in the user population for describing and retrieving information. Once the project was complete we would return to the model and review how our learning changed the model, and decide what to do next.

Electronic records and document management programme

The history of records management in the DTI has already been discussed, including the trigger of the 2004 Modernizing Government target for the ERDM project. But there were also good business reasons for investing time and money in moving to electronic records. Like most organizations, a very large part of the information DTI uses to make decisions is generated internally – correspondence, visit reports, policy documents, briefing papers, and so on. This documentation forms a huge information base, covering all its areas of interest. But the constraints of paper make it hard to access information outside the local area. And a remit as diverse as the DTI's means that several different units might, for example, be in contact with the same organization or company at the same time for different purposes, and be unaware of each other's activity. At best this is inefficient, at worst it can expose the Department to embarrassment or even loss. A strategic business review of the way DTI operated identified the need for greater cohesion, and made major changes to the Department's organizational structure and way of working. It also emphasized the importance of sharing information and knowledge.

For records management purposes information resides in documents, held in files, managed by business units in registries. Traditionally registries and so file structures were based on organization units – who they were, not what they did. The result was considerable duplication – an average of 19 files on the same company – and a lot of effort in closing and opening files when the organization changed, which it did, and does, frequently. But although DTI changes its structure and the way it does business, there is an underlying continuity about the functions it discharges. So, logically, the underlying information structure should remain the same, even if different business units are discharging that function.

The DRMS project began a process of rationalization. It divided files covering operational activities from those covering administration, introduced a common structure across the department for administration and began the move to base structures for operational files based on function rather than the unit. So, by the time that the ERDM programme began, the following items from the architecture were in place:

- *Information policy* This was first written in 1989 and revised in 1993: it was clear this would need updating.
- *Taxonomy* We decided to base the taxonomy on the existing file plan. It had been something of a struggle to introduce the new functional approach in DRMS and it had been more successful in some areas than others, so while we believed it was sound we recognized it would need more work.

- *Roles* At the strategic level a senior post had been created for an information director to oversee the programme. At local level DRMS had reinforced the role of the record manager, particularly where registries had combined. However, this was still an area that was seen as low priority in the battle for resources, and needed further attention to strengthen it. Other roles existed to manage data protection and open government responsibilities. All of these roles were a small part of an individual's job. So there was an opportunity to bring several related roles together to achieve efficiencies and greater impact.

However, there were many more things that needed to be developed from scratch:

- *metadata standards:* to describe the data elements for documents and files
- *a thesaurus:* there were many to choose from, but none seemed to match exactly with what we required
- *processes and procedures:* for records managers and standard users
- *training courses:* for records managers and standard users.

Information management policy

The old policy had been based on five basic principles: information was a corporate resource; it was valuable; it needed to be reliable; and to be kept safe; and it should be managed in accordance with the law. We concluded that while these principles were basically sound they needed to be refined for the new conditions and a wider audience. The five became seven:

- DTI information is a corporate resource. It belongs to the Department – it does not belong to any individual or group.
- We will make our information accessible to others in the DTI community, except where there is a specific reason not to.
- We will adopt a consistent approach to managing information across the whole of the DTI.
- We will retain details of all the business activities we undertake on behalf of the Department.
- We will ensure that the information we create on behalf of the Department is accurate and fit for purpose.

- Everybody is personally responsible for the effective management of the information they create or use.
- In managing information we will comply with the relevant statutory and regulatory obligations.

These principles, which were endorsed by the Departmental Board, laid the foundations for the way that information is managed in DTI. They state explicitly that information should be made freely available to everyone in the Department, except where there is a specific reason not to. Examples are given of possible exceptions based on a test of the risk of harm caused to an individual, an organization or the Department by the inappropriate disclosure of the information. They also laid a personal responsibility on everyone in DTI for the effective management of information, which includes the need to record what they do and keep information accurate and fit for purpose. The principles were deliberately written in simple language so that they could be used widely in guidance and training material for all staff.

The information management policy goes on to define different types of information: documents, electronic documents, records, electronic records and ephemera. It states that DTI will follow the appropriate published standard wherever possible, specifically the National Archive standards on electronic records and the Office of the e-Envoy metadata standards. It then has specific stated policies on:

- *security:* consistent with the DTI information security policies
- *storage media and file formats:* as far as possible to be system independent
- *metadata systems:* must define and hold metadata, and wherever possible these should be automatically generated from within the system or the information itself
- *versioning:* where required should be part of the metadata
- *modification and disposal:* each system must have a policy on the circumstances under which data can be modified or destroyed, by whom, how and what records of the changes should be kept
- *intellectual property:* permission must be obtained for the storage of non-DTI information
- *archiving:* transfer from one system to another

- *information management responsibilities:* of action officers for creating, selecting, receiving, adding metadata and storing information
- *compliance:* accountabilities with the policies.

The information management policy is the foundation of information management in the DTI. For the first time it sets out explicitly in a series of statements how information should be managed in the Department and assigns responsibilities for this. It also sets out the relationship with other elements in the architecture as shown in Figure 13.2.

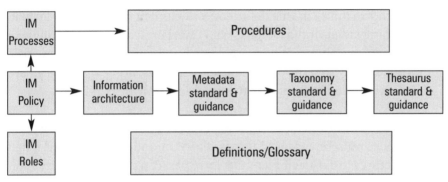

Fig. 13.2 The information management policy and its relationship to other elements in the information architecture

Taxonomy
There are many different interpretations of what a taxonomy is and does. In DTI we defined it as

> The structure and labels that describe the content of the DTI information space.

The ERDM taxonomy is a hierarchy made up of three main elements:

1 *The record plan* This provides a framework for organizing records by business function and activity, as represented by information series and themes. It is an exact translation of the same structure in the paper world. The purpose of the record plan is to provide context to the folders and documents, to aid retrieval and to aid the management of the records,

for example for retention or disposal, or movement of classes of records when responsibility for business functions change.

2   *Folders* These group together documents related to the same time-limited task or transaction. They equate in the paper world to files, but they can be either a virtual collection of electronic documents or a physical collection of things, or a mixture of the two. In the case of physical items the electronic folder would contain the metadata, including a location for the physical material that would be stored elsewhere.

3   *Documents* These are items of recorded information. Although the word 'document' might be thought to imply a particular format (textual information), in this definition a document can be in any format, including video, audio, database or PowerPoint, or it can be a physical item such as a photograph or a geological core sample. What distinguishes documents from the other elements of the taxonomy is that they have content, while the record plan and folders provide context.

The taxonomy describes the relationship between these elements, so an information series must represent a business function, and must be closed if that function ceases to exist. A folder must form part of a theme within an information series. Because a folder is time or task limited it should cover a discrete area, and should contain a manageable number of documents so as to enable the story to be read. When a folder becomes too large, physically or electronically, it should be closed and a new part opened. A document must be contained within a folder.

The taxonomy also includes guidelines on naming conventions for folders and documents. In summary, these are designed to aid retrieval for those who know that the record exists as well as those looking for information on a particular subject but who do not know what records exist. The guidelines go into some detail, which was reinforced by the change programme through training and help-sheets. But it has proved one of the most difficult areas for users. The battle against 'Industry – General', 'Miscellaneous' and 'April report' goes on!

Metadata

The definition in the ERDM programme for metadata is

> Structured data that describes a Document or Folder and is used to retrieve or manage that Document.

The DTI requirement for metadata was that it should:

- support the requirements of the DTI's main business processes by helping to ensure that relevant information can be retrieved effectively and efficiently
- satisfy regulatory requirements such as the Public Records Acts and the proposed Freedom of Information Act
- facilitate exchange of information with other government organizations, the general public, industry, and non-government organizations such as trade associations and lobby groups
- be simple to use and capable of being implemented in departmental information systems.

We reviewed a number of standards before deciding to base the standard on Dublin Core and, where additions to the core elements were needed to cater for specific needs, to base these on proven models developed by cognate bodies such as the National Archive, National Archives of Australia and the UK Government Metadata Standard (e-GMS) being developed by the Office of the e-Envoy as part of the Government Interoperability Framework (e-GIF).

We assigned different metadata elements to different record types such as folders, electronic documents, e-mails, scanned documents or physical documents. Wherever possible metadata was captured automatically by the system, either from its own resources (author, date created) or from already supplied information (title). Only four elements for documents are mandatory, and three of these are automatically supplied. The user has only to identify the folder to contain the record. Once a record has been checked in, the metadata cannot be changed by the user, but only by an authorized information manager, who must record having done so to preserve the audit trail.

Thesaurus

The DTI had some experience in the past of managing thesauri, and we were well aware of the difficulty of managing a large complex list of terms and producing something users could actually apply. We decided, pragmatically, to limit the use of keywords to folders to enhance retrieval at that level, but to make them a mandatory metadata element. This does not provide adequate support for content searching, but the search engine in our chosen ERDM software does not support greater sophistication. We plan to move in time to a universal search engine across the information space, and will then develop the thesaurus further.

Again, a key principle was that the thesaurus should wherever possible follow existing standards. There were four main concept areas covering DTI activities, and corresponding lists were identified to cover them which were relevant:

- DTI topics, where we used the Government Category List developed by Stella Dextre Clarke for the Knowledge Network
- business sector, where British Trade International had developed a list of markets and sectors
- geographical area, where we adopted the Foreign and Commonwealth Office authority list
- administration where, in the absence of a UK standard, we adapted the Saskatchewan Administrative Records System (SARS).

These were the basis for the core list of terms. But each business unit has a particular language, which staff use all the time to describe their activities, and selected local terms were also included. The list is controlled, with a management process to add new terms. Users pick terms from the list to index files.

Roles

The Information Management Policy defined key roles in the management of information so as to provide full visibility of accountability and responsibilities at corporate and local levels in the Department.

Ultimate accountability for the DTI's information, as with the rest of the management of the Department, belongs to the Permanent Secretary, with a member of the Departmental Board having particular responsibility for overall information management strategy and policy. The Information Director provides specialist advice and guidance to the Board and is the principal representative of the DTI on matters relating to information management. This person has specific responsibility for defining and promulgating information policies, standards and procedures for the man-

agement of information resources (thus including all information architecture matters), and also for monitoring and ensuring compliance with
these procedures. This person also has responsibility for delivery of information services, including the Library, intranet, DTI publications directory
services and translations.

At local level, each senior manager in charge of a business unit has delegated responsibility for the effective management of information created
and received in that unit. The policy recommended that he or she should
create a new post of Information Manager, which because it combined the
previously scattered responsibilities for records management, data protection, open government and IT security should be resource neutral. The
information manager should be a middle executive grade, to ensure both
sufficient understanding of the unit's business, and authority to apply
standards and procedures. Both information managers, and any support
staff, would be approved by the central compliance unit, receive special training and have administrator rights over their parts of the ERDM system.

And finally the policy restated that all staff are responsible as individuals for managing the information they create, receive or use.

Processes

Also flowing from the policy was the definition of key information management processes. There were a number of specialist processes relating to
particular tasks, including those around Freedom of Information, data protection and the appraisal and review of records. Similarly there were
processes around the management and approval of folders, thesaurus terms
and movement of areas of the record plan. These processes were owned by
particular specialist roles, some at local level, some at the centre.

However, perhaps of more interest in an architecture context, was the
definition of processes for ordinary users. We selected a number of units
and analysed their existing processes for managing information. At a surface level there were many different practices, and everyone said they were
different, but there was a remarkable consistency in the underlying processes. All units created documents, both electronic and paper, edited them,
sent them by e-mail, received documents from others both inside and outside the DTI, stored these documents in one way or another, retrieved them
for reference or reuse at a later date, and often ultimately destroyed them.
A significant subset of users managed these processes on behalf of others

in a secretarial or team support role. This high degree of commonality allowed us to create a recommended model of information handling processes to use both in the design of the system and to inform training. In only one area – prosecuting lawyers preparing material for court – did we find a process that was significantly different from the core model.

Skills

The final architectural element developed through the ERDM programme was information management awareness and skills for all staff. This is key, not only to the success of the ERDM programme but also, in our view, to the department's achievement of its objectives. DTI is predominantly an information processing organization. It takes in requirements from ministers, customers, other stakeholders and Europe; then through defined processes of policy development, consultation, problem solving and so on it turns them into new legislation, supports initiatives, gives advice and guidance, and even provides practical things like export licences. Getting better at delivering the Department's policy agenda therefore depends in part on getting better at finding the right information at the right time, and using it effectively. In the private sector lawyers and consultancies increasingly recognize that their knowledge is their long term future, and invest heavily not only in systems but also in training all their staff to be effective information managers. I would argue that a fully developed information architecture needs to include information literacy programmes, which not only provide the basic skills in storage and retrieval but also teach staff how to evaluate the reliability of what they find and its fitness for decision making.

This larger agenda was, however, beyond the scope of the ERDM programme. We focused more modestly on two key areas – the ability to:

- describe information effectively so that others can find it
- search for, and retrieve, information relevant to the searcher's enquiry.

The training programme was designed around delivering these key outcomes and comprised three separate training interventions:

1 About six weeks before their unit was due to go live all staff were invited in groups of between 12 and 20 to a one hour briefing to explain the bigger picture of what the ERDM programme was seeking

to achieve. It sought to answer questions people might have, invited them to express their hopes and fears, and also what benefits they wanted from the system. The output from these sessions fed into the benefits programme and was used by the later sessions to try to make the training more relevant for the individual units.

2   Three weeks before going live everyone attended a half-day work-shop in groups of 15 looking explicitly at information management issues. The groups discussed what a good title looked like and demon-strated through simple exercises different strategies for organizing and retrieving information. Then the week before going live all staff attend-ed a formal hands-on course in groups of ten to learn how to do their jobs using the system. This training was mandatory – those who did not attend were not authorized to use the system – and was based around the process models described above, using real life examples drawn from the unit.

3   Our experience was that users usually forget most of what they have been taught in training courses when they get back to their desks, so we included follow-up refresher training. Two weeks after going live floor-walkers provided follow-up clinics. And once the roll-out was completed we offered refresher training, tailored to the topics individual groups needed.

The evidence we have is that we have been successful in the first of our objec-tives – the quality of document titles has improved, as users now see why 'April project report' is insufficient. However, a significant number of peo-ple carry out searches at a basic level only, with most searches comprising single title words, and little use being made of saved searches. It is in this area that we need to concentrate future efforts.

Conclusion and next steps

I have tried to describe above how the DTI used a major project, its elec-tronic records and document management programme to flesh out its theoretical information architecture. So far, our approach has proved robust and, based on the key principles expressed in the information management policy, we have been able to develop a sound taxonomy, metadata schema and thesaurus. We have also addressed roles and processes, and begun to develop both a recognition of the relevance of information management and some skills in the DTI user population.

The next step is to go back to the architecture and assess which elements now need development. The taxonomy was developed around the file plan. But there are many other information sets with their own taxonomies, some quite closely related such as the Freedom of Information Publication scheme and Information Asset Register, others more remote like the internet and intranet, or the library catalogue. Can we have a single taxonomy describing the entire information space? Probably not, but it might be possible to link taxonomies through a central classification schema so that each was fit for its particular audience, but had an overall cohesion. The whole content area also needs development, first to develop a map of existing resources, then perhaps through a unified taxonomy, to check for and fill gaps. And, there is a lot more to do on the skills agenda to develop this crucial competence.

So far, we have found the architecture approach to be a useful way of organizing and prioritizing activity in the huge field of information management. The challenge is to make the approach relevant, and not to become bogged down in theory remote from actual business benefit. By taking it step by step and developing the architecture through practical projects we believe our approach has enabled us to make rapid progress, and to turn the architecture into a sound blueprint for the finished construction.

Reference

Cabinet Office (1989) *Managing Information as a Resource*, London, HMSO.

Chapter 14: a case study

Building a business taxonomy
A work in progress

RUTH MCLAUGHLIN
Information specialist, Southern Europe

ANGELA GREENWOOD
Knowledge management expert, Southern Europe

Our beginnings – informal communication and Windows Explorer

The company started as a small specialist European consulting firm, with its main office in a southern European city and several satellite offices throughout Europe and Latin America. At that time there were some 200 employees. Networking and internal communication were good, and thus information could be passed informally without too much difficulty. As the company grew, so the library developed from being run by one person in 1996–7 to having five staff by the end of 1999. This growth put a great deal of pressure on the then existing system of sharing of tacit knowledge and informal networking using the Windows Explorer shared network drive.

Initial attempts to improve this situation by organizing and classifying the Windows Explorer shared folders helped. It offered a simple classification structure and was open to the library staff as well as all consultants in the main European headquarters. However, it was not adequate to meet the demands of a growing multinational company, and a more organized, accessible solution was needed.

Lotus Notes

The shared network drive was followed by a set of web-enabled Lotus Notes databases at the beginning of 2000 based on the former Explorer folder browsing structure. This worked well on a European level where the whole company, not just staff in the central office, had full access to the library's material. All documents were stored in a number of separate databases (depending on their document type and content).

Classifying material in these databases consisted of assigning an industry keyword, selected from a controlled list. This list was not organized in a tree structure, but rather was a simple list that accepted broader sub-industries at the same level as higher-level industries. For example, Financial Services and Banking had equal status. Generic documents would have been placed in Financial Services, with more specific material placed in relevant folders such as Personal Banking, Mortgages or Credit Card Facilities, if that was their main area of coverage. Country or geographic region was also included, again taken from a controlled list.

To begin with, the Notes databases worked very well for external documents as consultants already knew the structure from Explorer. The drilling down was not deep and they could access material off-site, via the web and Lotus Notes. This helped the library to manage the growing amount of material held. Unfortunately, there were some drawbacks to this organization. For example, all documents had to have appropriate file names applied, and any material sent to us had to have file names changed to conform. All external material had to have at least three fields filled in manually and, in addition, all the old external documents that we had had to upload en masse (from the network) did not have any of this process applied to them unless there was additional time to change them, thus making them almost totally redundant.

For our internal documents we had a separate Lotus Notes database and again the taxonomy had to be filled in manually, without a control list. This meant that the terms entered depended totally on the person creating the record, and different terms, spellings or even misspellings could be added. This led to a completely inconsistent and imbalanced taxonomy, which was hard to use and not very useful to end-users.

In September of the same year (2000), the merger of our company with another from North America meant that there was a need to have databases that could be used and updated efficiently on both sides of the Atlantic. As our collection expanded exponentially so the need for one single repository became more urgent.

Beginning to put information in order

From this need to incorporate our holdings and make them accessible to all, it was decided that a global document repository should be constructed, with a controlled vocabulary. However, at the initial stages of our taxonomy construction we failed to undertake adequate and necessary homework and research, and the steps we did take were insufficient fully to encompass the problems to come.

Steps to investigate possible taxonomy structures began in August 2001. A roadmap was built of what we believed to reflect the current information holdings, revealing the interrelationship of subjects and how certain sub-verticals might interrelate, for example in the growing trend in Electronic Banking, and thus the cross-over between Financial Services and Technology, both of which had previously been separate concepts.

This was followed by a brainstorming session in September 2001, concerning basic sublevel terminology:

- Consultants were asked to help and were selected by sending an e-mail to a group of known library users, specialized in one industry. Those that responded worked on this industry for one afternoon.
- They were given a time limit (which overran considerably) to write down all terms they could think of that related to particular facets of their specialist field.
- They were then asked to arrange all their terms into 'families', and to agree their placement. Where several terms had the same meaning, they had to choose a preferred term, for example, *fast food* or *junk food*.
- Things that no one could agree on were placed in a 'widows and orphans' pile
- For very few of the terms did a clear 'winner' appear. Major disagreements ensued as to what should be the preferred terms. No further feedback was provided by participants.

After this experience, no more brainstorming was undertaken by, or with, consultants and the library did not carry out any further analysis or background research of any of the other industries.

October and November 2001

In October 2001 the basic top levels of a proposed browsing structure were formed. These were heavily based on the Windows Explorer and the slightly revised structure of the Lotus Notes databases. The information was sorted by:

- internal information (and divided by industry and sub-industry)
- external information (again divided by industry and sub-industry)
- company information (external and sometimes internal information on specific companies could be found here).

This basic structure was kept, with some cleaning in certain areas, together with proposed expansions in other areas, to allow for the imminent creation of the companies client base, and hence the material held on some industry verticals. Each area was to have an individual taxonomy, but to be visible on the same user interface. This was decided as most of the external content could be organized by industry (as they had been in Lotus Notes), while the internal content was organized by 'field' or horizontal, meaning topics that spanned more than one industry, such as Customer Value Management or Market Research.

At the end of these assessments, a basic thesaurus had been created to three levels in most industries, giving a skeletal view of the top level, including preferred terms for these levels, for external information.

November and December 2001 – using a document management system provider and a taxonomy provider

In November, an example taxonomy for our main vertical was sent to us for review by a document management system (DMS) provider to see if it would suit our needs. This company (from which we had recently bought a document management system) also provided some pre-built taxonomies. However, it was decided that this sample was neither deep nor representative enough for the specialist material we held, and thus another company would be used to help us build a taxonomy suitable for all our material.

After research by our management team, a taxonomy provider company was contracted to help us construct our own taxonomy. The decision to use the taxonomy provider was based on the fact that it was compatible with the DMS provider that we had already contracted, together with their tagging system editing tool.

A conference call was held with the taxonomy provider at the beginning of December, explaining the organization of our internal and external documents and they were given the basic top-level structure to look at. The aim was that the taxonomy provider would help us to construct our own taxonomy.

In January 2002 the staff from the taxonomy provider came to the office for one week, and were again given the basic structural information of our taxonomy so that the provider could begin an initial crawl of all the documents we held. We met the staff for 30 minutes every morning for one week, while they went through the material. In this process the external and internal data were crawled separately and a geographical taxonomy was also created. We worked with the staff to direct the flow, but only the top levels were really tackled, and it seemed that only a simple structure was created based on the elementary data that we had provided, rather than anything new.

At the beginning of our meetings with the taxonomy provider staff we wanted to see how they could help with both sets of documents but because of budgets and time constraints we decided to focus on our external content and do just one feedback loop for our internal document collection. (External material accounted for over 20,000 documents while we had only about 2000 internal documents!) In addition there were some doubts over whether internal documents (mostly in PowerPoint) would actually have enough 'meat' in them for relevant hooks to be made.

After one week the taxonomy provider staff left, and their initial output (a 'starter file') was introduced into the DMS by the IT department, where librarians had access to review it. We began working on the 'bundle files', and the whole repository of the company's digital library was crawled. Library staff then checked the results by drilling down in the taxonomy structure provided to see what concepts and tags (words that had hooked) had been created. Bad or irrelevant tags were deleted or modified. In addition, actual documents that were located in those particular folders were checked, to verify the relevancy of the documents contained. Three different librarians were responsible for checking and correcting different verticals and a one-week schedule was worked out for reviewing, editing and correcting the files, and giving feedback.

All levels of each different vertical's taxonomy had to be opened, copied and pasted into text format – full paths had to be given to the 'folder' that each text document referred to and a good or bad rating for each term was given. If 'bad', then marking for *delete/move to/use . . .* had to be provided. This was very time-consuming, mind numbing and sore on the eyes. All corrections made by the librarians were added to the original taxonomy file by the taxonomy provider's knowledge engineer, and the output of these corrections was returned to the IT department to be introduced anew into the DMS, where librarians could begin another round of corrections.

After a couple of feedback loops, it was discovered that the crawl was allowing 'noun phrases' of three to four words, which increased the number of hooks being returned as relevant parts of the taxonomy. When this was discovered in the sixth week it was decided that only specifically approved single words or compound phrases could be allowed from the previous crawls – this was to limit the number of hits returned and improve the quality of the material hooked.

For the internal document's taxonomy we decided to keep the hooks up to three or four words as this gave better results; this was because of the way in which our company writes documents: authors often use similar words and catchphrases, and consequently many relevant hooks were made.

For the external document's taxonomy the final file, which was provided in the eighth run, used only selected single and two-word noun phrases, which began to make the taxonomy much cleaner.

This whole process lasted for six weeks; during this period we had in particular to deal with:

1   *Linguistics*
    • *which language?:* selecting a preferred language, for instance US or UK English?
    • *same meaning but many words:* multiple terms for one subject – choosing preferred terms ('mobile', 'wireless' or 'cellular'; 'Hoover' or 'vacuum cleaner'; 'Kleenex' or 'tissue'; 'diaper' or 'nappy'; this was not necessarily related to the US–EU English language problem!
    • *same word but different meaning:* subtle differences in English, and the use of nouns that have different meanings in US and EU English, for example 'shop' and 'store'; in the UK 'shop' is a generic term,

in the US it means 'boutique' or refers to more specialized shopping; we also came across many differences in the use of terminology in financial services classification, health and insurance, because of the differences in European and US industries
  * *multiple languages:* not only UK and US English, but many other languages.

2 *Getting a balanced view*
   We realized the importance of taking a uniform approach to the data, but this was not easy to put into practice. Some librarians were including terms that they knew about in the industry files they were working with, but were ignorant of other terms that may have been necessary for the same category. Often the body of information for all verticals was not sufficient to draw on to create a full and complete taxonomy. While some verticals had mammoth amounts of information to trawl through, others had produced only 15 terms in total.

3 *IT problems*
   There were large bundles of unhooked documents (those that did not fall under any part of the taxonomy) that could not be explained – we were finding large sections of material that should have easily hooked in more than one vertical but were not appearing at all. The reason for this is still not clear but it seemed to be that the format of the document was not compatible.

After the final improvements to the taxonomy (the reduction of noun phrases) with the taxonomy builder, the eighth run produced an end file. Unfortunately there were some communication problems at this point as in order for it to be usable for our DMS provider we also needed a starter file. As a result the last run of information we had was useless, other than as a guide for the librarian working with the next stage of the process, editing tags, in the tagging system editing tool of the DMS.

The next stage – working with the tagging system
Getting started – taxonomy and material introduced into the DMS

The external taxonomy was imported into the DMS, implementing the taxonomy, applying it to our holdings and structuring the material for the intranet. It also allowed editing of the tags ('hooks' or terms) with a tagging/weighting editing tool. The hooks (the single words or noun phrases) which tagged documents to be put in different folders of the taxonomy all had values; these values contributed to the relevance of the hook. At this point it was discovered that only one taxonomy could run at a time. To be able to work in parallel with the internal taxonomy, we would need to have another server, running independently. Consequently, only one taxonomy was launched, limiting the usefulness to the end user.

As stated above, the end file produced in the eighth run could not be used so, before going live, the taxonomy was to be edited manually, to try and bring it more in line with the results of the eighth run end file. For this, the taxonomy was opened in the tagging/weighting editing tool; each vertical was opened down to the very last hooks to be edited. This involved deleting irrelevant hooks, or changing the value weighting. If the value weighting was increased, the hook needed to appear *fewer* times to be considered relevant – if the value was lowered, it needed to appear *more* times. The hooks could also be given an auxiliary value, meaning that in themselves they would not hook a document, but if they appeared with other terms in the same folder and in the same document they would contribute to the placement of a document in the taxonomy structure.

Problems after launching the tagging system

When the tagging system was fully launched with the taxonomy some major problems came to light:

- Generic documents were appearing in every branch of the taxonomy, as they had enough hits for every category to appear, although they may not have been strictly relevant to all the branches.
- All publishers' names had been removed as hooks when they automatically appeared as noun phrases while creating the taxonomy; however, the recurrence of 'business types' as part of publishers' names (for instance XXX Media, XXX Financial Services or XXX Technology Research) meant that, although these documents were usually *not* about Media or Finance or Generic Technology, they still appeared in these folders of the taxonomy.
- Some publishers have a list of all the industries they publish material for at the back of their publications. This was sufficient to have another

set of documents (all from the same publisher) appearing in all the folders for the industries mentioned at the back of their reports.

- Documents with graphs and charts (or little text) were not appearing at all, or not where they should have. The text contained within these reports was not sufficient for the taxonomy to place them in any folders, or they were being hooked into the wrong folders.

Some of these difficulties were reduced (but not eradicated completely) by editing the weightings, rather than further changes in the tags, hooking the documents. But a lot of the problems remain. They are 'works in progress' for the IT and librarian team working on this. Checking the quality of hits involves monitoring of the intranet taxonomy, as users see it, to review where documents are being placed, then reviewing the tags, which are hooking these documents to particular folders.

Conclusions and lessons learnt

Following management decisions both the DMS provider and taxonomy provider were introduced with little or no previous warning to library staff. These hasty decisions led to many misunderstandings and misconceptions on both sides.

One of the key lessons we learned through this process was the vast difference between the US and European company information structures and that no matter how much the management changed the direction of the company's service offerings our taxonomy needed to have a firm and consistent structure on which people could rely. This issue was never completely resolved and was even exacerbated by the fact that people who were asked to provide input all became 'experts', with their own opinions on how the taxonomy should be structured.

Ultimately, the conclusion of library staff involved in this project was that a great deal more preparation was needed, with time to research and build an accurate taxonomy to meet our needs, but still with room to grow and develop with the company. This preparation would have reduced our problems considerably. In addition to this, once the taxonomy had been implemented, more time for testing would have been invaluable to ensure a smoother rollout.

Despite the experience being something of a baptism of fire for all library staff, IT and management involved, a lot was learned, very quickly;

now everyone is much more aware of the library's needs. The project is still a work in progress, with scheduled weekly meetings between all involved. We hope that the taxonomy will be 'completed' some time before the end of 2003 . . . when the next major revision should begin!

Part 4
The user interface

Preface to Part 4

While it may appear that we have downgraded the user aspects of IA by placing this part at the end of the book, this is not our intention. We consider that this is the logical place for this subject, after the parts dealing with the building blocks to IA. This is because we feel that the user interface should be considered only after the information that is to be retrieved and displayed has been thoroughly analysed. However, the user interface has to be considered in the overall IA planning, and must not be seen as an afterthought. In practice, the user interface aspects of IA will form part of the iterative process by which the IA is implemented.

The case study described in Chapter 17 in some ways wraps up most of what has been covered earlier, as it has a substantial section on the design and testing of the interface. The environment was challenging, bringing together a number of dissimilar websites into one coherent system with the added complications of differences in language, culture and work practice. The driving force behind this implementation was, and still is, a common navigation scheme – 'findability', to quote Morville. At one level this is what IA is striving to achieve, a common structure, but the requirements of different user groups must also be taken into account. The successful IA is one where compromises have been accommodated but the result is coherent.

B. M.
A. G.

Chapter 15

Interfaces

Expressions of IA

JANICE FRASER
Adaptive Path, USA

Introduction

The past five years have brought countless changes in the way that information is distributed, shared, accessed and understood. The web as a medium excels at providing access to vast stores of information, and the difficult challenge of designing the structure of that information, both visible and non-visible, has provided interesting employment for many of us over the years.

In this chapter, we're going to talk about the design of individual web pages. In his book, this is what Jesse James Garrett (2002) calls 'the Skeleton' layer of a website – it's the concrete manifestation of conceptual architecture structures and functional specifications.

This chapter will provide you with a set of ideas about the relationship between interface design and information architecture. I'll be introducing three general page types – the hub, the content list and the facet browse. I've chosen to explore these types because they incorporate the most fundamental elements of contemporary information architecture practice – taxonomy and metadata, user task research, contextual navigation, and a page's relationship to high-level site sections.

ReliefWeb: a case study

This year, I've had the good fortune to work on a website for the United Nations. The site is called ReliefWeb, and it's an information resource for humanitarian relief workers worldwide. ReliefWeb is the first source for up-to-the-minute information for the humanitarian aid community about earthquakes, floods, famine and other natural and man-made emergencies. The ReliefWeb team publishes more than 2500 documents per month from more than 900 sources.

Adaptive Path and its partner Mule Design were brought in to revise the information architecture. The project had two information management goals:

*   to organize information and navigation according to user priorities in order to provide users with quick retrieval of relevant material
*   to make obvious the breadth and depth of information, resources and tools available on ReliefWeb.

Throughout this chapter, we're going to explore how the user interface of specific pages is helping ReliefWeb meet these goals.

Applying user research: the hub page

In the past couple of years, information architects have woken up to the value of using conceptual user research at the start of the design process. Contextual inquiry, a research method made popular by Karen Holtzblatt and Hugh Beyer (1997), is fairly broad and aims to develop a holistic view of how users work. Task analysis research is similar but focuses on detailing the steps taken to accomplish a specific task. Both approaches enable designers to develop a model that illustrates how users think about and approach their work. This model, called a 'mental model', can take any number of forms, from detailed diagrams to simple outlines.

For ReliefWeb, our research involved hour-long telephone interviews with representatives of three important user types. Our hope was to understand the activities each participant does to accomplish their job, so that we could begin to match those activities with the information resources available on the ReliefWeb site. Typically, we use this type of research to develop a high-level architecture – the 'tabs', if you will – that closely matches the user's tasks and goals. With this project, though, we found a few interesting facts that altered our approach:

- When retrieving information, users across all types often think first about country.
- Within the context of a country, they may want to find all sorts of information, for instance:
  - what has been happening recently in that country
  - funding for humanitarian aid, such as appeals and contributions
  - background information, in order to start working in an unfamiliar country.

While these findings had implications for the overall site structure, their primary value was at the interface level. These tasks essentially formed the requirements for a 'country' page that would act as a navigation hub for the various kinds of information that users are seeking within that context of 'country'.

The mental model illustrated in Figure 15.1 organized more than 150 tasks into groups, such as 'Understand specific humanitarian topic', which in turn were collected into goals, such as 'Gather information'. This method of illustrating a mental model, which was developed by Indi Young, clearly shows the most important user tasks that a website must support.

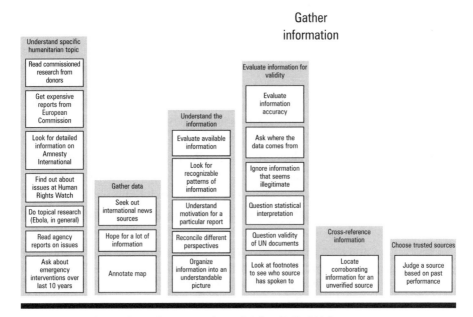

Fig. 15.1 A portion of a mental model for ReliefWeb

What is a 'hub' page?

To understand what I mean by hub, think about airport hubs – a central location from which you can get shorter flights to a very wide variety of destinations. This configuration enables airlines to provide a service to a greater number of destinations in any given region. A hub interface on the web is a central point from which you can get to a very wide variety of information about a specific topic. These pages provide a more or less complete overview of the content available.

Hub interfaces show up on a wide variety of sites. Take, for instance, the website for software company PeopleSoft, which we discuss later in the book. For any one of PeopleSoft's products, a person might want to learn about the features or customer case studies, see product demonstrations, read press releases, find out which other products it connects with, and so on. The user mental model for PeopleSoft showed that most visitors first orient themselves by finding a specific product, but from there they might be looking for many different kinds of information. This indicated that a hub might be the most effective way of them finding it.

The current hub page for a PeopleSoft product includes almost 50 links organized into four quadrants: highlighted product features, links to product information (press releases, demos, and so on), links to the components that make up the product and links to the various bundled 'solutions' that include the product. User testing showed that this 'hub' configuration enabled users to develop an accurate understanding of the product-related content and they were able to navigate quickly to useful information.

This concept is corroborated by usability research that was done for product information company Epinions. Like the PeopleSoft team, the Epinions designers observed that their visitors would navigate quickly to a topic that seemed generally to match what they were looking for, hoping to find links there that would get them closer to the specific product or information that would meet their needs. The Epinions team called the behaviour 'dive and bounce', and used that as a guiding principle to drive the rich contextual linking that has since characterized the Epinions site, and hub pages as a whole.

Figure 15.2 shows a PeopleSoft product page, which is a hub that provides access to more than 50 information pages and further product pages.

Fig. 15.2 A PeopleSoft product
page

The ReliefWeb country page

ReliefWeb has a very different audience and mission from those of People-Soft or Epinions, but a similar design challenge. Our research showed that most users want to move quickly to the country that they're interested in. From there, the set of interests is fairly diverse. Using the mental model as a guide, we can identify at least six distinct tasks that users consider within the context of a country:

- learning about new emergencies that might warrant humanitarian relief efforts
- staying up to date with events in the location
- staying up to date with the sector of the humanitarian field that they work in, such as housing or healthcare
- monitoring contributions and appeals for funding of humanitarian relief efforts
- gathering information in advance of travelling to the country
- learning about jobs and training.

Like the PeopleSoft site, ReliefWeb has organized a page that provides and links content pointing to this disparate range of topics related to the central concept of 'country'. This page, even more than the home page, is the nexus of the website, providing a complete view of all the content that the site offers and providing what is essentially contextual navigation to filtered views of every major site section. Figure 15.3 shows an early wireframe diagram for the ReliefWeb site, which shows a wide range of links for the country hub page.

Fig. 15.3 An early wireframe diagram for the ReliefWeb site

Applying taxonomies: the list page

The simple list page. We encounter it every day – airline flights, search results, news stories, press releases, programme listings. Lists are wonderful interfaces for enabling users quickly to evaluate a large number of items in order to identify and choose the few that will be useful. Well-designed lists are densely packed with information and structured to make that information easy to scan. Designing a good list is hardly simple, though. Designing a good list requires good librarianship.

The importance of librarians in the field of information architecture was established by Peter Morville and Lou Rosenfeld when they founded the pioneering web IA company Argus & Associates. Morville and Rosenfeld saw that, in addition to understanding business requirements and user goals, designing effective websites must also involve deep examination and classification of a site's content. Morville and Rosenfeld hold advanced degrees in library and information science from the University of Michigan and have proved that the principles that make content findable in the physical world also make content findable in the digital world. On his current site, www.semanticstudios.com, Peter Morville writes, 'Interface stands on the shoulders of infrastructure.' Nowhere is this more transparently true than in a list.

Think about the characteristics of a list. Sometimes a list has columns. If you search for flights on the Virgin Atlantic website, for example, you'll see columns for departure city and time, arrival city and time, flight number, and which class (economy or upper) the seat is in. The Google search results list foregoes the columns, but also includes several bits of information for each listing: title, description, category, URL, size, and so on. In either case, it is easy to scan down the list and choose items that match your criteria.

Each of these lists is constructed from metadata, revealing the conceptual foundations of the information space that the website describes. The list interface can only be as useful, understandable and feature-rich as the metadata scheme from which it is drawn. Compare the flight information lists from the three airline interfaces shown in Table 15.1.

Table 15.1 Comparison of three flight information lists

Virgin Atlantic	Orbitz	United
	[Price]	[Price]
Flight number	Flight number and airline	Flight number
Departure city		
Departure date, time	Departure date, time	Departure date, time
Arrival city		
Arrival date, time	Arrival date, time	Arrival date, time
Cabin/fare type		
	Stopover cities	
	Total flight time	Number of legs
	Number of stops	

In each list, the product being described is the same – a flight from London to San Francisco. But the lists are very different:

- Virgin doesn't show price, but it does show whether the ticket is for economy or upper class.
- Orbitz shows the most information, including total flight time, stopover cities and number of stops.
- United shows a very small set of information; instead of the number of stops, it shows the number of legs in the flight.

Why are they so different? Is one better than the others? Could the companies have designed the lists differently? That depends.

Virgin is famous for its upper class service, so showing class might be valuable to its users. Orbitz appeals to a broad audience that is very sensitive to price, so it prominently features price and offers a range of information to support a variety of user preferences. But why would Orbitz show 'number of stops' while United shows 'number of legs'? What's the difference? Obviously, they communicate the same message ('this plane will land once in another city before you reach your final destination'). Maybe they're different because of the audience – United appeals to the frequent flier, Orbitz to the mass market. Possibly. But the difference is also in the metadata – Orbitz and United are exposing different attributes, and a list can only expose the metadata that exists in the database.

ReliefWeb list page

ReliefWeb is at heart a massive document repository. Humanitarian aid workers check the site several times a day to watch for new emergencies around the world. With more than 80 new documents published to the site each day, it can be a challenge to design an interface that will enable users to find documents of interest quickly. The best way to allow users to scan through a large number of documents is clearly a list of some sort. To figure out what sort of list would work best for ReliefWeb, we started by looking at the metadata, to understand what facets were available to use in constructing a meaningful list. They included:

- date published (the date ReliefWeb published it)
- date created (the date it was published by the original source)

- headline (which includes subjects)
- content type (map, peace accord, situation report, news story, and so on)
- country (which country the document applies to)
- emergency (if the document applies to a specific emergency)
- sector (which segment of the humanitarian field the document applies to)
- subject (keywords).

Obviously, it would be unwieldy to show all of this information for every listing, and numbers of items in a given list can be large. To manage this scale of information, we needed to prioritize the facets somehow.

Our first task was to separate the facets that would be useful for broad sorting from those that would be useful for understanding and choosing specific items. From our research, we knew that country and emergency were primary points of orientation, so we divided those from the list and decided to give those views a separate page. From there, we identified that people would make choices based on headline (which communicates subject information) and date (which provides chronological context). Content type was an unusual facet, because it could be used for both broad filtering and item selection. The remaining facet, subject, was redundant to the headline and more appropriate for a search interface.

The resulting scheme for organizing the facets looked like this:

```
REDIRECT BY:     country, emergency
FILTER BY:       sector, content type
SORT BY:         headline, content type, date published
NOT USED:        subject
```

By approaching the list design task first from the standpoint of metadata and comparing that with the user model and a general understanding of human behaviour, we were able to establish a direction for the interface quickly.

Figure 15.4 shows early wireframes of ReliefWeb's Latest Updates list page, which allows filtering to manage the length of the list and sorting to facilitate item selection.

Go to Updates by country or emergency

Select documents of interest to you:

Sources
☑ News & Media
☑ NGOs
☑ Governments
☑ UN
☑ Academic & Research
☑ Other

Sectors
[All ▼]

Document Types
[All ▼]

Show all documents

[GO]

❶
June 2003 Updates

			Results 341-360 of 600
DATE POSTED	SOURCE	TYPE	‹ MORE RECENT | OLDER ›
4 Jun 2003	WHO	Sit Rep	This is where the two-line headline will describe what is in this document

Fig. 15.4 Early wireframes of the ReliefWeb Latest Updates list page

Working the metadata: facet-based search

I give special thanks to search expert and Adaptive Path founding partner Jeffrey Veen for introducing me to the Sears example.

The logic for a list interface essentially says: 'Start by showing all documents, then let the user reduce and sort that list by certain criteria.' This is more or less a hard-coded search query. There's another special instance of search that has emerged recently – a kind of advanced search that exposes all of the meaningful facets and values embedded in the metadata as criteria for a search. This idea has been around for a while, but a few sites, like American retailer Sears.com, have turned it into a sophisticated interface that exposes the architectural underpinnings of the site to resolve difficult problems of findability.

Sears is, among other things, a leading retailer of major appliances for the kitchen – dishwashers, refrigerators, cook-tops, and so on. They carry a huge inventory with hundreds of models for each kind of appliance. Choosing the right appliances from this large collection is one of the most important goals for Sears customers. The Sears solution is a page that exposes all of the facets of the appliance that might be useful when a consumer is trying to narrow the wide selection to a manageable few. For instance, in the refrigerator section, users can select their preference for brand, colour, energy use, width, overall height, capacity, ice maker type or price.

Users can type in a maximum or a minimum price, select from a small number of options for each of the other facets, and then click an action button to 'find a match'. The results are displayed on a list page, where users can select up to four products for the side-by-side comparison of detailed specifications that will help them to make a final selection. Say, though, that you selected stainless steel for colour, 21 cubic feet for capacity, and US$400 as your maximum price. There isn't a refrigerator on the planet that matches those criteria. Instead of simply providing a 'zero matching results' message, the Sears site again ups the usefulness by itemizing how many refrigerators matched each of your selections. From there, you can change the selection and search again.

Instead of presenting hundreds of products for users to browse through, Sears exposes relevant metadata through a custom search interface; see Figure 15.5. Figure 15.6 shows the results of a search where there are no products that match all the searcher's options. In this case it is easy to see that price was the constraint; increasing the maximum price to US$1100 results in eight matches.

The point is that content and categories are not the only tools in the IA toolbox. The attributes and values that are attached to content in the form of metadata are equally important when considering how to build interfaces that serve users.

The ReliefWeb facet search

Designing the advanced search for ReliefWeb was an in-depth study of designing for facets. One of the characteristics that makes the Sears example work so well is the limited number of values for each facet:

- brand – 8 choices
- colour – 6 choices
- energy use – 2 choices
- width – 5 choices
- overall height – 7 choices
- capacity – 7 choices
- ice maker type – 2 choices
- price – text entry.

Search by Feature ▸ Refrigeration: Top Freezer Refrigerators

331 Top Freezer Refrigerators exist in this category.
- To narrow this list, select **only** the features below that are **important** to you.
- In general, the more features you select, the **higher the price** will be.
- To **view all** items without narrowing your search,
  click **Find Matching Products**.

▸ **Please Select a Brand:** (Select all that apply)
☑ No Preference   ☐ Frigidaire   ☐ Galaxy
☐ GE   ☐ Kenmore   ☐ KitchenAid
☐ Maytag   ☐ Whirlpool

FIND MATCHING PRODUCTS

▸ **Select by Color:**
⦿ No Preference
○ Almond
○ Black
○ Off-White (Biscuit, Bisque)
○ Stainless Steel
○ White

FIND MATCHING PRODUCTS

▸ **Energy Star Compliant:**
⦿ No Preference
○ Yes

FIND MATCHING PRODUCTS

▸ **Select by Approximate Width:**
⦿ No Preference

Fig. 15.5 Sears' custom search interface

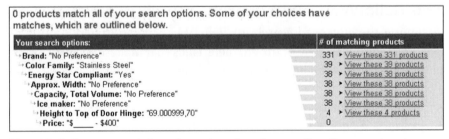

0 products match all of your search options. Some of your choices have matches, which are outlined below.

Your search options:	# of matching products
Brand: "No Preference"	331 ▸ View these 331 products
Color Family: "Stainless Steel"	39 ▸ View these 39 products
Energy Star Compliant: "Yes"	38 ▸ View these 38 products
Approx. Width: "No Preference"	38 ▸ View these 38 products
Capacity, Total Volume: "No Preference"	38 ▸ View these 38 products
Ice maker: "No Preference"	38 ▸ View these 38 products
Height to Top of Door Hinge: "69.000999,70"	4 ▸ View these 4 products
Price: "$____ - $400"	0

Fig. 15.6 Sears search interface showing the results of a search where no products meet all the search options

By comparison, the most important facets for ReliefWeb can have hundreds or thousands of values:

- country - 180+ choices

- emergency - 1000+ choices
- source - 900+ choices
- content type - 15+ choices
- sector - 10+ choices
- subject (keyword) - 100+ choices
- date - our discretion to define date ranges.

The sheer scope of this metadata model forced us to think systematically and creatively about the interface options available to us. A simple form with radio buttons and checkboxes wouldn't serve for a website of this complexity. As with the list page, we started by looking for patterns in the facets. We first identified that several facets describe document topic - what is it about. We grouped these together.

Source – 900+ choices
Date – our discretion to define date ranges

TOPIC-RELATED
Country – 180+ choices
Emergency – 1000+ choices
Content type – 15+ choices
Sector – 10+ choices
Subject keyword – 100+ choices

Next, we looked for hierarchically related attributes, which might allow us to shorten some of the longest lists:

Source type (5–10 choices)
 → Individual source (100+ choices per type)
Date (our discretion to define date ranges)

TOPIC-RELATED
Region (5 choices)
 → Country (<60 choices per region)
  → Emergency (<20 choices per country)
Content type (15+ choices)
Sector (10+ choices)
Subject keyword (100+ choices)

So, for instance, if you choose Africa, you next see a list of about 60 countries from Algeria to Zimbabwe. If you then choose Algeria, you see a list
of about 12 emergencies. By establishing hierarchical relationships among
the various facets available in the metadata scheme, we reduced the maximum number of choices from the thousands to, in most cases, fewer
than 100. From there we played with various configurations of drop-down
menus (which, unlike pull-down menus, remain open until the user clicks
the mouse), pop-up boxes, link lists, and other devices. The end result is
a hybrid interface that integrates aspects of browsing through a hierarchy
of facets, in order to search for an individual document.

To manage the breadth of content available on ReliefWeb, we provided
a robust search interface organized around hierarchical facets; see Figure 15.7.

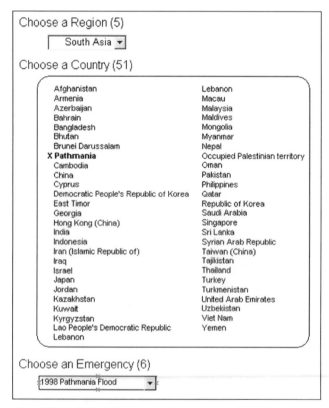

Fig. 15.7 ReliefWeb search interface showing the
countries within South Asia

Conclusion

User testing and iteration will continue on the ReliefWeb site for several months before they (and we) are satisfied with the outcome. The challenges of managing such a large, diverse and important information source have caused us to re-evaluate how we approach the task of interface design. In most cases, like those described here, the solution lay in the deep conceptual structures of architecture.

Peter Morville of Semantic Studios is fond of saying, 'findability precedes usability', and that has become something of a mantra for us. Rather than fearing the number of clicks it takes to get somewhere, we have focused instead on the ease with which users can identify the correct choice at every step. In some cases, that preference has led us to create interfaces, like the hub and list pages described here, that are almost purely navigational. Situations like these are important reminders that the 'rules' made popular by so many gurus are now more than ever subject to redefinition in the context of real situations.

References

Garrett, J. J. (2002) *The Elements of User Experience: user-centered design for the web*, New Riders Publishing.

Holtzblatt, K. and Beyer, H. (1997) *Contextual Design: a customer-centered approach to systems design*, Morgan Kaufmann.

Chapter 16

Guru interview

MARYLAINE BLOCK interviews GENIE TYBURSKI

Marylaine Block* interviews Genie Tyburski, Web Manager for the US law firm Ballard Spahr Andrews & Ingersoll, LLP, and the creator of the respected legal research site, The Virtual Chase (www.virtualchase.com/index.shtml).

MB   Did you set out to be a law librarian, or was that a happy accident you turned out to have an affinity for?

GT   During my first day at Drexel, I remember filling out a questionnaire that asked, amongst other things, what kind of librarian I wanted to be. Imagine my dismay when 'a good one' wasn't one of the choices. I had no idea there were different types of librarians. Six weeks later, I landed a part-time cataloguing job at Community Legal Services (CLS), an organization that provides legal services to the poor. About six months after I started, the director of the library resigned and recommended that CLS hire me to take her place. This rendered me speechless. I barely knew the basics of librarianship. I knew absolutely nothing about law. She spent her last two weeks on the job giving me a crash course in civics, basic legal resources and Lexis.

* Copyright, Marylaine Block, 1999–2003; reproduced by kind permission. Marylaine Block is the producer of Neat New Stuff, ExLibris and many other library-related electronic information resources. She has lectured widely on library-related topics; her website is at http://marylaine.com.

I was in the right place, at the right time, with a saint for a teacher. I learned to love the subject matter years after getting over my introduction to USCCAN [United States Code and Congressional Administrative News].

MB Tell me about your early days on the net, and how you came to build The Virtual Chase. What inspired you to add the various components of it?

GT I first traipsed around the net during 1992 or 1993, when I discovered it by accident after connecting to the library catalogue at the University of Utah. We have a Salt Lake City office, and I was looking for a book for one of our lawyers. What I found was so much more interesting!

By early 1996, there was enough legal and government information available that I thought it was important to try to keep on top of it. Also, the potential of the hypertext mark-up language intrigued me. And I thought, 'This is like WordStar. I can learn this.'

I hardly had a five-year plan. Wanting to write, as well as to share information about the legal and government documents available and to learn HTML, I launched what was then Genie Tyburski's home page. Four months later – during October 1996 – I renamed the site, calling it The Virtual Chase.

At that time, it offered rudimentary versions of the current Legal Research and People Finder guides, along with a couple of short articles reconstructed from a column I used to write for the GPLLA [Greater Philadelphia Law Library Association] Newsletter.

For the most part, I initially added content that I had used during in-house research training sessions. Both the securities resources page in the Legal Research Guide and the Company Information Guide started as in-house presentations. Later, as I began to conduct hands-on seminars for local library and internet groups, I added resources that helped me teach the classes. Both Government Resources on the internet (now archived) and Legal and Factual Research on the internet were visual aids for the classes.

Today, a lot more planning goes into what to add to the site. At about 600+ pages, it's big. Sometimes I feel like I'm running in place just to keep all the links fresh. That's important, and yet I know as I respond to your question, that some of the links are dead.

More than just the links change. The substance of what I write may change. Therefore, when inspiration strikes, I have to consider, how often is change going to affect the content? Can I keep up with it? And equally important, is the new content in line with the purpose of the site? I know from the e-mail questions I receive that many *per se* litigants, for example, use the site. If the content helps them, that's a nice side benefit. But we exist to help legal professionals, and I don't want to lose site of that goal.

MB   Are your firm's lawyers using your website?

GT   I'm confident that our lawyers use The Virtual Chase. In addition to the referrer logs, which reveal the domains that refer visitors, they often talk to me about it. One day, I put information about a competitor's website in the Legal Research Guide. It's a good site, and I spoke highly of it. Later, when I ran into one of the partners in the hallway, he said something like, did you have to include information about that site? I replied that I did. The site qualified on all counts for inclusion in the guide. He nodded, and then grumbled good-naturedly, 'Yeah, but did you have to call attention to it by giving it a "new" icon?'.

They're paying attention, and using the site. They mention it to clients and at CLE seminars. They also let me know when a link goes bad!

One of the funniest stories I have to relate about our own use of the site is, a partner once called me seeking copyright permission to provide handouts at an upcoming CLE seminar! Of course, I'm happy she called because I learned about the seminar and that she was going to talk about The Virtual Chase. But it is her – the firm's – intellectual property.

MB   Any thoughts on the way your website's popularity has changed your life?

GT   Let me count the ways. I never lack for work – payment perhaps, but not work. There's always an article or a presentation in the works. And I have met so many interesting people, some of whom have become close friends.

It has expanded my horizons. When you work for a large law firm in a fairly tight-knit legal community, it affects your point of view. Sometimes for the better, sometimes not. The Virtual Chase has put me in touch with lawyers and librarians all over the world. I learn about differences - different procedures, laws, cultures, experiences and opinions. I enjoy this interaction.

At the same time, managing a website is a 24/7 job. It seems that when bad things happen, they happen at the most inconvenient time. For example, I recently spent most of a weekend cleaning up a mess caused in part by some errant JavaScript I uploaded for a new navigational menu. I hadn't anticipated trouble, because I tested the menu on our secured development site. But when I uploaded it to the public site, the code duplicated itself in about 50 or 60 pages, which caused display and load-time problems.

MB What is the thinking that goes into a major redesign and reorganization of a 600+ page website?

GT Let me say up front that I'm no expert in web design. Content I understand and, like any librarian, I'll muddle through something that's hard to use if it has the content I'm after. But not everyone is a librarian. Design is as important as the content, because the content is meaningless if it can't be found.

The Virtual Chase was long overdue for an overhaul when I decided to undertake this task several months ago. I had put it off for a long time, because I was looking for an assistant. That process took a little longer than I anticipated, but I'm happy to announce that a recent Drexel graduate joined our ranks. He will assist, at least part-time, with the development of the site.

While I was interviewing folks, I began to read about web design. I subscribed to Jakob Nielsen's usability newsletter (http://useit.com/) and purchased several books, including *Don't Make Me Think* [New Riders Publishing, 2000], *Information Architecture for the World Wide Web* [O'Reilly, 2002] and *Web Word Wizardry* [Ten Speed Press, 2001].

With the help of our web host, I also created a secure site for development purposes. I am able to put many of my less-than-brilliant ideas to rest there.

Next, I talked to people. I talked to lawyers to try to understand how they looked for information at the site, and what frustrations they experienced. I tried talking to librarians, but they're too nice. They would only give me positive feedback and encouragement.

I also talked to a couple of folks with technical expertise. The newly arrived staff member, who studied interface design and usability at Drexel, made several suggestions. One may have saved my social life. He said: 'You really have to learn how to use cascading stylesheets [CSS].' This is ancient history in web design, but I hadn't taken the time to explore it.

A systems administrator at Penn State, who helps me manage the listserv for TVC Alert, suggested several ideas for improving the online version of TVC Alert.

All that was left was to put these ideas to work. After learning CSS, which took only a few hours, I re-created the site map. It may still need work, but it helped me organize the site from the viewpoint of the visitor. Next, I made several other minor design changes, and created a new navigational menu.

Finally – and I'm still doing this – I have to strip all the formatting from all 600 plus pages, so that the stylesheets can do their job. That takes the most time. Fortunately, when I redesigned the site a few years ago, I had – again on the advice of a technically savvy friend – incorporated server-side includes. This allowed me to make design changes to the header, which contains our logos, the menu and the footer, which contains copyright information, without actually having to edit each page individually. When I do something right, it's usually by accident, or on the advice of a friend.

MB   Thanks for taking the time to answer my questions. I always learn interesting things from you.

Chapter 17: a case study

Designing a worldwide experience for PeopleSoft

JANICE FRASER
Adaptive Path, USA

CAMILLE SOBALVARRO
PeopleSoft Inc., USA

For most large companies, creating a unified experience for their vast public website is a difficult challenge – so creating a single worldwide experience platform is unthinkable. PeopleSoft, Inc. is a leading provider of collaborative enterprise software. More than 4700 organizations in 107 countries run on PeopleSoft's integrated business applications, which include customer relationship management, financial management, supply chain management, and more.

In just 24 months, PeopleSoft and Adaptive Path systematically brought together more than 20 dissimilar web properties to create a unified worldwide messaging, customer support and lead-generation system. The new sites share a common information structure and navigation scheme to ensure that visitors become oriented quickly. In the same way, visual continuity strengthens brand perceptions and usability and shared content strategy ensures that the company is speaking with one voice around the world; a centralized template-based publishing platform has reduced maintenance time and freed staff for more strategic work.

This case study describes which techniques were most helpful in creating an experience system that was flexible enough for broad application worldwide, circumvented (or survived) the inevitable internal company politics, and above all provided a satisfying experience for users.

The One Site Project

The PeopleSoft One Site project had four explicit goals:

- to increase the number of sales leads generated
- to provide a superior user experience and decrease time to information
- to decrease the website maintenance work load, particularly within the satellite offices worldwide
- to provide a messaging platform that would support major corporate marketing programmes, as well as localized marketing efforts.

Inherent in these goals was a broad range of lesser requirements. For example, the project entailed implementing a content management system (CMS), creating an authoritative product taxonomy, and eliminating redundant and outdated content. At the same time, it was essential that the designers and architects remained sensitive to the diversity of needs among the 70+ project stakeholders. The design solution could be successful only in the long term if it were flexible enough to support local and departmental idiosyncrasies while preserving the continuity of the user experience.

Staffing the project

The One Site initiative was divided into two one-year projects, which launched in December 2001 and 2002, respectively. Adaptive Path provided pre-design user research, stakeholder research, goal alignment, information architecture, navigation, interface, interaction design and some usability testing services. Another agency, Department 3, provided visual design support.

By the implementation phase, each project grew to include the entire website staff of 21 people, with additional support provided by the IS development team. Other external vendors were added periodically to provide card-sort testing, usability testing, competitive research and a best practices survey. Though not technically 'project staff', more than 75 stakeholders from around the company and around the world participated in the design process.

Incremental development

The One Site project was undertaken in one-year increments. During 2001, PeopleSoft relaunched its three most important web properties: public website, customer extranet and partner extranet. This project focused on creating an architecture, design and technical platform that could be broadly extended to PeopleSoft's many other web products. In 2002, PeopleSoft used that platform to relaunch the company's 18 local websites around the world.

The end result was not 21 separate websites, though, but rather one website that appears in varying ways depending upon the user's relationship to PeopleSoft – login, language preference and country selection.

The first successes are often the most important ones. PeopleSoft succeeded in the One Site project primarily because the organization was predisposed to do so: the web team had a strong leader who was able to set up the project for success. She worked with her team to establish a long-term vision, advocated to senior management for funding, empowered her team to take action and set reasonable but firm deadlines.

Year 1: Three sites become one

The goal for the first year was to develop an experience platform that would be broadly extensible across a large number of similar sites.

The basic outline of the process was this:

1 Get funding approval.
2 Select the content management platform.
3 Interview stakeholders.
4 Identify and gain executive alignment around business goals for the site and the project.
5 Research and map user tasks and goals.
6 Research inventory and map site content.
7 Compare content to user tasks and goals.
8 Define architecture.
9 Define task-based navigation.
10 Compare information architecture to business objectives.
11 Validate architecture through card-sort testing.
12 Develop classification schemes for PeopleSoft products and the industries that the company serves.
13 Develop wireframe diagrams.
14 Validate wireframes through usability testing of paper prototypes.
15 Develop visual design templates.
16 Validate visual design through usability testing.

17 Prepare content for migration into the content management system.
18 Eliminate redundant, outdated and trivial content.
19 Implement the site.

This process took ten months and launched in December 2001.

Three particular steps were critical to the success of this project:

1   *Process Win #1: Developing a visualization of the user's mental model based on primary research* To understand users' needs and goals, Adaptive Path conducted a research study using techniques based on ethnographic inquiry. The goal of the research was to understand how users go about the task of purchasing and implementing enterprise software. We conducted 21 ninety-minute interviews with people from three user groups: prospects, customers and partners. The transcripts from these interviews were analysed to identify and diagram patterns common among participants within a particular user group. This diagram provided a comprehensive 'mental model' for each user type. Each model clearly illustrates in great detail the goals and activities common among individuals in that group. The models provided a rational basis for our subsequent navigation and architecture work.

2   *Process Win #2: Involving stakeholders in substantial and inclusive ways* In all, more than 75 stakeholders were included in the process. They were drawn from every level of the organization and a broad cross-section of functional areas, from the chief marketing officer (CMO) to customer service representatives to product managers. Each stakeholder was interviewed by Adaptive Path to establish business objectives and to understand the business context for the work. Subsequently, PeopleSoft senior leadership was included to ensure broad alignment around project and website goals. Finally, selected stakeholders were invited to participate in collaborative design and architecture sections. By soliciting and managing stakeholder input strategically, the project team was able to satisfy real stakeholder and business needs, while avoiding politics in what was otherwise going to be a rigorously user-centered design process.

3   *Process Win #3: Frequently checking the effectiveness of design decisions* Throughout the project, PeopleSoft took every opportunity to vali-

date the work including card sorts and various usability tests. After each round of validation, adjustments were made to the designed solution. By investing in validation often, the design team was continually able to move forward with a high degree of confidence. Throughout the process, these checks also reminded us to be open-minded and flexible. This proved helpful as the system inevitably evolved. The success of the final solution supports the wisdom of this approach.

Year 2: International rollout

Because the infrastructure was already defined and proven, the process for the second year was theoretically much simpler, emphasizing prototyping over primary research. The complexity came in sheer scale: instead of three sites, this project adapted the original design to 18 sites around the world. The sites represent a range of markets, resources and offerings. A successful solution would have to balance the requirements of each country and region, as well as PeopleSoft's strategy as a whole.

The specific goal of the project in the second year was to extend the core system that had been developed earlier (navigation, architecture, content strategy, visual design, templates and publishing) to support a website of any size in any country in which PeopleSoft does business now, or may want to do business in the future.

The expectation going into the project was that providing a standalone website for each country was no longer in the user's best interest. In order to develop a full picture of PeopleSoft's products and services, a visitor to the old sites needed to winnow through both the country site and the main dot.com site. By collapsing all of the worldwide content into one system, visitors are now able to traverse easily back and forth among all of PeopleSoft's content – country-specific and global content, local-language and English-language content.

The existing country sites varied widely in their sophistication, maturity and staff support. Large sites in the UK and Japan included not only a vast amount of translated content from the US site, but also original information to support local market positioning and programmes. By comparison, the PeopleSoft sites in developing markets had very small amounts of content, but big hopes for future growth.

Looking inward

As with the relaunch of PeopleSoft.com in the first year, stakeholder interviews provided an essential tool in creating a satisfying user-centered design. This may seem an oxymoron, but exhaustive stakeholder interviews provided the most cost-effective means to understand the differences between the site as implemented for the US market and the site as it should be implemented for local markets worldwide. Moreover, understanding and adoption of the new system within the local office would be critical to ensuring a positive user experience – and the best way to guarantee acceptance is to meet needs. We took great pains to understand the perspectives and concerns of the country-based PeopleSoft staff who would be our champions once the new system had been launched.

International marketing can be a very sensitive subject within a corporation – different countries have different needs, resources and market sizes. Larger markets fear lowest-common-denominator solutions, and smaller markets fear they'll be ignored in the interest of optimizing for the regions providing the biggest return. Corporate websites are the most visible expressions of global marketing plans, which makes their development particularly touchy.

Working with PeopleSoft, Adaptive Path talked to 50 stakeholders around the world (including PeopleSoft headquarters) about their goals, objectives, processes and resources. In a relatively formal research process, these discussions were structured around a discussion guide, which was distributed to participants ahead of time. The conversations were transcribed and the responses analysed to reveal recurring themes that became the focus of our efforts going forward.

Looking outward

For the 2001 PeopleSoft.com project, Adaptive Path had used a primary research study to develop a mental model for prospective customers of enterprise software. That effort has proven to be a long-term investment. Preliminary inquiries into the continuing relevance of the mental model and the information architecture that was developed from it revealed that the processes of purchasing enterprise software were consistent around the world.

Still, we suspected that international prospects had different specific information desires from a corporate website. Working with colleagues at

Easability, Adaptive Path designed a survey to understand what kinds of information prospective customers were most often seeking, and in what languages they would most prefer to see that information. The findings validated the existing mental model and stressed the importance of translating detailed technical information as well as marketing materials.

Building the new design

The sustaining relevance of the mental model meant that the existing information architecture would indeed work internationally, allowing the team to move quickly into the design phase. The task, then, was simply to make minor adjustments to the navigation and page templates from the 2001 launch of PeopleSoft.com to suit the varying needs of an international audience. In all, only five new templates were required to support all 18 worldwide country sites.

The interface design task began by looking at best-of-breed global sites from companies like IBM and HP. By seeing other solutions and comparing them to the PeopleSoft requirements, Adaptive Path extended the existing page template design to incorporate elements such as language translation and cross-navigation between local and global versions of content. PeopleSoft's in-house visual design team used visual language from the new PeopleSoft.com to turn the first round of wireframe diagrams into a functional prototype quickly.

Testing and launching the new design

To ensure the effectiveness of the new designs, Adaptive Path co-ordinated and oversaw usability testing in Tokyo and Paris, working with local agencies Ion Global and Design For Lucy, respectively. The results from the testing lead to some design changes, after which began the formidable challenge of implementation, translation and migration.

Only four months after completing the high-level design, the in-house team at PeopleSoft launched the new international sites.

Success factors

Among the key success factors for this launch were decisive leadership, a clearly defined and well-evangelized goal, relentless management of scope, deep in-house knowledge of the key disciplines required to build the site, well-chosen vendor partners, solid content management technology and very hard work.

In order to be able to launch on time, the web team applied nearly 100% of its resources to this project alone. Both the 2001 and 2002 implementations owe a great measure of their on-time success to the fact all site content was 'frozen' – that is, unchangeable – for periods preceding launch. This allowed the team to focus exclusively on migration. Some content was frozen for weeks, some for only days, depending on the time sensitivity and priority of the content. This required not only the foresight and management of the web team, but also the support of key content providers for all sites.

An important risk factor in the first phase of the project was the concentration of knowledge in a very few people. This placed an excessive burden of effort and stress on a few individuals. It also reduced the degree to which the larger group perceived its stake in success. Significant efforts were made to avoid this in the second phase of the project. Although not entirely overcome, the project responsibilities, perceptions of ownership over the work and commitment to success were more evenly distributed.

The development organization reported that clear documentation of requirements – site diagrams, page wireframes and detailed design specifications – were critical success factors. This documentation, they say, allowed developers to spend less time clarifying requirements and begin development sooner.

Solution details

Since corporate websites often grow organically and management is often decentralized, growth occurs without the benefit of common standards for visual design, information hierarchy and interaction modelling. Users who interact with these companies are subject to very different experiences depending on what they try to accomplish at these sites. PeopleSoft's approach was to unify their sites in order to create a brand experience online that would be consistent across all likely user scenarios.

The PeopleSoft One Site project had four over-arching goals. Point for point, the implemented solution addressed each goal fully:

1 *Goal* To increase the number of sales leads generated.
   Outcome In 2001, the PeopleSoft website produced a record number of sales leads.

2   *Goal* To provide a superior user experience and decrease time to information.

    Outcome Testing against usability benchmarks from previous years shows strongly positive results. Users have had consistently positive reactions to the changes. Likewise, the new system, with its consistent worldwide experience, has measurably increased users' opinions of PeopleSoft and its products.

3   *Goal* To decrease the website maintenance workload, particularly within the satellite offices worldwide.

    Outcome The centralized web department can now manage layout, visual design, navigation and information architecture for vast quantities of pages on the main sites and worldwide through a very small number of templates. This has eliminated tremendous redundancies within small, resource-constrained offices outside the USA. At the same time, distributed publishing through a content management system ensures that stakeholders have retained control over the content that they 'own', while freeing those same departments of design and production burdens. As a result, PeopleSoft anticipates an increased ability to support local marketing initiatives worldwide in 2003.

4   *Goal* To provide a messaging platform that would support major corporate marketing programmes, as well as localized marketing efforts.

    Outcome In the new system, certain pages are controlled by the corporate office and appear on every site worldwide. The corporate marketing department has reallocated translation budgets to ensure that the most important marketing messages appear in a variety of languages. Thus, customers visiting any PeopleSoft URL will see a consistent set of messages regardless of locality. At the same time, the new templates provide ample opportunities for the worldwide offices to promote local marketing initiatives, add locally relevant pages and sections, promote country-specific customers and partners and innovate with novel content.

Strengths and shortcomings

As a direct result of the One Site project, the web is recognized internally to a much greater degree than in previous years. This is largely as a result of its success as a source of business inquiries.

Nonetheless, there were (and are) areas of the web managed by organizations outside the central web team that have not yet implemented the new corporate web standards. The PeopleSoft team continues to evangelize to these groups, both directly and indirectly, by demonstrating the benefits of adoption and attempting to understand and integrate their needs into the standard experience platform.

Next steps

In 2003, the web team will continue its work to extend the PeopleSoft user experience platform. Inevitably some detailed requirements were postponed from the first projects, but they have not been forgotten. PeopleSoft has continued to prioritize and undertake projects based on available resources.

Index